JOHN WEIR PERR

THE SELF

IN PSYCHOTIC PROCESS

ITS SYMBOLIZATION IN SCHIZOPHRENIA

Foreword by C. G. Jung

UNIVERSITY OF CALIFORNIA PRESS

BERKELEY AND LOS ANGELES : 1953

UNIVERSITY OF CALIFORNIA PRESS
BERKELEY AND LOS ANGELES

CAMBRIDGE UNIVERSITY PRESS
LONDON, ENGLAND

COPYRIGHT, 1953, BY
THE REGENTS OF THE UNIVERSITY OF CALIFORNIA

MANUFACTURED IN THE UNITED STATES
BY THE UNIVERSITY OF CALIFORNIA PRINTING DEPARTMENT
DESIGNED BY ADRIAN WILSON

FOREWORD

As I studied Dr. Perry's manuscript, I could not help recalling the time
when I was a young alienist searching vainly for a point of view which
would enable me to understand the workings of the diseased mind. Merely
clinical observations—and the subsequent post mortem where one used to
stare at a brain, which ought to have been palpably wrong yet showed no
sign of abnormality—were not particularly enlightening. "Mental diseases
are diseases of the brain" was the *axioma,* and told one just nothing at all.
Within my first months at the Clinic, I realised that the thing I lacked was
a *real psycho-pathology,* a science which showed what was happening in the
mind during a psychosis. I could never be satisfied with the idea that all
that the patients produced, especially the schizophrenics, was nonsense and
chaotic gibberish. On the contrary, I soon convinced myself that their productions meant something which could be understood, if only one were
able to find out what it was. In 1901, I started my association experiments
with normal test persons in order to create a normal basis for comparison.
I found then that the experiments were almost regularly disturbed by psychical factors beyond the control of consciousness. I called them *complexes.*
No sooner had I established this fact than I applied my discovery to cases of
hysteria and schizophrenia. In both cases, I found an inordinate amount of
disturbances, which meant that the unconscious in these conditions is not
only opposed to consciousness, but also that the former has an extraordinary
energic charge. While with neurotics the complexes consist of systematically

split off and arranged contents, which for this reason are easily understandable, with schizophrenics the unconscious proves to be not only unmanageable and autonomous, but also highly unsystematic, disordered, and even chaotic. Moreover, it has a peculiar dreamlike quality, with associations and bizarre ideas as they occur in dreams. In my attempts to understand the contents of schizophrenic psychoses, I was considerably helped by Freud's book on Dream Interpretation, which had just appeared (1900). By 1905, I had acquired so much reliable knowledge about the psychology of schizophrenia (then called "Dementia praecox"), that I was able to write two papers about it. My *Contribution to the Psychology of Dementia Praecox* (1906) had practically no influence at all, since nobody was interested in pathological psychology, except Freud, with whom I had the honour of collaborating for the seven subsequent years.

Dr. Perry, in this book, gives an excellent picture of the psychical contents with which I found myself confronted. At the beginning, I felt completely at a loss in understanding the association of ideas which I could observe daily with my patients. I did not know then that all the time I had the key to the mystery in my pocket, inasmuch as I could not help seeing the often striking parallelism between the patients' delusions and mythological motives. But for a long time I did not dare to assume any relationship between mythological formations and individual morbid delusions. Moreover, my knowledge of folklore, mythology, and primitive psychology was regrettably deficient, so that I was slow in discovering how frequent these parallels were. Our clinical approach to the human mind was only medical, which was about as helpful as the approach of the mineralogist to Chartres Cathedral. Our training as alienists was much concerned with the anatomy of the brain, but not at all with the human psyche. One could not expect very much more in those days, when even neuroses, with their overflow of psychological material, were a psychological *terra incognita*. The main art the students of psychiatry had to learn in those days was how not to listen to their patients.

Well, I had begun to listen, and so had Freud. As he was impressed with certain facts of neurotic psychology, which he even named after a famous mythological model, I was overwhelmed with "historical" material while studying the psychotic mind. From 1906 until 1912, I acquired as much knowledge of mythology, primitive psychology, and comparative history of religion as possible. This study gave me the key to the understanding of the deeper layers of our psyche and I was thus enabled to write my book with the English title: *The Psychology of the Unconscious*. This title is slightly misleading, for the book represents the analysis of a prodromal schizophrenic condition. It appeared forty years ago, and last year I published its fourth revised edition under the title *Symbols of Transformation*. One could not say that it had any noticeable influence on psychiatry. The alienist's lack of psychological interest is by no means peculiar to him. He shares it with a number of other schools of thought, such as theology, philosophy, national economy, history, and medicine, which all stand in need of psychological understanding and yet allow themselves to be prejudiced against it and remain ignorant of it. It is only within the last years, for instance, that medicine recognizes "psychosomatics."

Psychiatry has entirely neglected the study of the psychotic mind, in spite of the fact that an investigation of this kind is not only important from a merely scientific and theoretical point of view, but also from the standpoint of practical therapy.

Therefore I welcome Dr. Perry's book as a messenger of a time when the psyche of the mental patient will receive the interest it deserves. The author gives a fair representation of an average case of schizophrenia, with its peculiar mental structure, and, at the same time, he shows the reader what he should know about general human psychology if he wishes to understand the apparently chaotic distortions and the grotesque "bizarrerie" of the diseased mind. An adequate understanding often has a remarkable therapeutic effect in milder cases which, of course, do not appear in mental hospitals, but all the more in the consultation hours of the private specialist. One should not underrate the disastrous shock which patients undergo when they find themselves assailed by the intrusion of strange contents, which they are unable to integrate. The mere fact that they have such ideas isolates them from their fellow-beings and exposes them to an irresistible panic, which often marks the outbreak of the manifest psychosis. If, on the other hand, they meet with an adequate understanding from their physician, they do not fall into a panic, because they are still understood by a human being and thus preserved from the disastrous shock of complete isolation.

The strange contents which invade consciousness are rarely met with in neurotic cases, at least not directly, which is the reason why so many psychotherapists are unfamiliar with the deeper strata of the human psyche. The alienist, on the other hand, rarely has the time or the necessary scientific equipment to deal, or even to bother with his patients' psychology. In this respect, the author's book fills a yawning gap. The reader should not be misled by the current prejudice that I produce nothing but theories. My so-called "theories" are not figments but facts that can be verified, if one only takes the trouble, as the author has done with so much success, to listen to the patient, to give him the credit—that is humanly so important—for meaning something by what he says, and to encourage him to express himself as much as he possibly can. As the author has shown, drawing, painting, and other methods are sometimes of inestimable value, inasmuch as they complement and amplify verbal expression. It is of paramount importance that the investigator should be sufficiently acquainted with the history and phenomenology of the mind. Without such knowledge, he could not understand the symbolic language of the unconscious and thus he would be unable to help his patient in assimilating the irrational ideas that bewilder and confuse his consciousness. It is not a "peculiar historical interest," a sort of hobby of mine, to collect historical curiosities, as has been intimated, but an earnest endeavour to help the understanding of the diseased mind. *The psyche, like the body, is an extremely historical structure.*

I hope that Dr. Perry's book will arouse the psychiatrist's interest in the psychological aspect of his cases. Psychology belongs as much to his training as anatomy and physiology to that of the surgeon.

C. G. JUNG

ACKNOWLEDGMENTS

In the depths of a psychic turmoil such as that described in the following pages, a person experiences ideas and feelings so implausible, distressing, and apparently unacceptable to the rational world around him that he ordinarily has an inclination to have the entire episode kept in the closest secrecy by those to whom he has entrusted his confidences, and preferably put out of mind after it is over. If this impulse were universally obeyed, our science would shrivel and die for want of nourishment by experience and its communication. My profound appreciation and thanks go then first of all to the patient, who, with her family, consented to let her experiences and fantasy productions be recounted and used for this discussion. My fondest hope would be that these reflections on her disorder might eventually prove to be of some help indirectly to others in similar straits in the future.

My most sincere gratitude goes to Doctor C. G. Jung, not only for his foreword, his many hours spent on the manuscript, and his helpful notes of comment, but even more for the rich discussions I have been fortunate enough to hear from him concerning the deeper reaches of psychic processes.

I wish to express by indebtedness to the Rockefeller Foundation for a fellowship, which made possible study and research at the C. G. Jung Institute in Zurich. This volume would not have been possible without this assistance.

To John Jennings I owe much for his patient labors in editing a somewhat complicated manuscript. I am indebted to John Goetz for his able handling

of technical details in the publishing process, to Adrian Wilson for his
creative touch in designing the volume, and to Jane Bendix for her skillful
line drawings. My thanks go also to Professor Donald McKinnon and Dr.
Joseph Wheelwright for their generous time and interest.

I am grateful to my colleague on the hospital staff for his part in the work
of assembling the material of the interviews and the records quoted in
the text.

I am indebted to the following publishing houses for kind permission to
use copyrighted material. In passages from the first three books below, I
have made my own translations since the English-language editions have
not yet been published.

The Bollingen Foundation, New York:
   Psychologie und Alchemie, by C. G. Jung
   Psychologie der Uebertragung, by C. G. Jung
   Gestaltungen des Unbewussten, by C. G. Jung
   Contributions to Analytical Psychology, by C. G. Jung
   The Integration of the Personality, by C. G. Jung
   Psychological Types, by C. G. Jung
   Modern Man in Search of a Soul, by C. G. Jung
   Essays on a Science of Mythology, by C. G. Jung and C. Kerényi
   Myths and Symbols of Indian Art and Civilization, by Heinrich
     Zimmer
Dodd, Mead & Co., New York:
   The Psychology of the Unconscious, by C. G. Jung
   Collected Papers on Analytical Psychology, by C. G. Jung
Rascher Verlag, Zurich:
   Psychologie und Alchemie, by C. G. Jung
   Psychologie der Uebertragung, by C. G. Jung
   Gestaltungen des Unbewussten, by C. G. Jung
Rhein Verlag, Zurich:
   Eranos Jahrbuch, 1948.
Constable & Co., Ltd., London:
   The Migration of Symbols, by Eugène Goblet D'Alviella
The Macmillan Co., New York:
   The Golden Bough, by Sir J. G. Frazer
   Primitive Secret Societies, by Hutton Webster
   The Sacred Tree, by J. H. Philpot
The Art Quarterly, Detroit:
   "Suggested Origins of the Tibetan Mandala Paintings," by Schuyler
     Cammann (Spring, 1950)
G. Bell & Sons, Ltd., London:
   Prelude to Chemistry, by John Read

Pantheon Books Inc., New York:
  The Divine Comedy of Dante Alighieri, translated by Lawrence Grant White
The Clarendon Press, Oxford:
  The Dialogues of Plato, translated by B. Jowett
  Serindia, by Aurel Stein
The Dial Press, New York:
  Plato, the Man and His Work, by A. E. Taylor
Appleton, Century, Crofts, Inc., New York:
  Selections from Early Greek Philosophy, edited by M. C. Nahm
Kelly and Walsh, Ltd., Hong Kong:
  Peking, by Juliet Bredon
G. P. Putnam's Sons, New York:
  Religion of the Veda, by M. Bloomfield
Museum of Navaho Ceremonial Art, Santa Fe, New Mexico:
  Hail Chant and Water Chant, by Mary Wheelwright
The Viking Press, Inc., New York:
  The Bible of the World, edited by Robert Ballou

I am indebted also to Dr. W. Y. Evans-Wentz for his personal permission to quote from his books *Tibetan Yoga and Secret Doctrines* and *The Tibetan Book of the Dead*.

I wish equally to express my apology to other schools of psychoanalysis, psychiatry, and psychology for an almost total omission of their points of view. I feel that much work is urgently needed to bring into some more workable relation the findings attained from these quite divergent standpoints. My apparent neglect of them here is not a statement of my lack of interest in them or lack of respect for them, but a necessary delimitation of the discussion for the sake of clarity. The task of setting forth a study of the comparative definitions of the self and of psychotic process would require further volumes, more years of work, and considerable prowess in handling theoretical constructs dispassionately.

J. W. P.

CONTENTS

ILLUSTRATIONS

PART I

1 INTRODUCTION

To understand what is meant in analytical psychology by the "self," it is necessary to call to mind some of the background of Jung's general approach to the study of psychological experience, for out of this arises the great difference between what Jung means by the "self" and what is commonly designated elsewhere by this term.

One of the most fundamental reasons for the wide difference in psychological theory is, of course, the variety of methods of conducting the scientific study of psychic processes at a high level of complexity. Obviously, the basic rule is to collect the data of experience and observation, classify them and find regularities, thus making formulations as faithful as possible to the nature of the observed phenomena, and to test their validity by the prediction of events arising out of certain known conditions. In clinical work with human patients it is not possible to set up ideal experimental conditions, once considered necessary for properly scientific treatment of a subject, for a certain group of phenomena cannot be studied in isolation from the general context of the life situation. The result is that the data of observation have become the whole array of spontaneous psychic events in their own natural setting, not in limited test situations but in complicated real ones. Consequently, accurate description here requires an emphasis upon the consideration of the processes at work in the organism operating as a whole, in the fullest complexity of internal and external conditions. Furthermore, account must be taken of all that occurs, leaving out no category of phenomena by arbitrary prejudice. Ideally, the holistic approach requires that every event that occurs in the organism be related to every other in their significances, just as is the case in the complex interactions of the factors in blood chemistry. In the mental experience of man, then, this would require careful and accurate observation of his irrational as well as his rational behavior and products.

These principles are so familiar as to be platitudes to scientists, yet just here is the point at which cleavages occur in the evaluation and practice of scientific method in psychology. Sexual or interpersonal problems have come to be regarded as fair meat for scientific study, but those emotions and notions that come under the heading of mythical or religious are apt to be suspect unless reduced to the terms of the sexual or interpersonal, even though such experience has been central in the dynamics of the molding of history and culture. It is truly remarkable that although the majority of cases of catatonic schizophrenia show delusions of a religious nature, at least in religious symbolism, few psychiatrists or psychologists take this material enough into account as the data of observation to try to draw real meaning from it. The religious nature of these delusions is in the blind spot of the conventional scientific eye of our generation (itself conditioned paradoxically by the modern development of presuppositions concerning its religion).

An exception has been Jung, in that he dared to take seriously what he saw, despite the condemnation he quickly earned from his profession—which labeled him a mystic and no scientist—just as Freud had dared do in the psychosexual field. Significantly enough, the result has been that Jung, through his respect for the wholeness of man's mental experience, has been the one to arrive at the discovery of the processes that are at work in the psyche effecting man's wholeness—the "individuation process," as he calls it. He has fashioned a psychological hypothesis that is in the truest sense organismal and thus in harmony with the most advanced scientific tenor of the day. For careful analysis revealed that it was just in the "religious" or mythological symbolism that the spontaneous processes concerned with wholeness lay hidden, and that if they were not taken in their own sense the point was missed and thus the key to the understanding of development was lost.

Thus for analytical psychology the term "scientific" does not designate the choice of subject matter, as to what is or is not acceptable for scientists to study, but rather the method, the manner in which the study is made, and the conclusions drawn. A thoroughgoing investigation of the unconscious must necessarily lead into all sorts of strange material, since its products are all those creations and concerns of mankind in the irrational or esoteric Analytical psychology has not hesitated to assemble the whole array of these unconscious products in whatever domain the fantasy of man has chanced to play: dream, vision, folklore, primitive mentality, superstition, religion, mysticism, myth, and such protosciences as astrology, alchemy, and healing ritual. Analytical psychology has grouped phenomena and classified, by making comparative studies, and thus sought out the regularities, and then made formulations. The terms used to designate the phenomena and processes were not chosen in accordance with preconceptions borrowed from other scientific disciplines, since the field was virgin territory and the investigator must be faithful to its own peculiar sense, just as any new science has had to break free from the blinding influences of the network of contemporary presuppositions.

The concept of the self cannot be understood unless all this is borne in mind, nor can the various contents of the psychoses in general. It is even safe to say that one reason why psychology has not progressed further in its penetration into the meaning of the psychoses is that these obvious principles of scientific operation have not been generally respected.

Several decades of research on the lines indicated above have resulted in a change in the concept of symbols. Gone is the day when a psychiatrist could have the satisfaction of interpreting such and such a symbol as standing for such and such a thing—for example, that tree equals mother or phallus, or that mountain equals woman and its trees the pubic hairs. The appreciation of the real significance of the unconscious symbol now requires far more subtlety of insight and respect for what is not yet known. We must now recognize, with greater deference for hidden meanings, that certain symbols appearing at any time represent specific leading aspects of the totality which are activated at that time, seen in their dynamic interplay of balances and oppositions and transformations and leading toward the goal of fulfillment of that totality. Each unconscious entity can be understood only in its interrelation with other psychic events that accompany, precede, or follow it, and only in the context of the over-all process of development. This is in accord with the organismal principle in that the images of the libido cannot be understood apart from the total pattern, only in relation to which they have their inner sense and function.

This view is apt to evoke a feeling of impatience with such vagueness about symbols, since it is hard to be concise and definite with such an approach; yet it is certain that the interpretations made will be truer to the facts of the situation, which are immensely complex. For the psyche is an organism in process of growth, and the primordial images show themselves to be the organs that operate to carry this out just as those of the plant or body do; they apparently represent entities as existent in themselves as the heart or the liver, and as interdependent.

Without this basic viewpoint the content of a psychosis appears to be only wishful fantasy play, whereas with it layer upon layer of subtle meaning can be probed. Certainly without it the material produced by the patient here discussed would evade comprehension. It is usually a matter for surprise to discover that Jung has said that when studying a psychotic disorder the psychiatrist must always ask himself where the process is going, to what end. For in such profound derangements we are dealing with the eruption of the deeper levels of archaic elements, which have to do altogether with the developmental process. In these levels we do not look for causes in the fortuitous circumstances of early infancy, as if the psyche were only an inert lump of raw material molded solely by the hands of caprice, so much as for ends toward which the psyche as a living organism is striving—namely, for its self-fulfillment in its several aspects and functions.[1]

To gain such an insight into the significance of the process, we must be able to think dexterously in terms of the symbols of the unconscious and feel quite at home in the elusive fluidity of its irrational imagery. Otherwise we could not see where the process is heading or where it stands at the time, nor would we be able to assist the patient through the process and back to consciousness. In an acute catatonic schizophrenia, for example, the psychiatrist usually has only the chance to cope with the unconscious in its own context, since the ego consciousness has been fragmented or pushed aside or engulfed by a flood of highly energic and archaic unconscious contents, thus surrendering its usual role of perceiving and relating to these elements. In this state the patient is lost as in a jungle, and it is important for the psychiatrist not to be equally unfamiliar with these surroundings but to have his bearings and even his map with him. It makes a tremendous difference to the patient to feel that someone can cope with all this chaotic matter that overwhelms his mind. In the present case the therapist did not try to calm the patient's delusional fears by taking the stand that they were unreasonable; rather he urged her carrying the fantasies further toward their objective. There was unconscious work to be done. A knowledge of comparative symbolism not only acquaints the therapist with the meanings of what he hears, but it is also a means of helping the patient at certain stages to get a working relation to, and thus a defense against, the potent archaic processes.

With this general orientation to psychic material analytical psychology struck upon the phenomenon of the "self." Here the "self" is not a theoretical construct, as in some present-day psychologies, rationally conceived and reasoned out. On the contrary, it is an entity of highly irrational character, which when activated is found already delineated and symbolically represented in the unconscious; it is then recognizable in all the various kinds of unconscious products, including psychotic delusions such as those presented here. It has been discovered entirely by the empirical methods of observation and classification just discussed, as is true of any of Jung's

---

[1] For notes to chapter 1, see p 161

concepts of unconscious contents. They are in this respect quite different
from those of psychoanalysis, whose "censor" and "superego" are perfectly
justifiable theoretical designations of categories of events observed during
the course of an analysis but are not seen portrayed as such in the psyche's
own symbolic self-representation; when we look here for them, we encounter complexities that no longer permit the rationally satisfying sim-
plicity of the theoretical constructs. These empirical concepts, on the other
hand, are based on the realization that psychic entities depict themselves in
the unconscious imagery. The beauty of these symbolized entities is that
they are not just thought up but are experienced, and are not built up as
ideas but seem to have a life of their own as organs of the mind.

Symbols in the form of the squared or four-pointed circle can be said
now, after some decades of experience with them, to represent the self as the
totality of the psyche, embracing both conscious and unconscious components and therefore superordinate to the ego; they depict a nuclear structure in the unconscious, acting as a directing center to the processes of the
psyche as a whole in its progress toward self-realization. (More extensive
definitions are given in Part I, chapter 8.) This is the hypothesis built upon
observations of the work of the symbols, but the symbols themselves reveal
actually existing entities with nothing hypothetical about them but rather
substantially experiential. Equally matters of fact are the experiences of
countless generations with these same symbols, which have in many ages
and in many places led men to draw conclusions about their meaning, for
the symbol is accompanied by its effect upon the conscious mind. The bulk
of the comparative material presenting man's experience of the self, however, is of a religious or esoteric nature, since the feelings associated with
this image are marked by a distinctive aura of awe, of respect for an unknown influence that can be deeply moving, powerful, or frankly overwhelming. Is it, then, to be said that this concept of the self is only mystical
speculation and not fit for science? That would be like declaring that
anthropologists are of primitive mentality. If the image of the self happens
habitually to impress human beings in a particular way, that is not the
doing of the scientist studying them, but it does oblige him to make careful
investigation of why and how this interesting circumstance comes about.

In the present discussion I shall start with only a few essential assumptions, to let the material speak for itself as much as possible, yet at the same
time to render it meaningful to the reader who is not acquainted with its
nature. These assumptions concern the nature of the symbol, which is
fundamental to any kind of grasp of the contents of the psychosis presented
here. The first of these assumptions is that the symbol is meaningful.[2] If we
insist on adhering to the notion that these images are only façades and dis-
guises for the supposedly real (infantile) intention behind them, then we
are halted in our tracks as soon as we embark upon any investigation of

them. If we are to study symbols and symbolic processes objectively, then it
is clearly more profitable to begin with the supposition that they represent
something and not that they are deceptive substitutions for other wishful
presentations of a quite different nature reached only via the theory. This
is only to say that we need to approach the material with a modicum of
naiveté, taking a certain kind of image as being what it is intended to be
and as suggesting the meaning that it is intended to suggest. Another assumption derives from the fact that symbols of the unconscious appearing
at other times and places equally have this quality of meaningfulness;
therefore the comparative study of them can be of help in achieving an
increased sense of their import. Finally, akin to both of these is a third
assumption—that as the image represents an entity of the psyche, so the flow
of images through a process represents a process of the psyche. We have only
to take note of the emotions that accompany these fantasies to realize that
they are highly dynamic and are concerned with the energics of the libido,
its flows and differentiations and transformations. The generally prevalent
symbolic images taken in this sense will be referred to as archetypes.[8]

In this way I shall present the material itself as factually as may be con-
sonant with intelligibility, by summarizing the fantasy formations and com-
menting on them briefly, so as to bring into relief their essential features and
developments. In so doing I hope to convey a direct sense of the reality of
the symbolic process apart from any prejudices arising out of psychological
theory. From these actual events, then, certain general conclusions will,
in chapter 6, be drawn concerning the nature of such a process. The extensive array of parallels arising out of the comparative symbolism will thereupon be summarized as further empirical material. Only at this juncture
will the hypotheses of analytical psychology be called upon, in chapter 8,
to account for these events and conclusions and parallels. With this theoretic
armamentarium the material will, in chapter 9, be attacked anew to wrest
from it some understanding of its meaning, by analytical interpretation.
Part II consists of a compilation of data and comments to expand and
elaborate some of the observations on symbols briefly mentioned in Part I.
For some more practically oriented readers it may hold less appeal, whereas
for others interested in this kind of study it may prove the half that offers
most information. For this reason the material is separated into two parts,
so as not to overburden the development of either the clinical or the sym-
bolical discussion with the content of the other.

By this general plan of procedure I hope to clarify and maintain the distinction between the facts and the theory, between emotional events in the
patient's experience and interpretive ideas in the therapist's experience. A
science needs more to cleave anew to the objects of observation than to
cling overlong to its evanescent hypotheses.

2 THE CASE HISTORY

The material from a case of catatonic schizophrenia with paranoid trends here presented shows strikingly how spontaneous and true to form the universal symbols emerging from the unconscious can be. It is only natural to suspect of most of the material from ordinary analytical experience that it may have been influenced by the preconceptions and guidance of the analyst, even though in reality this influence is not the determining factor in symbol formation. Here in this case there was no analysis, and the symbols of the self came straight out of the patient's delusional fabrications, with no influence whatsoever from the therapist's part or from any previous knowledge of such symbols or their meaning on the patient's part, and they speak their own meaning from their own context with unmistakable implications. The drawings and the formulations of intuitions are crude and simple, but for this very reason they are the more convincing.

The following is a condensation of the history from the hospital records. (A more detailed account of the case history is given in the Appendix.)

The patient was a twenty-seven-year-old married white housewife whose hospital stay lasted seven and a half months. She was admitted in the spring with a chief complaint of depression and periods of agitation of two and a half months' duration and fears of being poisoned.

The family history was essentially noncontributory, except that the maternal grandmother, mother, and patient all had similar traits of willfulness and superficiality of standards as well as an interest in Christian Science. Early personal

9

history described left-handedness corrected to right-handedness and occasional stuttering. Little or no relevant information was obtained concerning her infancy. She was shy and seclusive at puberty, but later made friends well. She did well at school and at jobs. The patient was the partner to urge the marriage, three years before admission to the hospital. She had a baby a year before admission, whom she raised efficiently if a little too unfeelingly. The medical history mentioned "nervous stomach" and a tendency to asthma. In personality, she was of bland, outgoing disposition superficially, liking friends and good times; on occasion she had periods of moody worry and "nervous stomach."

Half a year before admission she became engrossed in Christian Science. The onset of symptoms followed a laryngitis, which she first tried to remedy by Christian Science. This method failed, and as a result she had feelings of guilt. She became depressed and agitated and sleepless. She first suspected her mother of poisoning her baby's food, then accused others in the family. She became self-accusatory, convinced that she had had illicit sexual relations. She was admitted to another hospital several times for electric shock treatments, which had only temporary effects.

On admission, physical examination was essentially negative. Mental status revealed characteristic signs of catatonic schizophrenia· posturing, negativism, muteness. She was disheveled, confused, preoccupied with sexual matters, and she complained of significant odors, fears of being poisoned, and being watched and talked about.

Treatment consisted of ambulatory insulin TID, which had a good effect within the first two weeks.

1st episode

3 THE INITIAL DELUSIONS

guiding?

critique

The patient's delusions are best summarized in paraphrase rather than quoted directly in full, for the sake of the tempo of the discussion; since there was an evolution in the later fantasies, they are presented period by period. Considerable coaxing and encouraging were necessary to get the patient to carry the thread of her thought at first, which otherwise tended to skip and wander from point to point in fragmental fashion.

2nd week. Condition dazed, confused, withdrawn, thought fragmental.

She is being poisoned, watched, talked about, and spied upon. There is another half of her here, in the form of another woman by the same name (actually nonexistent). She worries about her father's sexuality, suspecting he is homosexual.

3rd week. Condition improving, more cheerful, lucid and coherent, but still bewildered by her ideas.

She is being framed for a murder, and this is punishment for her bad life. She heard eight shots. She has died and is resurrected, and she and the others here live in the afterlife, which is in the world, death is only a planting, and you cannot be killed, but come back the same. The smells are the reincarnation. She has extraordinary powers, being responsible for everything that happens and controlling all deaths, the sun and moon, and the weather. So she must be punished. There is to be a great election, her father running for an office; there are two sides, the mother's and the father's, which are connected with the sun and moon, and the world is divided into opposite camps, waiting for her to vote. She is on the fence, at the center; all the world has come to see her, and she hides from them. She holds it all up, also the circle of traffic is tied up for the same reason. Her father wanted her to come on a Pacific cruise, being also in Dutch, but she blocked that too. She is Churchill's daughter; also she is a hermaphrodite, like her father. She is accused of having an illegitimate baby, from the injection needles; she imagined a Negro was the father, and that her other, dark half was foisting the child onto her. She has many dark halves around here. She has a million ideas, and is at the center of all of them; this is like her being such a self-centered child.

These delusions are a most graphic and revealing account of the structure and mechanism of this patient's psychosis, as later discussion will show. In cases of this sort, however, it is of distinct advantage to both the therapist and the patient to have recourse to the method of intuitive drawing to clarify what is happening: to the therapist, so that he can get a more clear representation of what is being apprehended in these fleeting images; and to the patient, so that she can get a sense of objectification of the inner contents from which she must detach herself. Since it was important to know what symbolic form her feelings of being "at the center" would assume in visual representation, the therapist considered this a good place to begin to get at the heart of things as directly as possible.

Drawing 1, produced on the 21st day, was begun when the therapist asked: "Could you just show here your feeling of being at the center with the whole world around you, waiting?" At first she was somewhat nonplused, but she embarked upon her undertaking directly without apparent over-all plan, merely representing herself first and letting the rest grow as it seemed to want to. A second therapist recorded what she said as she drew. During the process her manner was instructive. At first she was hesitant and vague, but as the pattern grew and she got into the fantasy she became quite enthralled, jumping ahead to each new step with an excited enthusiasm and with the air of making great effort to solve a problem of representation of a most important idea. At the end she seemed very pleased with her work, but was slightly dissatisfied in not having resolved a certain contradiction in its form. She afterward referred to the design as "a picture of my ideas and feelings." It should be stressed that in no way was any suggestion made by the therapist as to what form to give the images, though he did frequently encourage the patient to keep at her task, since concentration tended to dissipate into chatter.

Drawing I (21st day). Condition improved, but withdrawn and moody; by now she disbelieves many of her delusions.

She used to think that there were two sides, her father's and mother's, with the sun and moon connected somehow, and that she controlled everything. She says, "I guess I love me. I am in the center and people are all around me. I am in a circle," this being a sunny and sun color. She is two personalities, the red and black for her gay and her quiet side. The people "who stick up for me" are in the next ring, father and husband in green, mother in orange, being nice colors. The next circles depict her progress from ward to ward, and as she draws she rehearses the delusions she had at each, thus reviewing the whole psychotic episode. The first, in yellow, is her sunny mood in the good ward, on arrival. The next is when she was getting upset, in purple, in OT and the intermediate ward where she had her disturbing fears. The third ring, in brown, is the disturbed ward, where she was most at odds with people. These colors thus get progressively "gloomier." Then comes a ring of six petals in different colors, depicting her "wild" and "mixed-up ideas." The outer ring shows the father's and mother's world, on either side of the fence, father's in red, the mother's in the gloomier blue and purple. The green square is the hospital grounds. Bands of policemen are shown by 16 black marks in the brown circle, and four detectives in four black marks on the petals, placed apparently by her father to help her out. She uses every color in the box for the traffic that tries to circle around and which she ties up. There are two gates, at the upper corners. She is uncertain how to make the traffic go, feeling it should go around, and break up, and also go up to her at the center, so she feels dissatisfied at the end. She concludes, "I tie up the whole world because I am ruling them. Everyone lives in Utopia."

Only the main outlines of the delusions will be discussed in this section, merely enough to bring into relief the chief thread of the developmental evolution at work in the psychotic process. In a later section a more thorough treatment of the principal symbolic themes will be undertaken.

If some reality can be conceded to the symbolic images, so that they can be taken as representations of entities of the unconscious psyche, then it can be said that the patient had identified with an image that was clearly of a different order than her ego. She felt that she was responsible for everything that happened—for all deaths, and for control of the sun and the moon and the rain; she was, quite simply, a deity. Also she was at the center, which seems to be the position of this cosmic omnipotence and of balance of opposing forces. To keep to the material and to avoid putting hypothesis first, this center will be referred to temporarily as "central archetype."

The delusions revealed the domains upon which the patient's ego-consciousness was trespassing. She said that she had already died and was resurrected and living in the afterlife, which is to say that the ego had died to the world of reality and found itself in the "other world," the "beyond," the "land of spirits," the inner world of the unconscious where the "immortals" have their being (see Part II, § 32). Expressed another way, that other world like an odorous vapor invaded the life of the here and now, which then became an intermingling of the world of time and the world of eternity or of conscious and unconscious. In it she identified with its most powerful element, the central archetype. She was tortured by fears that she was being poisoned, "framed," and punished for her all-powerful, central position of responsibility. The problem of the psychosis here, as is usually the case, seemed thus to be the mistaken embroilment of the ego in these powerful machinations of the unconscious images in their cycles of death and rebirth.

Encroaching upon the realm of the archetype also here involved a painful embracing of the opposites. She was distressed by the awareness of "the yes and the no" in her, the light and the dark, gaiety and quietness, life and death, and feminine and masculine. Since it is the ego's task to cope with its world rationally, it cannot take upon itself too much the function of sustaining paradoxes and the burden of tension issuing from them, as the irrational symbol is designed to do. Such tension was vividly portrayed in the patient's feeling that the whole world was divided into opposite camps, surrounding her at the center as the point of union, watching and waiting— waiting for her to make her choice. To contemplate this predicament with genuine empathy is to catch a sense of the most unbearable hell of tense balance; one move from her and the whole world would be set in motion again as if by an atomic fission. This intolerable situation established one of the problems for the symbolic process to work through.

That the two halves of the world should be perceived as the father's and the mother's might at first seem grotesque, but the idea is based upon another collective representation like the others. That the world or even the cosmos is thus divided into opposite principles ruled by a male and female being—or sun and moon—is a notion as old and universal as mythology itself. In these fantasies of the patient, the parents were subjected to the same disproportion as the ego in being elevated to rulership over the opposites throughout the world, akin to sun and moon. The contents of the personal and impersonal constituents of the psyche were deeply confused, and from this confusion came the impression of grotesqueness. This is the infantile view of the world, in which all meaning is still embodied in the actual parents and all potential conflict is withheld in the inert paradise of family-bound unconsciousness.

Drawing I, then, is a depiction of the patient's state of identification with the image of the deity—the central archetype. In this design we recognize without question the pattern of the squared circle defining the center, the symbol alluded to in the introduction. How closely the characteristics of the symbol here parallel those of its traditional forms elsewhere will be discussed more fully in a later section, after the patient's full series has been presented (see Part I, chap. 7).

The problem was thus stated symbolically in delusion and in plastic image. This was the point at which it must be asked, From where does the healing process come? From the therapist? From the patient's conscious will and understanding? From the regimen on which she is placed? It will shortly be seen that the therapist proceeded on the hypothesis that it came from none of these, but that it was initiated in the psyche itself by the spontaneous effort of the unconscious to strive toward wholeness and one-ness. Thus it became evident, as is usually true of catatonic schizophrenia, that the disorder is a natural process working in its own strange way toward a goal of greater consciousness, even though it may end in disaster more often than in success if it is left unaided. In the life of the body, after all, man is well accustomed to the failures of the "vis mediatrix naturae."

critique - good

4 THE DEVELOPMENT OF THE PROBLEM

In the ensuing account of the interviews with the patient not much emphasis will be given to the role of the therapist, since the principal focus of attention is the spontaneous emergence of the central archetype and not therapeutic technique. Justice would not be done to the material, however, by leaving aside the question of how much the therapist's activity might have produced effects upon the unfolding of the unconscious productions. Of subliminal influences, of course, there may have been any number; but of manifest ones, certainly few. The therapist said little to the patient, because, like so many catatonic schizophrenics, she was too autistic to give much heed to his comments. Also for scientific reasons he wished to avoid disturbing the material by interpretations. While the patient talked, the therapist usually made only brief remarks, which were intended to assure her that what she brought forward was both acceptable and meaningful and that it would be honored as her vital emotional experience. Many of his responses were merely interjections of encouragement for her to pursue her gropings in the dark reaches of her fantasies and associations. Somewhat more explicit on his part was his verbalizing back to the patient the affective meaning she herself gave to her imagery, so as to stress its importance and help her feel it.

As so often happens, the patient developed a strongly toned transference as soon as she realized that the therapist was giving acceptance and recog-

16

nition to her disturbed preoccupations. She tended to feel guilty about this love, but he encouraged her to honor her feelings and recognize in them the important psychic content that lay hidden in them—namely, her own potential of development appearing from day to day in archetypal form.

During the following week the patient's fantasies were carried a step further, as follows:

4th week. Condition cheerful, lucid, coherent, habits neat.

The voices and odors still persist, and she remains preoccupied with the ideas that have been besieging her, but is less uncomfortable with them. About the poisoning she is more definite than before, saying it started with the conviction that her mother was poisoning the baby's milk. She relates previous fantasies that she was an illegitimate child herself, the mother on the loose because of the father's hermaphroditism; also that she was hermaphroditic because that was what the former ward was for, and that she was sent as a man to the "men's gym." She feels again a 17- or 18-year old attitude, wanting dates and romance, but also reacting with guilt because she is so straightlaced; these are her two sides again. She is being turned into a man, but also having illegitimate babies, one by a former doctor, also through needles.

She draws a diagram of her ideas of death and rebirth, as cyclic phases of gloomy dark and gay bright colors [not reproduced for discussion]. The body died and they celebrated her funeral, but she always came back since she could not be killed. Her soul will always live. The grave is black but the afterlife is yellow.

She expresses feelings of love for the therapist, finding "something spiritual" about him, as if he were "a saint or something."

She had a dream (on the 23rd day) that the two friends she grew up with were in the ward dining room with her sitting around a table together; the maternal uncle was about to die of cancer of the throat, and his mother was there, too.

The therapist suspected the possibility that there might be a pattern of interest in the image of the table with the three friends, so he again asked the patient to try to show on paper her feelings about this group. This led to Drawing II, in which the problem of a fourth component of the squared circle presented itself.

Drawing II (24th day).

She makes five attempts before she achieves what she wants in the sixth. It concerns the three friends, herself (A) as the effervescent kind, the second (B) as more calculating, the third (C) as blunt; the latter wants to take the second away from the patient, thus a rival. She starts with herself "at the center of attraction again." She puts herself in a cheerful color, yellow, the color of the sun, "which is important"; also she has a second color, green (in parallel), making a plant leaf. Her rival (C) is another leaf in blue, on the left, and her friend (B) in orange on the right; the rival (C) tries to draw the latter (B) away to her side, thus she (B) is reduplicated, making four leaves in all. They are enclosed in a circle, the world they grew up in together. She experiments with colors, dissatisfied. Finally, in the sixth attempt, each has her two sides: the patient is in yellow and green; her friend (B) is in orange and purple-brown, and her rival (C) is in blue and purple. The world is drawn in grey. Since some people think of the world as square and some as round, she adds square corners as the future life, in contrasting pairs of light and dark colors, as the light and dark sides of the afterlife. Then the sun and moon as again the lighter and darker side, and as up and down, the sun an orange triangle, the moon, a yellow crescent, the former making a blossom, the latter a base.

It might at first seem far-fetched that such a drawing should follow out the theme presented in the dream, but it should be remembered that the dream concerned three friends at a round table with four places, one of the friends (B) dividing her loyalties and thus occupying two places. It was a first approach to the realization of a fourth element, by the clumsy device of reduplicating one friend (B) to make her fill out the third and the fourth places, thus continuing the synthesis of the central archetype. The interview illustrated the patient's sense of the importance of getting four elements into the structure and of attributing the right colors to them. (This is brought out in the transcript of the interview in the Appendix.) The design has several layers of meaning: the personal associations, of the three friends of the patient's earlier life; the plastic form, of a four-leaved plant with a crescentic base and triangular flower; and a more mythical foundation, of cosmic features—a sun being born like a budding blossom out of a matrix of four double (that is, eight) elements arising from a moon contained in a circle of the material world, which again is held in the square of the spiritual world. Once more the figures of her personal world are merged in confusion with those of the archetypal one.

The main thread of the delusional theme is still being carried, which consists of what occupies the center, of this life and the afterlife, and of being planted in death and growing in new life. Again the squared circle is used as the vehicle for working out the problem. This time it fairly teems with polar opposites, but the nightmarish quality has gone. There is an impression of tenderness and beauty in the design and of the quiet, sure growth of a flowering plant. It is true that the first drawing was also a blossom, with its six petals, but here in place of hospital wards the setting is the adolescent world, and instead of mixed-up ideas and police there are rival friendships. Most important, though, is the fact that the inflated and split ego at the center has been replaced by a new factor, the triangular sun arising as a newborn blossom out of the living structure of her early relationships. At the start of her work on this drawing, she commented that she would be at the center again, since she was the center of attraction always; yet while she was drawing, the unconscious made another statement that countermanded her former prejudice, putting her off to one side and making the sun the center of attention. Hence the burden of the world-wide division into opposites no longer lay upon the patient to sustain and to decide, but was now represented in the impersonal sphere of this world-other world, light-dark, sun-moon, perhaps day-night by implication, above-below, and leaf-leaf in a state of tension between right and left. The patient's clinical status was much improved at this time as well, so the change in the feeling tone and content of the design is indicative of this factor with fair accuracy.

Since it was difficult to obtain the patient's associations with the colors and the friends, it is impossible to render a complete account of them. A few observations might, however, be significant here. She started with the remark that "yellow is cheerful and is the color of the sun," which is "important," and proceeded thereupon to identify it with herself; this was when she intended to show herself as the center of attraction. In the end, however, it became the color of the moon and of her own lighter side. In our culture the moon traditionally symbolizes the feminine principle, and the sun the masculine;[1] the patient's feeling that the sun and moon were connected with the father's and mother's sides of the world confirmed this symbolism. In its position at the root the "earth" aspect of this feminine symbol is also designated, out of which the plant structure grows and culminates in its gold sun blossom, suggesting the "spirit" aspect of this masculine symbol sublimated out of its feminine opposite as "matter," thus attaining the polarity of blossom-soil as sun-moon and spirit-earth. She was very unsure of her identity, however, and of the difference between the connotations of these opposites in respect to color, that is, to feeling tone. The color red is, as she herself noted, conspicuously lacking, but on the other hand it makes its appearance furtively as a component in the brown and purple of the friend B's dark side. It seems certain that blue is a color that, since she attributed it to her rival, she sensed as contrary to her own nature, which was red in Drawing I in her state of identification with the center.

In her delusions the appearance of the new illegitimate baby of her dark half and by a Negro man was an integral part of the psychotic process in this phase. When the theme of the new birth is encountered in dream and fantasy, we are usually able to find in the patient's general psychic context at the time the manifestation of some new form the libido is taking, giving a new dynamic relation to the central archetype.

The atmosphere of something strange and forbidding was conveyed by the patient's comments while doing the next drawings (III and IV) on the topic of the cancer in the dream.

[1] For notes to chapter 4, see p 161.

Drawing III (26th day). Condition the same as above, but there is a sense of greater apprehensiveness.

She begins by associating the cancer with the uterus and the illegitimate baby. She draws an outer square as the disturbed ward, and a dark blue circle in it as the baby, dark because illegitimate, large because "a major thought." Concentrically within it is a black circular center as the cancer, "a horrible thought." The whole would be on a black background, so nothing would stand out, all only unpleasantness and gloom. The uncle is a seclusive, depressive man.

Drawing IV (26th day, same interview).

She suddenly becomes fascinated with an image in her mind, of blackness with moving "white thoughts." She draws a square field, and in it fragmental white lines like rivers flowing, terminating rivers. She becomes engrossed and somewhat dazed as she draws, and does not finish it.

We might ask: Why should the cancer be associated with the baby? Was this just a stray notion in a confused mind? In dream symbolism a tumor often represents the negative aspect of a new potential like this. The sense of it is not far-fetched, for the essential characteristic of the cancer is its very primitive, undifferentiated, and rapid growth that makes the whole organism suffer. The new baby has these same properties together with the same connotation of evil and undesirability. The cancer appears as a kind of black chaos in the dying depressive masculine image (the uncle), and in the newborn one (the baby). The depressive quality of the whole group of symbols is indicated by the general darkness of all its story and portrayal, its chaotic character and amorphousness, and also the fragmenting effect (the rivers) so characteristic of the schizophrenic process. This revealed an important disturbing complex in the patient's disorder, which tended to pull her libido away from consciousness even as she talked about it, and which was operative at the time in initiating a new downward—that is, depressive and confused—phase in her clinical condition.

At this point a play of coincidence gave the patient occasion to reconsider her misconceptions; Easter came on the twenty-seventh day of her hospitalization, and she heard a sermon in the chapel on the subject of resurrection. This struck home, and she became deeply engrossed in ruminations on the meaning of death and resurrection in general, particularly Christ's. Concurrently with this came a marked improvement in her insight.

Drawing V (28th day). Condition· She has her "nervous stomach" again, which absorbs a lot of her attention. She hears no more voices, and suffers no more anxieties, but is tense.

She believes there is death only of the body, not the mind. She wants someone to explain religion. Christ could be any one of us, being like the power within us. She rehearses her former ideas of god-like power, and thinks she had these because she was always the center of attraction at home. She needs more interests and self-expression to put her imagination to use. She observes that in the drawings she is getting outside her circle. She agrees with the therapist that Christ is a symbolic being in our minds. Only the mind is real, not the body, and Christ is in all of us, he was in the tomb and has risen, and that happens to all of us. We can all be Christs.

She draws the pews and altar in the chapel where she was meditating over this. At the right she depicts her fantasies about the death and resurrection of Christ, beginning with a tomb. "I thought it could be any one of us; it needn't be Christ's life ... I think we could all be killed and planted in a tomb." We celebrate Christ's life because it is an ideal one which we imitate. There is no heaven, but we come back and "face it" here again, always enclosed in this life. She draws Christ come back, as a double triangle in red and black halves. Since he went through suffering, he is like us and is one of us; he is both cheerful and bad.

She realizes now that she is not at the center and laughs at the idea. No one person can see the whole world; that is why there are so many people.

Drawing VI (same interview).

She begins a second drawing in red, to represent Christ at the center and all the many people in the world. She realizes now that the traffic in Drawing I was trying to show the world full of people. They have good and bad sides. The ones who "give more" are to be bigger and redder, the nearer they are to Christ. He is the example, the symbol in us all, and his life is the model. He is at the center, "not me."

This touched, then, the central problem of the first delusions and attempt at the squared circle—her identification with the deity. Now, quite spontaneously and with the help of the accidents of the church calendar, she was grasping the relation of herself to the image of the divine being, that is, of her ego to the central archetype. It is very revealing that she should represent the resurrected Christ in the same colors—red and black—as those at the center of the world in Drawing I, which were then herself in her resurrected state. This is a further confirmation of the assumption made earlier that in identifying with the position of the center she was identifying with the image of the deity; she was most psychotic at that position, and least when disidentified from it.

Her reflections about the Christ image constitute a most significant insight on the part of a person coming from a background of relatively simple thought structure, a perception she would scarcely have pronounced with such conviction if she had not been entangled with a much overactivated unconscious. The concept that "we can all be Christs" has been a problem to Western minds before—that not only can man have in his own soul the experience of the deity but that he is then the embodiment of the deity, the soul that the deity needs in order to be born again into the world.[2] It is not in the scope of this book to go into these questions of religious psychology, except to point out that the patient is here struggling with the immense predicament in which any human finds himself when experiencing the depths of the psyche and the archetype of the deity in his birth, death, and resurrection. The tendency of naive minds under these conditions is to identify with this archetype and to suffer the inevitable inflation. Only with greater consciousness does an individual realize that this powerful factor is wholly other than ego, one to which he should be related and in tune without being engulfed by it. It can be said at this juncture that the patient's problem was basically a religious one, in the stricter sense that it concerned her relation to the real and potent but unseen powers in the psyche,[3] this being meant in the psychological and not the metaphysical sense.

By the gradations of the color red the patient intended to express the degrees of participation in this experience of Christ and Christian love by the various individuals in the world. She intended at first to differentiate the light and dark aspects of people, but in the final outcome the drawing gives the impression only of a bald straightforward statement, with no subtleties or complications, or even any oppositions of principles or colors. When the patient later gave her associations to the color red she named fire and emotion, and the redness in her drawing conveys this feeling of warmth, even heat. Fire is a symbolic image traditionally used to express the experience of that central archetype which Christ represented and with which the patient is now coming to terms.[4]

This is a great step for the patient to have made, to realize that the divinity is something other than herself, though in herself, and far greater than she, that she is only one among the many mortals in the world, and that her position in the great circle of the world is not central but off to one side. This was the beginning of a proper relation of ego to unconscious; but, as in most psychic experience, the progress was phasic, with cycles of progression and regression, of synthesis and dissolution, and during the next week her condition became worse. She had still to cope with the whole complex represented in the baby, the cancer, and the black square with the fragmented white thoughts; that factor was all black as this one is all red—the black as all-depressing and threatening as the red is all-inspiring and enlivening, and the two need to be brought into a working relation. She was given some brief instruction on how to regard the symbol as inner and not outer reality.

The interview of the following day found the patient plunged in the emotions of much more personal problems in contradistinction to those of the inner life.

? is she on medication?

Drawing VII (29th day). Condition apprehensive, anxious, serious, the delusional fears returning.

She has been crying, feeling again her guilt and fears of being framed; she
blames insulin for the myriad ideas and depression. She wants no more drawing,
but rather to solve her own problems. She has told her mother she wants to be
independent of her apron-strings and does not think her mother would let her
be, or her child or husband be. She rails with animation against her mother and
her false, superficial standards.

She rehearses the history of her relation to her parents, illustrating it in a series
of six diagrams; as a child she is a red circle with her problems as a black margin,
under the influence of two circles above, the parents. In the fourth (d) as a young
woman, she is a red circle surrounded by her many friends in all the colors in the
box, in streaming rays (which create the appearance of rotation, crudely). A
black outer circle suggests the war. She is independent of her parents' help in
her work that year. The fifth (e) puts the war at the "center of attraction," the
whole world being interested in it; then an orange ring for her sunny mood, a
purple one for the happy time she was having that year with her friends at the
shop, and an outer red one for her marriage which was happy and gay. She feels
the war, and not she, should be at the center, "because I'm a very small bit," but
the family is still centered around her.

In two final little diagrammatic gestures she shows her father, mother, and
herself as contiguous blocks of color, and with angry emphasis removes herself
from her mother by interposing the father and putting herself off at a distance.

It is scarcely necessary to comment on the importance of this rehearsal
of her life, for she made very clear all her resentment over not having been
granted her early freedom from bondage to the parents' overbearing love
and not having been given her chance to grow up. Characteristically, she
blamed the mother for her own infantile backward lagging, but at least she
squarely faced its existence as her problem. She worked out a solution in
the diagrams that is certainly effectual, for the emotions represented here
are vivid and are the factors actually undergoing the shifts indicated in the
colors. It should be noted that she realized the mistake of feeling herself to
be at the center and that she put there what was probably the first thing
that made her really aware of the smallness of her own little self-centered
world—the war. The upheaval of the war at the center is a theme that grows
in importance in the ensuing fantasies. Also important is the fact that her
means of winning freedom from the mother is to put the father in the position of separating agent; this has a special psychological significance that
will be discussed later.

During the fifth week the patient gradually suffered a return of her
former delusions.

Sixth week (early). Condition depressed, agitated, apprehensive, withdrawn,
preoccupied.

She is at the center again, everyone being interested in her and watching her and whispering about her. She is the cause of all that happens, and is hurting people and messing things up. They are accusing her, framing her, and poisoning her and her baby. She has body odors. They are giving her pills to change her into a man, and X-raying the results. She is in love with the therapist, but doubts he is a psychiatrist because she saw his picture in a magazine as an army officer. She demands interpretations, and minimal ones are given on the subject of how to take her fantasies symbolically, as inner and not outer realities. It is the mother who poisoned the baby. She is breaking up her home by falling in love with the therapist, "every inch a gentleman."

She had regressed again to the state of identification with the central archetype, with the associated feelings of guilt and responsibility for all that goes wrong. This time more was learned about the effect of the poisoning, that it had to do with her changing into a man, which would then result in a possibly hermaphroditic condition. It is therefore justifiable for us to assume that to be changed into the central archetype was equivalent to her becoming masculine, a conclusion already indicated in her ideas about the Christ figure's occupying the central position. Yet there is something hermaphroditic about this archetype also. The later discussions of the central archetype will go further into this question. This aspect is discussed in Part II, § 6, but for now it is sufficient to say that being poisoned meant again the ego's becoming unconscious and identifying with the masculine and central archetype, the medicine being the agent bringing about this dissolution of the conscious structure.

Later in the sixth week she produced an interesting image, on the day following the patients' dance.

Drawing VIII (36th day). Condition as above.

She draws her impression of her feelings at the patients' dance. She feels self-conscious with no one paying attention to her as they had at home. There is a base in layers of different colors as the crowd in the dance. She designs herself as a tree, above this base, walking in as "half and half again," one part cheerful, in red as the trunk, the other as leaves radiating out in dullish green, her "flairs for different things."

The tree, then, is another way of representing the center—that is, herself at the center in her condition of identity with that position. It has a circular eightfold pattern; half of her is in seven green leaves, and the other half is the red trunk as the eighth element connecting her with the crowd. It is significant that she chose red to play the role of axial bridge between her mind and the crowd mind, for it is the same she used to indicate the center in Drawings I and VI.

Drawing IX (41st day). Condition as above.

She insists that this was done as a "doodle" and can have no other significance than this; she did it the day before in her spare time when in an absent-minded mood, and no thoughts were being represented by it.

Alongside it is a figure with an oval center and rhomboid shape with strands between, strongly suggestive of a cell in mitosis.

Apparently the patient applied herself with some diligence to this drawing and elaborated a rather complex design. Her own estimate of the drawing need not imply its low value so much as her unconsciousness of its import; here is an entirely autonomous product that unfolded itself through her hand without the slightest effort of her mind to make it meaningful.

This drawing grew out of an attempt of the day before to start an image of herself at the center in red (the fact that the Christlike figure seemed to belong there only a short time before had lost its meaning to her); this is the red oval at the corner, penetrating into the enclosure. In the context of the drawing of the cell alongside it, there is here the irresistible impression of germination, of cells with nuclei, and their multiplication into an organismal pattern, thus taking up the thread of the process of the new birth, the baby and the cancer. Those two unwanted growths were earlier depicted as dark and foreboding and depressive; in this new manifestation, when the attention of consciousness is withheld from the theme, it is allowed to appear in its more pleasant aspect. Here the impression is given that the whole structure is encased in a black outer covering that seems to carry some of the old atmosphere of the former depressive connotation, as a shell that outwardly appears sinister yet turns out to contain within it the promising values of newly germinating life. Possibly the penetration of this by the red oval was unconsciously intended as a suggestion of fertilization initiating the growth, and perhaps the new structure was a corrective to her delusion of the day before that she was at the center, pointing out that not ego but this newly emerging life form was really the central element.

At the center are four symmetrical spirals in gold, in two pairs of different shades. Gold had pleased the patient in Drawing II, where it became the color of the central gold sun-blossom symbol in it. Again the central element is gold, fourfold, and sunlike. Around these are placed a ring of twelve spirals, of which four are in gray at the points of juncture of the inner four, and the remaining eight are in green. The emphasis on green is significant, for she later associated it to the growth of nature, and green is the color of the tree growth in the previous drawing. The sunlike quality of the central golden fourfold element is borne out by the twelvefoldedness of its surrounding circle, as will be discussed later.

At the start of the next week, the patient gave voice to many woes.

7th week. Condition superficially more cheerful, but her actual attitude is bitter and her mood depressed.

They are calling her homosexual. The poison is the "hate that destroys." All her life she has liked people, but now she is breaking up people's lives. They make her run the world and depend upon her, but find her weak and pick her to blame things on. She is the cause of the world's troubles, and she is alone against the world because they misunderstand her.

Here is the typical pattern of paranoid delusions—that she was ruler of the world but despised and blamed. But it becomes less and less possible to call the megalomania only a fantasy compensation for the feeling of inferiority and isolation; the inflation was also based clearly on her identification with the ruling center. She was being shamed for her hermaphroditism and homosexuality; when she was responsible for the world's ills she evidently referred to the world strife, which became a theme greatly elaborated in the fantasies immediately following. Thus she was a hermaphroditic world ruler who felt that her whole domain was becoming embroiled in a great destructive conflict, for which she was held responsible. The paranoid mechanism was the identification with the archetype.

It should be noted that the comment about the poison being "the hate that destroys" occurs in the midst of this context and refers to it. This was a most revealing statement. The significance of the poisoning theme is complex and does not permit of interpretation until the whole delusional series has been appraised in the subsequent comments and interpretations.

5 THE RESOLUTION

The opinions just described constituted a low point in the patient's feeling about herself and her status, and, as is usually true with such extremes, a turning point. A new theme was initiated now, meaning that the libido was activating a new area and appearing in a new symbol.

Drawing X (45th day). Condition still apprehensive and fearful but less depressed; she speaks with zest.

Her husband is a Red, a Communist; also perhaps the therapist is. She has ruled the world hitherto, and this is a revolt on the part of the lower classes who want to become popular and know the other classes. This explains her hunch that something has been going on around here, the patients and nurses are in on it. Also this is the meaning of the election; her mother is against the revolt and her husband for it.

She draws the two rival parties for the presidential election, in bright colors for their optimism; the Republicans are the upper class, the Democrats, the lower, fighting for world power. The Communists are a third party in green, for envy, off to one side, who want to come in and level it all out by taking the whole thing over, destroying both the parties. She is fascinated by this problem, and doubts that she can solve it. It is her two halves again, the two sides of a person; the parties are inside the mind. They have to compromise; no one party can take it all over.

From this it was clear that the present movement in the psyche came from its "inferior" parts, from "below"—a revolt by its "lower classes," so to speak; it was to be experienced in political symbols—in fact, in political projections. It was highly interesting that the patient was here in good enough condition to get a glimmer of insight into the fact that these were really projections of things going on in the mind, partly because the therapist tried to get her to look at her delusions as inner truths, and partly because drawing them on paper in these patterns allowed her to see that more than just world politics was involved. It was only fitting that politics should be the form of symbolization here, since she had had the notion of being placed in the position of rulership over the world when at its center; hence for her to get out of the identification with this role of the center and "off to one side" required a revolt by another aspect of her psyche to dethrone her and establish a new, balanced order.

This revolt came from the man—her husband—who may be assumed to be the carrier of an unconscious image for her. Thus her former obscure feelings and suspicions, that "there's something going on around here," had to do with a dim awareness of this movement of the unconscious to displace her ego from this pathological situation. The therapist also was implicated, which means that his influence was on the side of the unconscious movement from below; he too was considered of the upper class, hence the content of the transference embraced the opposites. The mother, on the contrary, stood for reactionism, no change, and thus perpetual unconsciousness.

Another interesting feature was the sense of deadlock between the two older parties, which she equated to the opposite sides of a person's nature. This could be broken only by the intervention of the third party, which thus played the role of a reconciling symbol.[1] She was right that "no party can take it all over," that is, that there would still be the tension of opposites but they would be superordinated and embraced by a third, more ample structure. This is green, which strives to possess; it is also the same color as the germinating fourfold and twelvefold design of Drawing IX, which seemed to have the connotation of the new life with its depressive, threatening exterior.

The next two days gave some illuminating personal context to the new movement in the fantasies.

46th and 47th days. Condition greatly improved, free of depression and fear.

She realizes she has not grown up yet, still under her mother's influence; she sees herself as gabbing and superficial, but knows there is more to her and wants to know herself at last. Since she pushed this aside before, it means a turmoil now. She likes the world again now.

Her former ideas now seem ridiculous, and she is not sure what is real and what is not. She now understands about not taking the symbols concretely. She

union of opposites

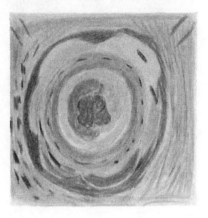

Drawing I

Drawing II

cancer

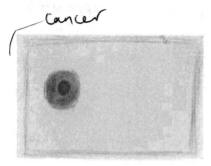

Drawing III   Drawing IV

Drawing V

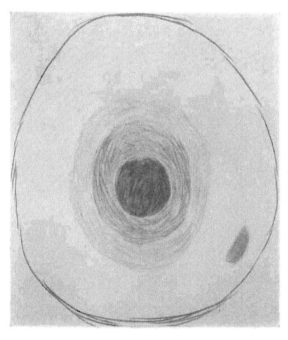

christ
at centre

Drawing VI

war at centre

self at center

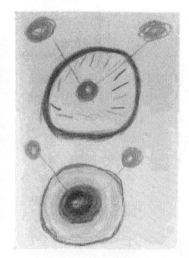

Drawing VII

Drawing VIII

Drawing IX

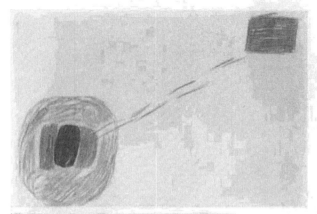

Drawing X

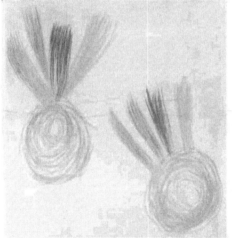

Drawing XI

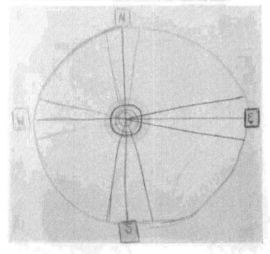

Drawing XII

thinks "the third party was a new life, a new birth," "the masculine and feminine parts of me creating a new baby." She draws these parts as adjacent squares in blue and red, respectively, with a round black spot in the latter as the new birth growing in the feminine part, which is bigger [not reproduced here for discussion].

The patient was thus swiftly regaining consciousness. She realized that it was now up to her to make something of her individuality independently and no longer to be satisfied with the mask of gaiety. The revolt was part of this question, for with the ego too much identified with such a mask and the personality only a collectively determined set of outward appearances, its opposite was becoming constellated and was leading the libido back into an activation of the unconscious, to draw the ego away again from this misleading identification and into an experience of self-realization.[2] If the personality is only a mask, its core is certainly infantile, embedded in the love and care of the parents. Yet just this infantile core is the real individuality that needs to be nourished and developed and differentiated.

The new creation—her individuality—had another attribute, then; it had been illegitimate baby and cancer, and then germination in a squared circle, and now it became the third party as "a new life, a new birth." It was still dark, and still threatening. A few days later (51st day; see below), she called the Republicans the mother's party and the Democrats the father's. This implied that the union of the feminine and the masculine parts of herself in creating the new baby was equivalent to the union of the mother's and father's halves of the world in giving rise to the third party, which was the new life binding up the conflicting halves into a new whole. It will be seen shortly what this new state consists of.

The therapist made it a point in the discussions of this phase to keep speaking in terms of the political symbols, since they were the substance of which the solution was going to be formed, and yet not to let them be taken too concretely, since this would encourage the loss of them again into the unconscious projection of which she was just getting free. It was a narrow path to find but essential to follow. The method was to encourage a way of carrying out the fantasy actively, as in the weaving of a fairy tale, as if it was true and yet knowing it was not. She needed above all to learn to think symbolically, so that she could attain a creative relation to the activated unconscious without being engulfed by it. The idea that the third party was the new life did not come from the therapist but was her own insight; the realization that the parties were segments of her own nature, on the other hand, was in line with the general attitude toward the symbols that was being promoted by the therapist, but she volunteered it here as her own understanding of the situation.

The next two interviews brought forth a group of spontaneous images that led to her long sought solution to the symbolic problem.

Drawing XI (50th day). Condition good, cheerful, friendly, sociable, free of
fears and depression.

She has been feeling fear but also confidence about the new life, and it has
occurred to her that there should be a fourth party, the Socialists. She draws the
four parties as four leaves of different colors emanating upwards from a point at
the edge of a green circle. She does not see how there can possibly be four parts
to the mind, and guesses the therapist must be crazy, too. But she feels this issue
is the crisis which she has always pushed aside and now must face. The four
remain in the world together and always will; each thinks it is right, and to
decide, there will be a great clash, a war, and the new birth will come from this.
But none can win, and they must learn to live together. "This is the hardest
lesson in the world," like a world war.

She draws a new version in which the four are side by side and not converging
in the point at the edge, which was herself; thus they do not clash here. When
asked what the ideal status would be, she said, "It would be where they were all
heading for one goal, all converging somehow."

This design is reminiscent of Drawing II, with its four plant leaves springing out from a common center, and its round world. The special gain in
this new production was that the fourth element was sensed as something
well differentiated from the other three, no longer a mere reduplication of
the third as in that earlier effort. Also there was an advantage in this political form of symbolism in that she was thereby brought into touch with
more universal experience, suggesting more what the collectivity of man
is concerned with and not only what she herself went through in her early
friendships. More scope was thereby given to the mighty, dynamic unconscious components of a collective order than could be satisfactorily expressed in terms of purely personal past events.

She was still at work on the theme of the green world, and she sensed
that the threefold state of affairs left in Drawing X by the reconciling
function of the third party was unsatisfactory; evidently the true nature of
the new birth arising out of the clash of the rival elements must be fourfold.
Only here the question was still unsolved: Where should the point of meeting of the four take place? She felt at first that it must be in the ego, since
naturally she sensed all this conflict in herself; yet she knew that the ego
was not at the center of the world then. She showed it at the edge of the
circle. She had an awareness of tremendous forces in conflict, involving her,
clashing in her, yet somehow going beyond her. So she changed her representation to show that these forces were enduring entities, not eliminating
each other by their strife, since none could be destroyed, but continuing to
live on together in a highly dynamic tension. The ego was thereby dis-
entangled from these superpersonal forces; it was not even given a place
in the second attempt.

Yet the question of where the four do converge, what their point of meeting might be, remained unanswered. This, of course, was the mysterious paradox she had not yet quite fathomed. This was an inner drama and a world drama, the four parties were the four parts of her nature, and there was a crisis at hand, one leading to a new birth—her own—yet somehow it did not all happen in her ego even though it seemed to implicate it immeasurably. It seemed to hint at the possibility of another center that was not her ego, where forces and events of these dimensions are handled. It should be well noted that this was the crisis that she felt she was meant to face all her life—and the most difficult lesson in the world. That is, the solving of this baffling problem would be an event of tremendous importance to her, accomplishing what had waited to be accomplished throughout her life.

In the eighth week she had a dream that threw some light on the theme of the poisoning.

She dreams of the poison, that it is called Thrivo, which is the name of a dog-food, but it is made to rhyme with a word for sexual intercourse.

The patient kept her mind on her problem conscientiously, both on the personal and the symbolic level, and worked out further conclusions by the time of the next interview.

Drawing XII (51st day). Condition the best to date, outgoing, friendly and clear in her thinking.

She says more about her former superficial gay surface, and her present awareness of great depths, like the bottom of the sea. On the therapist's recommendation, she told the other patients about her fears toward them, and they told her they liked her. She needs independence of her mother, and recalls that her husband helped her broaden her interests.

She resumes the problem of the four parties in a new drawing, as the four directions and quarters of the world, thus: Republicans, Mother's upper class, north, North America, orange; Democrats, Father's not caring about class, south, South America, green; the Reds, Husband's lower class and revolutionaries, west, China, grey; Socialists, believing in one level, one class, sociability and the brotherhood of man, a happy medium, east, Europe, red. She puts these in little blocks at the four points, and draws the round world, in which they all point in to the center again. They are joined by a purple cross also. There has to be a center to everything, and that is warmth. The sun gives warmth, but the war does too. They have the revolution first, at the center, so all colors converge here and it gets dark (black). They are all after the upper class to destroy it and level it off, just what she has been through. Then when it is quiet again it gets all warm and the sun shines; then the center is bright and yellow. Yesterday she put herself at the center of convergence, but she sees that was wrong.

In associating to the colors, she says of grey that it is "pessimism, rainy day, cool, nothing cheerful about it," but she likes it. Of red she says, "warmth, fire, blood, turmoil, feelings like love and hate." If it symbolized a psychological function, she says that grey might be thinking, which was never so important as now: she used to go on the assumption that fate managed everything and all was predestined, so that she never planned or thought things through.

When the therapist suggests the sun is like the god at the center where the ego has been, she agrees enthusiastically, that this is like her idea at Easter that Christ is in us all. "All people have a unity inside, the same experience in us all, common to everyone."

There might be some significance in the fact that the general impression given by this design is one of insubstantiality; it is skeletal, an outline without body, as if only a vague intuition of the meaningfulness of the pattern. In unconscious products the therapist likes to see such symbols filled out in full color, as if with conviction and even with devotion, indicating the interest and esteem the patient holds for its meaning. In her conversation she indicated the importance of the image to her, and she was sincere; but in the execution of it she betrayed what was probably her unfamiliarity and uncertainty with regard to its implications.

The therapist tried to keep her attention focused upon the theme by suggesting that another attempt might be helpful; but within a few days she began to lose the vividness of the experience and then began to regress again. (For the later clinical course, see Appendix.) This is apparently one of the regularities of unconscious happenings; it is tidal, and a forward direction of movement toward synthesis of structure is followed quickly by a falling away again of libido into regressive motion and dissolution, evidently to gather up elements left out of the structure hitherto. The phasic swings of the catatonic patients do not seem to be basically different from those of ordinary patients in analysis except for the violence and unconsciousness in the former.

The previous groping during the course of several weeks thus led to a remarkable set of spontaneous intuitions, culminating in the representation of the resolution of the conflict in the image of the sun wheel, one of the most ancient and universal archetypal images known. The patient did not know that the pattern of the circle and cross, with the sun at the center, had any symbolic meaning other than what she herself gave it, and she had never seen it used as a symbol. Although of course its resemblance to the compass is obvious, its evolvement and use are far more subtle.

The patient seized with alacrity on the therapist's few brief words about the deity as the sun-god at the center in pointing out the parallel to her Easter insight, which she had not mentioned during the intervening three weeks. To her this was the image of the "Christ within," the unity in all and common to all. This was her intuition of the meaning of the central archetype, as a being greater than the ego in its power and scope and universality, an impersonal nonego center, common to all, a "new life" of a "spiritual"

order. It is by no means well known today that in art before the seventh
century Christ was represented standing with arms outstretched surrounded
by the sun wheel; the sun wheel was also common to pre-Christian deities,
as further discussed in Part I, chapter 7. Least of all did the patient know
of these once familiar symbols or particularly of their significance in regard
to her own psyche and its turmoil in the struggle for reintegration. Yet only
through them could she bring about her disidentification from deity and
center. She was now able to behold this as a world that she was not controlling divinely but only experiencing as do other mortals, and to feel
this as a battle that she was not causing but only suffering as her inner
conflict, and this as a new order that was greater than herself.

The introduction of the fourth element here as the Socialists was rather
telling All the connotations with this party were healthy and reassuring,
and had to do with brotherhood and sociability and the leveling of class
differences. Relationship on a very human plane seemed to be the keynote
of this theme, which was reinforced by her new experiments in attaining a
rapport with the other patients. The realization of this new capacity came
hand in hand with the need to become independent of her mother, who had
served as a model for her pseudofemininity, the gay mask that had pre-
vented her from vital relationships or self-knowledge before. That mask
was the upper-class rule (the mother's party), whereas the revolt came from
the lower classes (the husband's party), the "grey, dismal" threatening unconscious that set in motion the whole train of events that finally gave the
patient her realization of her own individuality. The mother was the agent
of constriction in the superficial mask that would keep her unconscious;
the husband was the agent of the struggle for self-development, who helped
her broaden her interests. Her former infantility was again brought out by
her comments on her previous habit of expecting all decisions to be made by
fate, that is, leaving them to the unconscious as she had to the parents when
she was a child. Here, however, she sensed a new awareness of individual
responsibility, and no longer accepted the role of daughter or subject under
the rule of an upper class; for all classes could be leveled off, and she took
her place in the companionable society of adult persons.

The way was thus opened up to her to effect in experience a new mature
individuality. This suggests that there had been a transforming process at
work in her attitudes and emotional capacities. The essence of the symbolic
story here had been transformation, which is the chief feature of unconscious process: the four conflicting factions became a unity, tension and war
turned to peace, the black in which all colors are contained turned to gold,
and chaos evolved into order. It had also been implied in the theme of
rebirth running through the whole series of delusions. There was the planting in death followed by resurrection, and the new life was intimated in the
form of baby, cancer, Communist party, and chaoses, here evolving into this

cosmic order centered in the sun—the real rebirth. The infantile way of nestling at the center of the parental world had to be sacrificed, and a new center had to be brought to birth that would establish her own unique autonomy.

6 THE NATURE OF THE MATERIAL

The natural question at this point, after the extensive elaboration of these aberrations, is: What of it—What good has all this done her? We are, however, not entitled to conclude that if these questions cannot be answered satisfactorily the phenomena here are any the less valid. These sorts of experience are the data for scientific study of unconscious process, and our failure to understand the why and wherefore is a reflection of the inadequate nature of our knowledge, not our material. At the end of a long and bizarre process like this a better question to ask would be: What is it all about—What has actually happened? Also at just such a juncture it is important to think very carefully, weighing the most basic features, for here a little impatience with the bizarre might lead us to throw out the whole performance as curious but not worth our time.

A few essential facts stand out:

First, the patient represented her delusions of grandeur and persecution in a symbolic pattern quite spontaneously, without knowing the nature of the image she was producing. No therapist would recognize its nature either unless he was familiar with the comparative symbolism of this theme. Understanding the symbolism, however, he can instantly recognize that the image accurately represents the sense of the delusional opinion, or rather, that both the drawn symbol and the symbolic opinion vividly describe the psychic situation in which the patient finds herself at any time.

Second, there was a profound shift in the patient's thoughts about her position in the world, from one of fear-laden, superhuman rulership to one of simple human membership. Again, the delusions and the drawings reflected each other's meaning, since the overthrow of the ego from its position at the center involved delusions of a plot leading to world revolution and war. In other words, there was a process at work in terms of symbols, with changes toward improvement, and not a mere wallowing in idle play of fancy.

Third, when the patient synthesized a squared-circle design in which she was definitely a beholder and not at the center, her clinical condition was good and her thinking more clear. Her condition was worst when she was portraying herself and believing herself at the center; this state evidently involved feelings of godlike powers that consciousness cannot tolerate. Her state of mind was also one of forboding, confusion, and depression when she was representing the theme of black entities in delusion and drawing.

Fourth, the emotional tone implied in the delusions was varied but, characteristically, not expressed vividly or communicated effectively. Yet the variations followed a pattern conforming to that of the delusions and the drawings. Since the images in her designs and her speech paralleled her emotions, they can be said to represent the same dynamic phenomena that she was feeling, so that drawn symbol, symbolic opinion, and emotion all sprang from and reflected the same psychic entity at any one time. Here again there was a definite progress from fear, mistrust, dullness, and omnipotence at the beginning to friendliness, self-confidence, enthusiasm, and awe at the periods of clarity, with a series of other depressive and aggressive moods in the transition. Drawn and spoken symbols seem to assume more realness or actuality when they are associated so closely with emotion; for then they are recognized more easily as aspects of things that have effects, that matter because they have the power to disturb or to clarify.

Fifth, the symbolic problem consistently dealt with the patient's relation to the center, which also was consistently represented in a circle involving fourness. The theme was expressed in mythological, religious, political, familial, and other terms, but the most regular feature was the circular design that never pictorially described what she said it did except in a highly abstract symbolic way. This created the impression that the circular symbol came closer to expressing the essential central phenomenon than did the other fantasy products.

Sixth, these symbolic opinions and drawn symbols and emotions were meaningful to the patient because of their immediate impact upon her; again and again she emphasized that the images she was producing were interesting, or fascinating, or important to her, and they clearly contained more meaning for her than she could comprehend at the time. Hence her demand for interpretations.

Seventh, the images were also meaningful to the therapist, but for different reasons. Here the sense of their importance was the result, not of any immediate impact—by empathy—so much as of the modicum of knowledge of comparative symbolism the therapist had at his command. To his colleagues who watched the developments, and who did not have the same interest in symbols, they had no such meaning at first.

Lastly, because of this acquaintance with symbols, the therapist could communicate meaningfully with the patient even when she was quite psychotic, thus making a bridge of relationship for which the patient was grateful, since order then began to arise out of chaos.

These are the objective observations, before any psychological hypothesis needs to come into play to explain the nature of the symbolic theme. The drawn symbols have been referred to as the "central archetype" because of the patient's own preoccupation with the question of the "center." What now can be offered as justification for the claim that this is the archetype of the "self"?

In the first place, the patient's opinions told us much that identifies it in this way. She felt it as a cosmic order, "the whole world"; yet it was also a conflict within her. So it was an ordering of both her world and her psyche—in other words, it was the totality of her psychological field. The emphasis was upon the center, as to its function and identity. It seemed to her to be the focus of universal events, again in either her own inner world or the world generally, in a position of rulership over what surrounds it. Consequently at the center were elements considered of highest value, such as ego in its deified inflation at first, then the sun and moon surrounded by her closest girlhood ties, then the deity Christ, then the new life and golden germination, and finally the struggle for world power and the harmony of world peace presided over by the golden sun. Through the centuries sun and gold have been traditional attributes of divinity or divine kingship. She clearly saw that in the image occurred the paradoxical union of opposites: ego and its shadow half, mother and father, mother world and father world, party and party in rivalry, this world and other world, divine and human, friend and friend in rivalry, masculine and feminine halves, four parties in strife, four directions, war and peace, dark and light, and so on. Apparently the function of the symbol was to unite these contraries. In this there was always an associated feeling of satisfaction with the product and of its importance (the germination design excepted), which indicated relief in the finding of a central factor with a capacity to unite the opposites. There was an obvious sense of accomplishment, as in the solution of a problem or in the arrival at the goal of a long work. Finally, to repeat, when she was at the center she was badly inflated and disturbed, and when at the periphery or looking on she was clinically improved.

To sum up, then, the attributes of the central archetype as she experienced it: it was for her an outer and an inner world order, built around a center designated by a high valuation, by sun, gold, deity, or ruler; in it a new life emerged through a transforming process; in it the various opposites were united; the structuring of it was a goal of psychic work and suffering, engendering specific feelings of satisfaction and peace and fascination and awe. But these are precisely the attributes of the symbol of the self that have been described in the various times and places that the phenomenon has been experienced:. thus the phenomenon becomes as much historical as clinical fact. Therefore, to elucidate its nature at all adequately, the historical parallels to the patient's material should be cited as further empirical material upon which the psychological hypothesis is based.

7 AMPLIFICATION OF THE SYMBOL

During the past several decades considerable scientific work has been done on the study of the morphology and nature of the symbol of the quadrated circle. All possible sources, from primitive cultures to the most refined, have been examined for examples of any commonly recurring symbols and symbolic processes. In this way, just as with the early researches in any scientific field, the various phenomena have been found to fall into groups according to their characteristics and functions; that is, the data have been examined impartially, regularities found, and classifications made, such as the symbols of the Hero, the Great Mother, the Divine Child, and the death and rebirth, the quarternity, and the quadrated circle. Similar patterns have been found to occur spontaneously in the material of analysants, and these have been added to the compilation of data.

The use of these studies is twofold. In the direction of the pure science, there has developed an extensive knowledge of symbolic expression and its implications in the evolution of consciousness and culture. In the direction of therapy, this knowledge has proved indispensable for an adequate understanding of the meaning of the various symbols occurring in dreams and fantasies and for an effective use of them. In the latter use, the method for elucidating the meaning of the symbol has been called "amplification," which is the enrichment of the fantasy material by the analagous material of its parallels found in comparative symbolism.

An extensive study of the parallels to the patient's symbolism will be found in Part II. At this point I shall make only a few observations that I consider necessary to a realization of the validity of the patient's imagery.

The Asiatic mandala is similar in pattern and meaning to the patient's first design. The term "mandala" has been borrowed from the East to denote the entire group of similar images, marked by the quality of geometrical symmetry and basically forming a circle concentric with a fourfold structure such as a cross or a square. (Other numbers and their multiples may occur under certain circumstances, as mentioned at the end of this section.) The word "mandala" means "circle," especially a ritual or magic circle,[1] and in religious usage in the East it is a "symbolic geometrical diagram wherein deities are invoked,"[2] and also a "diagram of the universe ... serving as a frame for assemblies of deities or for their symbols."[3]

The patient first used the image of the mandala to denote the world and its center, where she was situated as deity; later she made a circle and cross as continents in four colors, with the sun at the center. The Asiatic form of the mandala (see Part II, § 14) was originally used in temples to establish the axial center of the universe symbolized in it; its central circle is the sun at the focal point of creation, and it frames a chief deity as lord of the universe. The square outside the lotus represents the earth; its gates are the four directions, designated by the colors yellow, green, white, and red—the same used by the patient. The outer enclosure may vary, being a circle (Plate I), concentric squares (Plate II), or a cross (Plate III). The form that seems historically earliest is one in which the circle and cross enclose the inner square and lotus, the limbs of the cross depicting the outside lands or continents (Plate IV).

At the center the patient first represented herself as a circle in red and black halves, torn between the father's and mother's halves of the world, associated with sun and moon. Another cosmic design found in the East, the Chinese "T'ai-chi" (see Part II, § 23), with a similar function of establishing the central axis of the universe, is a circle divided by an S-shaped line into red and black halves representing the great cosmic masculine and feminine principles, often designated by sun and moon.

In the patient's progress she went through a process of death and rebirth in the mandala, the infantile ego being overthrown at the central position by a revolt that then placed the sun or the divinity at the center of the world. In the East the mandala is used ceremonially in initiation[4] (see Part II, § 28), in which the novice sacrifices his ego personality and attains a realization of the supremacy of the divine consciousness; he is supposed to have a vision of the mandala in the sky with the gods enthroned in it, to identify with the deity at the center, to fight the demonic powers, and finally to identify the structure of his body with that of the cosmic mandala.

In the first drawing, the patient started by indicating herself as deity

[1] For notes to chapter 7, see pp 161–162.

(dual) at the center and proceeded to construct around herself the mandala as the world and the hospital, giving her imagination free rein. In another Eastern rite[5] (see Part II, § 15) the novice has a vision that constructs out of and around himself the mandala as the world and as the temple, in which he is at the center identified with the supreme god (holding his female consort in his embrace). Even the mandalas that are hung on the wall as an aid to meditation[6] are said to be only formalized versions of images that may be spontaneously experienced through active imagination on the part of the initiated Lamaists.[7] The mandala occurs in many other forms in the East (see Part II, § 16), thus assuming an importance that compels the conclusion that the theme is no matter of mere idle curiosity there but a fundamental and widespread expression of basic concepts and values.

The symbol of the quadrated circle is no less widespread in the West, but in our culture it does not have the refinement and integration of meanings of the Eastern forms. The most fertile elaboration of the quadrated circle occurred among the nature philosophers; to them the nature of matter was still unknown and mysterious, and thus it became the recipient of all manner of unconscious symbolic contents mingled with its qualities and processes by projection[8] (see Part II, § 17). Alchemy was essentially a system of projections. The squaring of the circle was a symbol of the alchemical "Work," which had essentially to do with differentiating and then uniting the four elements into a "stone" or "gold" (see Part II, § 18). For example, just as the patient, in the last drawing, found the world divided into four parties that were in a state of strife until brought together under the united rule of the golden sun at the center, so the alchemists found it composed of four warring elements needing to be united in the final gold, a solar substance. One commentary described a diagram[9] (see Part II, § 29) of a circle and cross containing an inner circle; the circle in the center is called a "mediator," making peace among the four inimical elements designated by the cross, for the mediator alone could bring about the quadrating of the circle. The symbol of this synthesis was sun or gold. The diagram is strikingly similar to Drawing XII and is reproduced in Figure 14.

Another symbol of the alchemical Work was what was called the "wheel," a quadrated circle having to do with the four directions, the four seasons, and the four elements, and being essentially an image of the rotating universe. The designs of these Western mandalas do not have the consistency of the Eastern ones, but are elaborated in many different ways[10] (Plates V and VI) (see Part II, § 18).

These brief allusions serve at least to indicate the existence and importance of the mandala theme in Eastern ritual and Western protoscience and the close analogy to the patient's material. Even briefer mention can be given here to the several functions of this symbol. To bring some order into the confusion of the great multitudes of related images, their various aspects can be grouped into categories.

The earliest and most widespread form is the sun wheel (see Part II, § 1)—the circle and cross, designating the sun, sun-god, or king—which seems also to be the historical basis of the Eastern mandala.

The supreme deity or divine man has customarily been pictured in the four-pointed circle (see Part II, § 2) sometimes surrounded by other sacred figures in some fourfold arrangement. The divine prototype of initiated youth has also been represented in the wheel, and in initiation ceremonies the drama of death and rebirth has been staged in the quadrated circle. The halo as the sign of holiness (that is, wholeness) is apparently derived from this use of the sun wheel.

The cosmos and its central axis, as well as the principle creating the cosmic order, are designated by the quadrated circle in various cultures (see Part II, § 3). It has been mentioned that in the Eastern mandala the diagram, the temple, and the world are intended to share a common axis, merged by a kind of inner identification; the novice shares in this identification during the initiation.

Another aspect of the mandala is its function as a protective enclosure (see Part II, § 4). Among primitives it is familiar as the magic circle drawn on the ground by medicine men for healing ceremonies or initiations. At higher levels of culture this circle serves to induce meditative concentration. Further variations on this pattern are sacred or legendary enclosures, such as the "garden of the philosophers" or the monastic cloisters for quiet retreat, and the familiar representations of the various forms of the "paradise garden" or "paradise city." Primitive and ancient communities have often been ritually founded on the ground plan of the quadrated circle, perhaps delimiting and protecting the precincts of hard-won culture.

Closely associated with the protective aspect of the mandala is its maternal character (see Part II, § 5). City and garden are often of maternal significance, but especially the lotus in the East and the rose in the West represent the generative aspect of the mother goddess that brings forth the divine child in its center. Both the flower and the child are mandalalike in form, and there are frequent allusions to the golden quality of each.

Important among the universal features of the mandala is its duality, as a representation of a union of opposites (see Part II, § 6)—heaven and earth, spirit and matter, sun and moon, god and goddess; the hermaphrodite or spherical androgynous being is a common designation of this duality.

Finally, the mandala possesses healing aspects (see Part II, § 7), often as a symbol of the panacea or drug of immortality, which also may be poisonous or harmful.

In its morphology (see Part II, §§ 8, 9, 10) the mandala is sometimes three-fold or fivefold, instead of the usual fourfoldness, but such forms are found empirically to have differing significances under special circumstances. Circulation or rotation is often a prominent feature of the image, as is also its high value as treasure.

It is highly interesting to note that each of the aspects of the mandala symbol mentioned above, drawn from the comparative studies, occurred also in the patient's material. She places the palm tree as well in the mandala series, which is in keeping with the fact that in the various mythologies of the ancient world the tree has the same significance as the mandala and is often placed in it or shaped in the same form (see Part II, § 12).

8 PSYCHOLOGICAL CONCEPTS

The universality of other symbols of unconscious experience led Jung to an awareness of the "primordial image" and to his formulation of the concept of the "archetype" and of the "collective unconscious." The term "archetypal image" designates a certain class of symbolic formations appearing in dream and fantasy and creative imagination, possessing the attributes of mythological aura and universality and functioning chiefly in the developmental and integrative processes of the psyche (see Part II, § 34). The clinical observations of many years of experience have repeatedly indicated that this symbol formation according to certain generally valid patterns is endogenous in the organism. The present patient's material demonstrates this point with striking clarity.

The occurrence of such preformed phenomena in psychic life is certainly baffling to the modern scientist who has become accustomed to think of mental experience as the product of the conditioning of the individual by his experience. To account for them Jung has hypothesized that the archetypes are instinctual in the sense of being unlearned, innate, and universal systems of preparedness. Where the instincts are propensities to act, so are the archetypes propensities to apprehend in response to certain kinds of typical situations in certain kinds of typical ways. The archetypes are not inherited ideas, of course, but are the inherited predisposition to form images and apprehensions in certain given ways. They are made up of imagery and emotion together,[1] and each thus carries a certain quantum of

---

[1] For notes to chapter 8, see p 162.

44

libido in specific form; they are thus the foci of meaning and motivation. Whether or how they might be inherited remains unaccountable, but the evidence points to their innateness. They seem to be imprints in the psychic structure that typify the most frequently and intensely used functions of the psyche.[2] The "collective unconscious," of quite different nature than the "personal unconscious," is made up of the whole array of the various instincts and archetypes.[3]

One of the major results of Jung's concept of the role of the primordial image in life experience is a wholly unique attitude toward and evaluation of the products of certain sorts of fantasy, especially when the content of the psychoses is concerned, which is largely collective unconscious material[4] (see Part II, § 34). The activity of fantasy that is induced by concentrated effort and work, as in the present patient's experiences, is neither a wholly free play of whim or of fiction nor an activity of mind merely determined by the infantile complexes and wish fulfillments, but is more a conscientious searching out and notation of the unconscious imagery as it actually exists and moves at the time.[5] The careful analysis of a consecutive series of such images generally reveals a process moving toward a goal, and the more the comparative material is familiar the more readily will the significance of the symbols and their developments be recognized.

Perhaps Jung's most significant pioneer work has been in bringing to light the most basic of the instinctive drives: the propensity toward psychic development and self-completion, along with its multiform galaxy of symbols and functions that come into play in this evolution of growth, which he terms the "individuation process."[6] This drive toward individuation is apparently a spontaneous urge, not under the leadership of the ego, but of the archetypal movement in the unconscious, the nonego, toward the fulfillment of the specific basic pattern of the individual, striving toward wholeness, totality, and the differentiation of the specific potentialities that are innately destined to form the particular personality in question. The unconscious is the matrix out of which these various qualities arise step by step toward differentiation in consciousness, which they approach first in symbolic guise until the ego learns to understand and incorporate them. In this unconscious matrix, then, the pattern of the wholeness of the personality lies hidden awaiting the hand of experience to stir it into activity; it is not an ego ideal formed by upbringing, but a dynamic urge emanating from the core of one's being, laden with affect and presenting itself to consciousness in terms of the archetypal symbols.

The term "self" designates this pattern of wholeness that thus represents itself in archetypal form. Like the other archetypes, it is nonego. Experience shows it to be not only a center of the psyche but also a circumference that encloses it; it is the center and delimitation of the totality of conscious and unconscious. It governs and structures the total psyche as the ego does its conscious contents.[7] Since it is constellated only under conditions of stress,[8] this phenomenon is apt to evade study under "normal" or experimental conditions. In Western culture it is so unfamiliar that the investigator must approach it with the cautious awareness that his knowledge of the psyche is still very limited indeed. The mandala symbolism discussed above shows itself to be the picturing of the goal toward which the integrative processes of the psyche work in manifestly purposeful fashion.[9] This symbolism clearly, as in the present case, represents the perception of a ruling center around which the many contrasting contents of the psyche tend to structure themselves into a pattern that is always unique, that is the "law of one's own being."[10] It reveals, then, an entelechy, the striving of the organism toward self-realization.[11]

The psyche, in its striving toward this objective, has the problem of differentiating itself from what is not itself—that is, from the general properties of human nature and human culture. Individuation acts as a ruling center gathering in a circumscribed circle about itself the contents of the psyche, selecting and rejecting what does and does not belong to the individual personality.[12]

In modern Western culture it is difficult for either therapist or patient to comprehend the relative functions of ego and self and the manner in which each tends to relate to the other. The various qualities ascribed to the self in all its symbolism—cosmic, divine, imperishable, irrational, paradoxical—point to its nature as nonego. It is felt rather to be a ruling factor with numinous qualities to which the ego is subordinate. It presents itself to consciousness with the incomprehensible paradox of possessing all the attributes of universality and yet more immediately designating the basis of an individual's own single uniqueness; it thus tends either to remain too distant and aloof or to approach too closely and to overwhelm. As an archetype and a supremely potent entity of the unconscious, it can raise havoc if a person is in the wrong relation to it. If the ego tends to identify with it, there is danger of the severest inflation and fragmentation of consciousness by the inrush of the large quantum of libido carried by it.[13] We learn to be guided by its organizing and directing influences but not to be identical with it, so to speak.[14] The present case study is essentially the description of the nature of the problem when the ego does identify with it.

Such, very briefly sketched, is the hypothesis attempting to account for the observed facts of the mandala symbolism as it appears in individuals and cultures. As sun or deity it is all-powerful center and nonego; as cosmos it is an ordered totality of incalculable proportions; as protective enclosure it is a delimitation of specific contents and an inducement to concentration of them; as mother and child it is the psychic matrix and the emergence from it of the ruling value; as union of opposites it is the embracing and reconciling of the many contradictory components of psychic life; and as healing agent it has the power to make whole or to destroy utterly.

9 INTERPRETATION OF THE PROCESS

The self, as a psychological entity that represents itself in the symbol of the quadrated circle, can be said to consist of a ruling center and an organizing totality. Although only a sketchy outline, the review of the symbolism and psychology of the self, in Chapters 7 and 8, serves at least to indicate the importance of the universal human problems, clothed in equally universal imagery, that the patient was having to face. That the relativity of ego and deity to the self comes to light spontaneously in an experience of the unconscious is made apparent by the difficulties the patient was having in grasping the sense of the inward reality of the deity image and of the images of cosmic and world events that seemed to be herself and yet not herself. She was entangled in archetypal images and processes of which she knew practically nothing, and hence toward which she had completely inadequate orientation.

A therapist, to be honest at this point, must ask himself frankly whether he is any better oriented to all this kind of material than his patient. He must do more than recognize that the imagery used is valid and meaningful. He must ask: Of what significance is the archetypal process in this particular person's psychic development? What took place here, and why did it happen at this particular point in her life? As stated earlier, no analysis was done on the patient. Consequently, any attempt at interpretation of the material must necessarily suffer from its scantiness; since, however, this is usual in the treatment of the psychoses, I shall present my interpretation for what it is worth.

47

The drawings came entirely as efforts to represent the delusions as the patient felt them at the time, and the process was not set under way or given any shape through the influence of the therapist. Rather it was a spontaneous movement of the libido at a crucial juncture in her life situation and development. In the interviews she herself described the nature of the crisis. She said that she had been hiding her true nature under a mask of superficial appearances, and that she had considered herself not adequately related to others. Her baby now called for the most genuine feeling and motherly response, and yet she found herself still a child in her own parental family circle. Her individuality had not yet been delivered from the mother, but it was imperative that at this point in her life it should have been. When the psychotic episode eventually passed, on the other hand, she was then deepened, mellowed, more genuine in her feelings and rapport with her baby, husband, and friends, and more mature in her relation to her parents. In other words, the most needed changes somehow came about, an outcome that has been observed of psychotic episodes if they are allowed to run their course.[1] The question thus becomes, if this is the overall need and effect, whether we can trace such a development through the material.

The opening delusions elaborated first the theme of death, in the ideas of poisoning, murder, eight shots, and planting in death; somehow associated with these presentiments was an insistent but unclear notion of a journey with her father in the Pacific. The whole situation was tinged with guilt, people accusing her and being about to punish her. These are typical representations of the regressive flow of the libido away from the role of conscious adaptation to the outer world and toward the unconscious, whose various maternal aspects are then constellated and become overpowering. The unconscious becomes first of all mother (poisoning), then death (murder and shootings), earth (planting), and sea (journey). The comparative symbolism of this phase gives indications that the regression was not concerned merely with the infantile incestuous wish but with the intent upon rebirth.

Poisoning by a mother goddess, along with her other means of giving renewal, is seen frequently in mythology (see Part II, 30a). In the tales of Isis or Medea, for example, she has poison agents among her healing and rejuvenating arts; these she can misuse, if it suits her whim, and turn in deadly deceit against her victim. This theme signifies that the maternal archetype contains a distinct duality, a creative and destructive polarity in her nature, exemplified in the very contrary aspects within the natures of such figures as Hecate and Kali as rulers of life and of death. Much as the members of the cults of the goddess customarily protested to her against her cruel trickery, so the individual under the spell of this archetype is

---

[1] For notes to chapter 9, see pp 162–164

inclined to hold the mother to blame for an evil intent against him; in the patient's initial situation this projection was quite obvious.

The killing and atmosphere of death are likewise a common theme in the archaic symbolism of the maternal archetype, usually associated with a disintegrative phase in the sequence (see Part II, § 30b). Kali exemplifies her annihilative role in resolving the whole of creation back into its unmanifest state, as Tiamat does in threatening the destruction of all that she has brought forth; yet both goddesses give life and substance to the cosmos. In the great myths of the dying and resurrecting god, the mother is agent of the sacrificial death, whether of Dionysus, of Attis, or of the Christ of medieval legend. Most lucid and helpful for an understanding of the significance of the death phase in the symbolic sequence is the phenomenon found in the alchemical system of projections under the term "blackening" ("nigredo"). This is the depressive, death-ridden first step in the procedure, specifically called "mortification" or "putrefaction," in which the opposites in their corruptible form must die and come to a new union through a kind of resurrection by distillation. One of the mythological representations of this stage is the death of a hero in the belly of his sister at the bottom of the sea, preparatory to his rebirth.

The earth aspect of the mother imago is better known, and it scarcely needs pointing out that fertility, birth, and rebirth are her principal functions (see Part II, § 30c). One example is Gaea the Great Mother, the nourisher who gives life to men and receives them back into her bosom at their death; another is Cybele, who promises rejuvenation of the spirit in man along with that of the vegetation in the world of nature. In antiquity caves and tombs were thought of as the organs of regeneration through the mother. The concept that in death man is planted as the seed to be reborn into a new life is familiar in Christian symbolism as it had been in Osiris worship; the Pauline epistle that is often read at funeral services (I Corinthians 15), describes the sowing of the corruptible, natural body in death so that the incorruptible, spiritual body might come to life. The alchemistic projections contained the same concepts of natural and spiritual bodies.

Finally, the sea is the maternal symbol par excellence (see Part II, § 30d), and has in many cultures been regarded as the procreative matrix and source of all life. It, along with the lotus, is an integral part of the imagery of the Divine Child archetype. For example, in the Christian mother cult the Virgin is called "Stella Maris," as Isis had been before her. The maternal role of the sea comes into play in the widespread mythological motif of the "night sea journey" of the sun hero who dies in the western sea and is devoured by a monster that transports him to the east, where he is born out of the sea again, rejuvenated, at the rising of the sun.

Thus, in the parallels to the patient's symbolism of the regression, the overpowering by the mother had to do with the aim of rebirth through her, for the generation of an "incorruptible, spiritual" form of psychic life out of the death of a "corruptible, natural" one. The sense of the motif seems to be that in order to change a psychic structure that has become inadequate for progressive development the structure must be resolved and its raw energic content liberated for a renewal of its form of expression. The libido is thus transformed from more primitive modes to more differentiated ones, or from instinctual to cultural ones, or from infantile to mature ones, or from rigid sterile ones to inspired fertile ones. The maternal role in this process of rejuvenation is one of destroying and re-creating, of dissolving and resynthesizing, of devouring and giving birth; the mother then represents the unconscious itself, whose role it is to transform the libido in this way.

Such death and rebirth of psychic structure were the function of the initiation ceremonies of primitive and antique cultures, whether by passage through the toothed maw of the ceremonial crocodile or by the lamentations over the lost deity in night processions or caves (see Part II, § 27). In primitive usage, the aim was to graduate from the child's state of dominance by the mothers into the status of manhood and its responsibilities of membership in the tribe; in antique forms, the intent was to cast off the ways of worldly man and enter the experience of the spiritual life. In either, there came a point at which the initiant identified himself with the deity or mythical or totemic being. For the archetypal personage alone has the qualities needed to carry through this transformation process, being the gradually fashioned representative of the age-old, often repeated ancestral experience of the problem of emergence from primitivity and infantility into individual consciousness. These initiations often took place in a mandala. But where is the connection between the regression of an individual patient and these religious ceremonies?

The common supposition of Freudian psychoanalysis is that the extreme regression reached by the schizophrenic is that which goes all the way back to the oral phase and primary narcissism of earliest infantility, and that the ideas of world power are derived from the child's wish for omnipotence vis-à-vis the parental setting.[2] We can see this apparent phenomenon in the present case in Drawing I, in the child-centered world surrounded by mother and father (and his adjunct, the husband). But more has already been seen as well: a regression back to archaic symbolic formulations of death and rebirth and cosmic structure; this, then, is the return, not only to the parents of early personal experience, but beyond them to the ancestry of past universal experience, first projected into the parents. As Jung puts it, "A return to childhood is always a return to father and mother, to the whole burden of the psychic non-ego embodied in the parents, with its long, momentous history. Regression means disintegration into the historical, hereditary determinants from whose embrace we can free ourselves only

with the greatest effort."[3] Being unconscious, the entire potential of wholeness and its symbolization are first found in a state of projection, and the
parents become the first objects to catch this imagery.[4] As long as this infantile dependence still persists, the family circle, then, remains the representative of the circle of the individual's wholeness, its components still
being found in that group.[5]

Such a regression brings the danger of a splitting up of the personality
so that the parts, so tenuously integrated, are drawn asunder and lost among
the powerful machinations of mythological contents. Dismemberment, the
archetypal foundation of the schizophrenic fragmentation, is depicted in the
mythological motif of the fate of the god hero,[6] as for example, Osiris or
Dionysus; it was no chance whim that led Nietzsche in his psychosis to
identify with the latter and sign himself "Zagreus." Beyond this danger to
the personality, however, the regression also brings with it the possibility
of an integration of the unconscious through experiencing its archaic components; the regression can then be, as Jung calls it, a "bath of renewal in
the source of life,"[7] the maternal waters of the unconscious, the matrix of
psychic life.

With this elucidation of the background setting of the patient's unconscious material, it becomes increasingly clear why she found herself thus at
the center of the world as it is represented in her first mandala.

First, in its infantile aspect, the patient was snugly embedded in the
charmed circle of the family, surrounded by mother on the one side and
father-husband on the other. This was indeed the infantile paradise, where
she was already swallowed in parental love and self-love ("I'm at the center
of attraction; I guess I love me"), and where she reigned all powerful in
her suckling's world, having renounced and died to the adult one. Here
all moral—that is, responsible—choice was forgone, for the balance of opposites remained inert as long as she refused to make her decision. The entire
condition was that of Eden before the eating of the fruit of the tree of
knowledge, which alone would cleave the opposites asunder by giving man
the awareness of the contrast of good and evil and all conflict and thus give
him consciousness. She was indeed guilty somehow, she said, but only in
the eyes of "them" who persecuted her; so far as she herself was concerned,
she remained in the innocence of the child. Moral awareness was the parental prerogative here, and so the father surrounded her with his detectives
and agents of the law; they alone had the fourfoldness of consciousness.
This was the image of the self in its "superego" aspect,[8] its most undifferentiated and primitive form, in which the potential of individual autonomy
was still projected upon the parents as rulers of the world.

These watchers, akin to the motif of the "many eyes" seen in some mandalas,[9] had the function of holding the patient in by forming the circle
around her. The entire pattern is a containing structure: the magic circle

discussed above, which is constellated when the personality is most in danger of scattering in fragmentation and losing all sense of its own limits amid the boundless reaches of the collective unconscious.[10] It creates, then, a kind of containing vessel in which the transformation process can take place safely in an ordered way.[11] Little wonder, then, that the concentric circles beyond the parental ones were felt to represent the hospital and her progress through it from phase to phase, each increasingly disturbed and deeper into the collective unconscious. The hospital was the place of initiation for her, the containing and protecting circle that tried to hold all alien forces at bay and to direct the therapeutic procedure of self-collection. In the language of the archaic mind, it would be a temple of healing or the sacred precincts, especially demarcated for the ceremonies of renewal by identification with the deity.

The lotus formed by the six petals carries similar connotations. It is, as explained elsewhere (see Part II, § 5), a symbol of the generative aspect of the goddess, the maternal womb in which the germination of the divine seed takes place and the redeeming hero is given birth into the world of men (see Part II, § 31); that is, the lotus and the child constitute the mother-son aspect of the mandala as noted above, with the meaning of the synthesis of a new form of the self and its appearance into the world of consciousness. The patient depicted herself, then, nestled at the heart of the lotus as the godling. This was in sharp contrast to the previous symbolizations of the mother in her devouring aspects, as poisoner, death, earth, and sea. This was her creative side, as the womb that gives birth. It was as gentle and pleasant in its appearance as the delusional associations accompanying it were violent and nightmarish. Thus, since in the midst of the terror and turmoil of the regression is found the promise of renewal, the whole experience has this dual nature. She called the petals her "mixed-up ideas," by which she meant her delusions—in other words, the contents of the collective unconscious; the latter is itself a maternal chaos (see Part II, § 25), like that "teeming womb," the "receptacle," the "nurse of all becoming" in the Timaeus, out of which arises world order.

The outer ring is the portrayal of the two opposing halves of the world as the father's and the mother's, which are associated with sun and moon. The connotations of this ring go beyond the family circle and the hospital to cosmic dimensions. That the world or cosmos is thus divided into opposite principles ruled by a male and a female being is a notion as old and universal as mythology itself (see Part II, § 22). Perhaps its most subtle expression is in the Chinese concept of Yang and Yin, whose balance throughout the cosmos is in constant alternation of ascendancy one over the other; in the Hindu, Vishnu and Maya (or Shiva and Shakti) represent the contrary principles of potentiality and actualization at work in the cosmic history of successive alternations of creations and resorptions of the

iniverse. More clearly than ever the patient indicated the nature of her
regression, with her projection onto the parents of the basic archetypal
oundations of wholeness. These archetypes are cosmic rulers—a king and
queen as carriers of the whole array of opposites in essence—as they are in
he alchemistic projections, where they are called Sol and Luna (Plate VII);
he same archetype underlay the patient's comment that they "seem connected with the sun and moon somehow."

It is tempting to suspect, though it cannot be confirmed, that the frag-
mentary delusion about being Churchill's daughter was an attempt to break
ree of the infantile, personal frame into which she had put these great
uling principles, and to reach for some sort of relation to the impersonal
ind the mythological. (Passing mention should be made of the fact also
hat a play on words in part determined the choice of this name.) Churchill,
regarded from the viewpoint of archaic apperception, was the ruler stand-
ng for the good, who led the global battle against the powers of darkness
ind evil. He was thus much closer to becoming a successful representative
of the archetypal principle than was her own, more ordinary, father. It is
ommon to find among schizophrenic patients the belief that they are orphaned offspring of royal or somehow notorious parents; the explanation
seems to be that they identify with the archetype of the primordial Divine
Child, who is characteristically born of the union of a cosmic pair and
abandoned to be cared for as an orphan by foster parents.[12] This is an arche-
ypal image of the self in its nascency; the nature philosophers expressed
his aspect of the image in the terms "infant," "orphan," or "son of the
philosphers" (see Part II, § 5). Identification with this image has the effect
of bringing the schizophrenic's consciousness to an awareness of the exist-
nce of his relation to the suprapersonal, archetypal parent figures of the
inconscious, thus breaking the restricted infantile frame of reference where
ll supreme rulership is in mother's and father's hands.

Through her regression the patient had become, not only the infant of
er own past life, but also the Divine Child, borne in the heart of the lotus,
ngendered by cosmic parents, and possessing extraordinary capacities (con-
rolling the sun and weather and death). She claimed that her former in-
antile personality had died and that she was resurrected; thus she had
become this infant deity. In other words, the return to the mother and the
death in her had already taken place, and she was now undergoing her
rebirth by identification with the god in the age-old manner of initiation;
or, psychologically, the libido had withdrawn from the ego consciousness
to the unconscious, where it had activated the archetype of the self and its
opposite polar aspects, and the self, by this shift of energy overweighting
he side of the unconscious, engulfed the ego. On this account, the patient
elt herself living in the "afterlife," that is, in the "other world" of the un-
onscious and its incorporeal spirit beings (see Part II, § 32); over that

world the parental images apparently divided their rule, again confirming their archetypal nature.

The next layer in the design of the drawing is the green square. This represents the hospital grounds, although the progress from ego to parents to hospital to world thus far might have aroused the expectation that at this point the next step might have been of an even more universal dimension. The actual hospital grounds are not at all square, nor do they have two gates any more than it has concentric rings, so the evident intention of this step was the squaring of the circle. This procedure made the pattern characteristically the mandala symbol, as described above. The best-known mandalas from the various cultural traditions cited above are representations of totalities at different levels merged into one: cosmos, citadel, temple, place of healing, and state of soul (see Part II, § 11). So although the patient's idea seems at first a bit grotesque, that the whole world should be in the hospital, it must be admitted that it is rather merely archaic and perfectly in keeping with symbolic notions of very long standing, whereby the ideal organization of world and community and hospital and soul are made one in the mandala. Her little aside that "everyone lives in Utopia" is an integral part of this imagery.

A most interesting feature is the last that the patient added to the design—the stream of traffic, into which she took care to put all the available colors. The mixture of all colors is an old symbol of the potential of wholeness; in alchemical symbolism, for example, the appearance of the "omnes colores" is a foreshadowing of the goal.[18] The rotation of this stream around the center is the equally familiar theme of the "circulation" or "circumambulation," which in alchemy meant the distillation process; this had to do with the evolution of "spiritual" subtle bodies out of "natural" coarse ones.[14] It therefore has the same sort of significance as the patient's idea of the death of her natural self and her resurrection in the afterlife. Further implications of the circumambulation are the defining of the center, or the activation of it, or progress toward it; the leftward, counterclockwise motion indicates its going in the regressive direction—toward the unconscious where the ego lay embedded in the self.

However, a few things went wrong for the patient in this circulating process. She felt quite disturbed that she had been holding up the traffic, and she bore this out in her inability to make the traffic do what she sensed it should do in the drawing. It should circumambulate, but it should also come to her at the center—like an impregnating stream—to start germination there; the simile is not amiss in view of the later development of this theme. (A less modern version of this archaic theme would be the serpent that coils around the center and starts it germinating.[15]) At any rate, she was unable to choose, and this indecision held up the circulation and arrested all progress.[16] The manifold opposites throughout the whole pattern are in even balance—and very tense balance—and in her regressive slumber in the bosom of the parental protection she was too inert to make a choice, for to discriminate thus is the function of consciousness. Instead she felt herself being drawn toward the hermaphroditic state of original undifferentiation, where masculine and feminine rule in equal measure.

The ego at the center, in its identification with the infant and its return to the mother, was split into its opposite components in red and black. This kind of dismemberment, evidenced by her autonomous alternations of mood from cheerful to depressed so characteristic of the catatonic, is to be expected at this juncture in the process. It is reminiscent of the Chinese "T'ai'chi," with its red and black Yang and Yin at the center, the alternating forces of light and life on the one side, and darkness and death on the other. In the circles around this were contrasting directions of progress. The ego went through hospital phases outward, whereas the traffic circulated inward toward the center. This was most important, for it was necessary for the ego to escape from its identity with the central archetypal role of the self; and the circulating stream of "all colors" was the representative of the self that ought to supplant the ego at that central point. In its outward progress the ego went through increasingly disturbed phases, in that it experienced more and more of the overwhelming contents of the collective unconscious, through the "mixed-up thoughts" out to where the parental images took on a truly archetypal universality. There the stream of all colors started its inward flow to initiate the germination of a new ruling factor at the center (see Part II, § 19).

Finally, the threefold and sixfold mandala seems to carry the connotation of incompleteness. Psychologically this incompleteness is found where there is a bias toward the rational or personal, as against the completeness that comes with an awareness of the role of the irrational and nonpersonal in the unconscious."[17] Such a triadic mandala is not necessarily abnormal—only incomplete; it tended to go over into the quadratic as the patient gained in experience of the unconscious process, as this series shows.

Among the same initial delusions was the corrective to the patient's identification with the child archetype, in the theme of giving birth to the illegitimate baby; since she dealt with it further in Drawing III, it will be discussed with that drawing.

The mandala of the three friends (Drawing II) did not belong to the delusions of the patient's deeply disturbed period as did the first one, but followed a dream of the night before the interview at a time when she was clinically improved. She depicted herself, no longer as infant, but as adolescent trying to make her place in the social structure of her community, the design being supposed to portray her "growing up together in the world" with her two neighbors. It was the phase, no longer of infantile narcissistic and receptive love, but of homosexual love. Here she was reaching out for her femininity, the self in its feminine aspect. This is the kind of bond that is kindled by the projection of the feminine image onto a partner; thence the striving, through the experience of these emotions, toward such a realization of her own femininity that she becomes accepted into the society of those who represent it. Such a homosexual tone is found in initiation rites of primitive boys, with the same function of proving the boy and introducing him into the adult world of manhood (see Part II, § 27); conversely, the initiation pattern can be seen in the unconscious imagery of homosexual patients. Here, in the situation of rivalry, the patient found it necessary to engender love so that she could bind a needed friend close to her, a state of affairs quite different from that of the passive-dependent bedding down in the parental protective love of Drawing I.

Why, then, the need for the vegetative and cosmic symbolism in the design? It can only be assumed that the patient's capacity for genuinely relating with affection and love—that is, her Eros nature[18]—was still unconscious and thus stood in need of being differentiated out from the matrix where all such unrealized potentials were still contained at the instinctual level. It is characteristic of any such undifferentiated functions that they are found in projection to the extent that they are still unconscious; a person is then to the same extent dependent upon those on whom they are projected to supply them. In the first drawing, the patient's Eros was still residing in the parents; but this projection had to be withdrawn and the dependency resolved and the Eros generated by the patient's own effort. This entailed the activation of all those archetypal foundations of the psyche among which it was still lodged.

In the present drawing, the homosexual love was a step along the way, but still a love between similars, still somewhat autoerotic in its aim of ego development. Mature love, on the other hand, has at its root the contrasts of opposites—male and female—and an aim that reaches out for the experience of what lies beyond ego consciousness. Only when the opposites have differentiated out, it seems, is there the capacity for real love, the Eros that strives to bring them into dynamic relation[19] (see Part II, § 6). This seems to be happening in this mandala. It represents the experience of girlhood friendships as a living thing, like a plant that grows and flowers, whose end product and beginning source constitute a pair of opposites, as sun is counterpart to moon, or as spirit is to earth, or as masculine is to feminine, or perhaps as sun god is to mother goddess. Here sun and moon are no longer the father's and mother's attributes in stalemate, but have a dynamic relation in the patient's own emotional experience of love.

The psychotic process in the schizophrenic is usually initiated by the need for the mobilization and differentiation of the function of feeling, which is so necessary in relating to the people and things of the world of reality, and which is the great lack in the life of the withdrawn personality.[20]

Feeling is the instrument of consciousness for discrimination of and adaptation of value—that is, for judgment by valuation. When it is missing in the conscious personality, there begins at the same time the process that is in general the psyche's way of making its readjustments. When the growing consciousness at any time runs into a dead end in its progress because a component necessary at the time for adaptation is only subliminal and unavailable to the ego for use, there occurs a damming up, and consequently an autonomous backflow of the libido to activate the unconscious and bring up the needed element, in a form that the ego can accept despite the opposition of the two standpoints.[21] The danger is that with this activation and constellation of the unconscious the entire collective unconscious is apt to follow in the wake of the element that is rising toward consciousness, and there is the great liability to identification with its contents.

The initial delusions and drawing show that this happened to the patient. The color red is customarily the one used to designate the quality of feeling, in that it naturally associates with warmth and passion;[22] this was the color she used for the light aspect of the ego in its identification with the archetype of the Divine Child. Her regression led back to the function that had been left behind in an infantile state of undifferentiation and dependency, but also back to the entire unconscious. The desired function was activated and came to awareness out of the depths, but with it came the nuclear archetype of the self; when she became the red oval—"warm" and "gay"— she was also divine. Its opposite, the black one, seemed to be her cold, depressive, withdrawn standpoint in which her feelings all sank out of sight, in deep inversion—that is, turned inward.

In Drawing II, however, her situation was different. Just as the theme was not infantile narcissistic love but active object love, so also she was not "at the center of attraction," as she expected to be when she began it, but at the periphery competing among friendships. The center now became the axis between the basic archetypal opposites—sun and moon—representing the hermaphroditic self. The color red is now only a half-concealed attribute of the shadow side of each of the friends,[23] that is, latently present in projection in the friendships but still to be made conscious.

The composition of the mandala suggests that it seems to be an end in itself to make it fourfold, to square the circle, to fill it with opposites, and to place the sun at the center as a flower.[24] The associations of this world and other world, or of lightness and darkness, are secondary to the fundamental urge to synthesize the structure of the symbol itself diagrammatically. These associations, however, also infer that spirit is generated out of nature: as with the sun-blossom arising out of the moon-earth, so for the patient the squaring of the circle has the connotation of the sublimation of a spiritual afterlife out of the corporeal natural life (see Part II, §§ 14 and 30c). This concept could be approximated psychologically by the paraphrase that cultural consciousness is generated out of biological instinct, as a subtle body out of a natural body or an active Eros out of passive narcissistic gratification.

The role of the transference here in this evolution is not to be underrated, for the "spiritual" pole[25] was apparently activated in its projection upon the therapist, in whom she therefore found some saintly qualities. In characteristic fashion it seems that the transference contained in projection the content of the archetypal potential of wholeness.[26]

The next drawing (III) took up the théme of the new life. At the very depths of her regression, when she felt herself most enveloped by her "mixed-up ideas" in the disturbed ward, which she represented by the lotus, the child motif appeared in several ways. She evidently felt each of these representations to be illegitimate, for she thought of herself as an illegitimate offspring of her mother, also as the daughter of the world figure Churchill; then the new baby was hers from an injection, yet foisted onto her by her dark counterpart, who conceived it by a Negro. The theme is thus by no means clear-cut, but it can at least be said that at the time when she was having the most fearful intuitions about death she was also fantasying a new birth, and that these came simultaneously with preoccupations about death and resurrection. It can be argued also that when she most felt herself to be the infant in the bosom of the parental circle, as well as the Divine Child, a countermovement in the psyche was producing the image of the coming to life of a new, dark child who was not herself.

The theme was reintroduced by the same dream as that from which Drawing II sprang. The image of the dying, depressive uncle and his cancer is as gloomy as that of the three girls is bright; together they seem to constitute opposite aspects of the synthetic process, the one having to do with death and darkness and masculinity, the other to do with growth and lightness and femininity. Of the former she makes a sequence of death and new birth again, since in Drawing III cancer becomes baby.

At this point—the day on which she did the two drawings on this motif —(III) the Negro baby, the depressive uncle's cancer (done in black), and (IV) the black earth's fragmental rivers all seem to merge into one major theme whose tone is disagreeable and depressing to the patient, even pulling her libido down into a mild confusion. This is again the phase of the "blackness," like the "nigredo" described by the nature philosophers, which they called the "terrible darkness of our spirit."[27] For example, one of these philosophers tells of the primordial matter, saying that it comes in lowly form, is water and passive-receptive substance, and emanates from chaos as a dark sphere; another says that it contains in itself the potential of the goal, the round stone, and is the black earth in which the gold is sown like seed.[28] There are accounts of the dark child as a "luck-bringing embryo" conceived by the conjunction of a virgin with a giant born in river waters; thus

formed is a black "mighty Ethiopian" who dies, is buried and reborn, thereby
giving rise to the stone.[29] These examples are only a few of the innumerable
variations in which the same archetypal themes are interwoven.

Any concise psychological formulation of this kind of black phase is
difficult to achieve; but it is none the less important, for in it lies a key to
the understanding of the depressive mood swings of the psychotic. This
phase seems mostly to concern the unadapted, unstructured raw material
of the psyche—its instinctual and emotional foundations from which are
distilled the elements that go into making an adapted, structured consciousness and its culture. This dark area is expressed in mythology as the maternal monster of chaos, in philosophy as the maternal void, or in alchemy as
the chaotic primordial matter (see Part II, § 25). To slip into the blackness
of the psyche is to regress from order into disorder, or from structuring into
destructuring, or from adaptedness to unadaptedness; it entails the sacrifice
of a conscious bias and a descent of its libido into its psychic substratum
to gain renewal by energizing needed contents and by raising them in this
manner to the threshold of consciousness, thus forming an integration on
a new level of development.[30] Conversely, a new form of structure or of life
given birth in this dark side would be a new leading value emerging from
the chthonic psyche into the world of consciousness.

Here the further evolution of the theme of the "new life" into the germination mandala (IX) and the struggle of the political parties (X–XII)
will give further elucidation of the nature of the new life as a symbol of the
self in both its dark and emergent aspects. The roles of the uncle's death and
of the conjunction of the dark male and female figures in creating this birth
will be discussed shortly. After the self has been shaped in an image in its
light and benign side (II), its dark and threatening opposite most frequently follows close upon it in the next dreams or fantasies (III and IV).
This is the "enantiodromia," the habitual turning over into the opposite or
the mutually compensatory play of opposites.

In the patient's Easter insight—that it is not she but Christ who died and
was resurrected and was at the center (Drawings V and VI)—was a return
to the light, spiritual side. Consistent with the gist of this whole phase of
her clinical course, she now more surely than ever put the deity at the
center and the ego out at the periphery as one among the adult community
of ordinary mortals. The imagery was even quite precise in its intent, for
in drawing the death and resurrection of the deity (V), she made him, in
the risen state, a red and black triangle, the same colors she had used to
portray herself at the center in Drawing I. More is learned of the connotations of these colors here: his descent into death is shown in the black rectangle (V), and his reign in immortal life at the center is in red (VI).
The risen Christ in red and black, then, shows that to her he is not all light
and spirit but that he has brought with him from the experience of suffering

and descent something of the dark and mortal—a union of opposites very necessary to his function of redeemer and reconciler of the natural world of men to the spiritual world of the deity. Her meaning in the red and black is practically identical with that of the Chinese Yang and Yin (see Part II, § 23),[31] thus further supporting the comparison of the center in Drawing I to the "T'ai-chi." Even closer in its implications is the Chinese companion concept of the two kinds of soul, the one immortal, spiritual, light (Hun), the other mortal, earthbound, and dark (P'o). The patient's designation of these as "my yes-and-no nature," or "glad-dismal," or "cheerful and bad" does not, of course, approach the Chinese in refinement of expression, but it is apparent that the intent is the same. On a higher level of expression is her perception that the Christ symbol is an "example" of a death and resurrection that we all experience; in brief, that is the function of the archetype (see Part II, § 29).

The patient in effect was reflecting on the meaning of the initiation process, which she was undergoing, in terms of the Christian archetype. The first initiation rite of Christianity is that of baptism, which Romans 5 and 6 expresses in terms that are certainly in the larger context here as well as in the context of the patient's ruminations (see Part II, §§ 27 and 30c). This epistle says that to be "baptized into Christ" is to be "baptized into his death," and "buried with him," and "planted together in the likeness of his death," the old, natural man being crucified with him, so that with him an initiate might be resurrected and walk in newness of life. The text goes on to a second point that is a corollary of this: there are two laws working in one's nature—the spiritual law of the mind and the carnal law of the members. The patient had been experiencing all this, not as ideas learned from reading the Bible, but as a deeply unconscious emotional turmoil that completely overwhelmed her; it is even more true that this Biblical passage was written from intimations of psychic process of the same unconscious origin.

In the process of the symbolic descent into death there is the fear that the ordeal may prove too overwhelming and that the psyche may be permanently damaged by it; it may be considered a good prognostic sign that the patient was not content to think of departing into a heaven away from reality but insisted that "we come back and face it here again." This she repeated on many occasions, and it represents the attitude that in the end did bring her through the work of the psychosis and back out of it into her real world.

As already mentioned, the impression given by Drawing VI is of a bald, bland statement of a half truth. Here is the light, "spiritual" side, the red, with no play of opposites whatever, just as the former drawings of the illegitimate baby was a one-sided statement of the contrary, dark aspect. However this may be, it does not detract from the importance of the perception that Christ is an image of the self, the center.[32] This was known also to the nature philosophers, who made the projection of this image into the goal of the Work, as Jung has demonstrated thoroughly in his discussion of the concept that the Stone, the One, Anthropos, Microcosm, and Christ, all have an inner identity.[33] It is to this image also that the Pauline epistle (Galatians 2: 20) refers as the Christ within (see Part II, § 29). Among these archetypal cosmic concepts it is not unusual to find that the center should be of fiery nature (cf., her associations to the red); for example, fire is at the center of the quadrated circular cosmos of the Platonists as well as at the center of the quadrated wheels of Ezekiel's vision.[34] The statement that to partake of the nature of the center is to take on the nature of fire is contained in the uncanonical words of Christ: "Whoever is near to me is near to the fire; whoever is far from me is far from the Kingdom."[85] The patient recorded this same idea in the gradations of the red according to the closeness to the center. A close parallel is to be found in Dante's *Paradiso* (see Part II, § 32). Looking into the eyes of Beatrice, he sees rings of light and, turning, he beholds in the heavens a central point of radiating light (divine) around which are nine concentric rings of fire consisting of souls; the closer to the center, the more rapid are the revolutions and the more translucent the flame of the ring, "because it shares its truth the most" and is "spurred onward by its ardent love."

The patient's later associations to the red of warmth, fire, and feelings, and the fact that here "the ones who give more" are in deeper red, suggest that by this theme she intended the meaning of Christian love. The idea of the inwardness of Christ is intimately bound up with the parable of the vine and the teaching that he is in his disciples and they in him inasmuch as they live in love.[36] As already mentioned, it was impossible for the patient to love when deified at the center; there she could only fear. But when she realized her participation in the community of those who shared the nature of the image of the deity, the inner potential, she could then develop and live the love belonging to it.

Her expression "Christ needs a great many people to see the whole world" comes from the same intimation that man has always had about his gods, that they depend on him: in ancient times they were thought to be sustained through man's sacrifices,[87] and in medieval times certain mystics said that God needed to be born anew in the soul of man.[88] We of today would restate it, in the language of psychology, that the archetype of the self stands in perpetual need of the effort of consciousness to bring it from the state of potentiality into actualization—that wholeness of the organism is an urge to be fulfilled. Similarly, in the individual this fulfillment of the totality will not come about unless the individual participates in vital relationship with his community.[39] It is commonly agreed that the predominant function of initiation rites among primitives is to equip the child in emotion and in knowledge to become a responsible member of the adult community of the tribe.[40] It could be expected equally that the archetypal heritage of the initiation process, which the patient was undergoing at this time, would bear the same features and serve similar ends.

From the atmosphere of Drawing VI, which was rather high-flown and removed from the patient's more pressing problem, she turned to the other direction—to the emergent new life in the blackness. This dark side, concerned as it is with instinct and emotion and the natural man, has to do with the materialization of psychic into concrete experience, to the same extent that the light side just discussed has to do with the disembodied mind structure of inner development. This actualization of the potential is the specific area in which the schizophrenic fails, and in which psychotic episode differs sharply from genuine religious experience, no matter how great the similarity of the symbolic expression in each. She thus proceeded immediately to deal with the strong emotions that lie in this dark area, and with the next interview another step in her initiation was undertaken. She was depressed and grieved over her bitterly resentful feelings toward her mother, and she announced her intention to deal with them. The reaction away from the disembodied, impersonal images and toward her practical, personal emotions was evidenced by her momentary wish to have nothing more to do with the drawings, since "I'm trying to solve my own problems"; fortunately, however, she realized that even these could be expressed through diagrams and that real results could be achieved in so doing.

In rehearsing the entire history of her growing up, she squarely faced the degree to which she had remained in an infantile relation to the parents. She rebelled vehemently against the regression expressed in the initial delusions and Drawing I, and saw to it that she found some way out from under the maternal domination. As mentioned above in the discussion of the symbolism of the return to the mother, although the mother is blamed for an evil intent to destroy the child, this intent originates instead in the child's own regressive backward lagging in infantility (see Part II, § 30a). However much the real mother may have domineered the child, in the grip of an unconscious maternal instinct to possess, the subjective factor that held the child so effectively under this dominion was the spell of the archetypal mother, projected upon and acted out by the real parent. This is the "mother complex." This archetypal mother, providing all the implementations of death and disintegration, also has the advantage of possessing the indispensable means of salvation from them—through rebirth, rejuvenation, and transformation (see Part II, § 30a–d). The patient was dealing with both kinds of mother: she had succumbed to the clutches of death and earth and the enfolding embrace of the real parent, and was now fighting free of the dominion of the latter at the same time that the "new life" was coming into being out of the archetypal mother. The freedom for which she was fighting was thus twofold—from the outer and the inner mother, a liberty of ego in the community and of spirit in the psyche. The severance of every sort of bond with the real parent is an integral part of the procedure of the initiation rites among primitives (see Part II, § 27), and is directed toward the liberation of the youth from all traces of childishness and weakness that comes from protracted maternal influence; he leaves the home forever, and no longer recognizes his family, but considers himself now the brother of the other initiated youths and a son of the tribal ancestors or totem.

In the mandala (Drawing VII, *d*) several recognizable features recur. The red is the ego at the center again, in the spiritual, developmental aspect, learning to love. The black encases the whole and represents the practical "problems to face"—that is, the coming to grips with reality, which the mother complex always prevents; this black is the same dark element just discussed—of the concretization and actualization of the potential through her emotional entanglements, which, in their state of unconsciousness, are found in projection as a disturbing "confused mass" or chaos. Around the center are the circulating radiations of "all colors"—this time as her friends, through whom she learned to enjoy a real community of relationships. The circulation of the periphery in the initial mandala (Drawing I) was the traffic that she later recognized as the people in the world (also done in "all colors"), and in the Christ mandala (Drawing VI) it was also the people (which she at first intended to do in "all colors"). Again it was apparent that the totality represented by "all colors" was a whole human community, and that the work of generating (indicated by its circulation") was toward the production of her capacity to relate; in Drawing VII, *d,* it was more personal in that it indicated the Eros experienced in her own friendships. Since it involved community and not only homosexual ties, it was again a step further toward maturity than Drawing II.

In the mandala (Drawing VII, *e*), at her place of work, a striking change takes place. The black changes places with the red and now represents a problem of world dimensions. The global war was a conflict of opposites on a scale akin to the cosmic. Chaos and mass destructiveness had become a collective problem, participation in which had given the patient's little world an enlargement of horizon. As a result the "center of attraction" could no longer remain the infantile ego in a parent-bound world; instead it became the great problems of all humankind—the tremendous dynamics of the psyche that arouse whole masses to conflict. From this point on she was primarily concerned with this kind of gigantic collective psychic factor and was ready to acknowledge that she was "just a tiny bit" relative to it. She enclosed the black central chaos in circles denoting her work, her friendships, and her marriage, which then serve as containers for the interplay of these tremendous forces. (That her marriage was in red again suggested that this color carried the connotation of Eros.) The "problems to be faced" were now internalized, and formed the center. The black global war was the same that occurred at the center in the last drawing of the series (XII); but between this encounter with the theme and that final one, there took place an entire differentiation of the elements that made up the conflict, so that a solution became implemented thereby.

The battle for freedom from the mother was her main task—the liberation of her still infantile individuality, lying heretofore behind the protecting surface of a mask of appearances learned from that parent. But since it activated very strong and very negative emotions, it was not surprising that it plunged the patient back into the depressive and confused darkness of psychotic disturbance. At this point, the conclusion must be drawn that she was still unable to handle the feelings that needed to become conscious; for they were disturbing, and the conflict they brought with them in their contrast to the "gay side"—the nice-girl consciousness—was too great to bridge. Further capacity for the reconciliation of these opposites was still needed.

In the illusion that the therapist was an army officer lies a hint of the location of the hostile feelings that were arising at this juncture. The soldier is a representative of a collective system of aggression. In being masculine, aggressive, and collective, and in a particularly intimate relation to the patient, he is unmistakably an animus figure.[42] In the woman's psyche the factor that initiates the process of distinguishing her individuality from the general participation in the relationships around her is the animus, which carries the masculine property of discrimination and separation as against the entangling and binding quality of the feminine.[43] Consequently she put the father in the position of agent of separation of mother from child, the father being the first carrier of the projected image of the animus of the child.[44] The fact that the therapist encouraged the outpouring of these feelings of hate went far to constellate this image and activate this function complex; but it was disturbing to the patient, for the therapist then no longer was the saint who reconciled all things in a spiritual unity.

It seems that in her regression this time she identified with the center in the aspect of animus rather than of infant. The poisons now were not so much from her mother's drawing her back to the family circle, but were in her doctor's medications designed to turn her into a man. Her worries about hermaphroditism stemmed not only from her intuitions of the androgynous qualities of the self with which she was identifying, but from her sense that in her make-up now was something masculine as well as feminine. This was the animus, still primitive and unadapted, and hence characterized more by aggressive than discriminating properties.[45] Thus she was disturbed by the perception within her of an impulse toward "hurting other people and messing things up." This is the direct counterpart to the Christ image, by whose influence people dwell together in love. The soldier image and the Christ image are opposing aspects of the animus, which holds within itself the potential of the self at this juncture, so that to identify with it is again to be at the center.[46] This identification with the animus, or in a man's case with the anima, is characteristic of schizophrenia.[47] Thus in her seventh week, the delusions were full of remorse for her destructive influence; the world depended upon her rule, but found that she was weak and was the source of all the world's troubles. In this condition she was incapable of love.

Just as she had been blaming her mother for keeping her infantile, so she attributed to the poison all her present difficulties—the depression, the myriad crazy thoughts and feelings, the guilt, and the whole suspicion of homosexuality. It was now both the medication given for healing and the potion that was insidiously turning her into a man. Here she was trying to express her feeling that something was being activated in her as if by an agency quite outside herself; this is the usual impression given by the autonomy of the function complex as it exerts its independent influences in the personality—in this case, the animus in this negative aspect.

Previously the external agency had been felt to be the mother—really the mother complex—whose effects she expressed in her fears of being poisoned by the mother. At that time she was finding death where love should have been—in the milk the mother gives her child; what should nourish only destroyed. The bond with the mother had been much too strong; it had given rise to an identification with the mother that only cloaked the daughter's own specific personality. Hence this love became a poison that kept her unconscious and infantile, and dissolved every individual effort of consciousness; it could only be felt as an evil, and her struggle for individuality necessitated a fight against it. Thus, the love that was so unconscious could only give rise to hate—"the poison is the hate that destroys," as she put it. As the aspect of any unconscious complex mirrors the attitude of consciousness toward it, appearing fearful if the ego is afraid of it or powerful if the ego feels weak against it, so here her own fearing hate toward the mother complex was felt by her as a threatening hate on the mother's part. In the early experiments with word-association tests in family groups,[48] it was demonstrated that a patient's paranoid feelings are most directed against that member of the family with whom he or she is most identified. The aim is, of course, the struggle for one's individuality, which is always threatened by identifications. In ancient tradition it has long been recognized that the factor endowing things with individuality and distinctness one from the other is hatred—the opposite of love, which makes all one.[49]

At this juncture the patient felt that the external agency was the poison that was turning her into a man. The dark new entity being brought to birth in the patient was the animus of discrimination, separation, or hate, which

would open the way for her coming into her own. That this new entity
was dual in its nature was further borne out by her later dream in which she
called the poison by the name of a dog food and made it rhyme with a word
for coitus. It was toxic, but nourishing to the instinct; it was hate, but gave
rise to selfhood; it was destruction, but engendered out of mother love; it
was the potion of a plot to masculinize her, but also her medication ordered
by the doctor she trusted. This is entirely in keeping with the general
symbolism of poisons, which can be at the same time healing mixtures and
destructive toxins (see Part II, §§ 7, 30a)—for example, the Christian "drug
of immortality," the alchemists' primordial matter, or the Aesculepian
serpent. The patient had just put her "nigredo," her "problems to be faced,"
at the center in the last drawing (VII), and it became in fact the beginning
substance of an entire synthesizing process that runs through the ensuing
fantasies. This beginning substance is a chaos of mass hatred and war, from
which four elements are separated and emerge from their clash in darkness
into a peaceful unity in the brightness of the ruling sun—at each point an
effort to seek the "new life."

The drawing of the tree (VIII) might at first seem out of place in a
series that is so consistently working out the problem just discussed, but
the contrary is true. The unconscious was constantly trying to define and
synthesize the center, and it might be anticipated to use the classical symbols
of this progress at each point. Her intention here was to show the relation
of the center to the group—that is, herself at the center in red, and the group
around her in many colors, as she had already done in Drawings I and VII.
She was psychotic again, and was identifying with the deity at the central
position of rulership in her delusions of this phase. Of all the symbols of
the central archetype, the tree is one of the most consistently and frequently
seen in the world's mythologies. It has not only the properties of the
mandala already mentioned, but is frequently seen placed in the mandala;
their equivalence is seen in Plates VIII and IX (see Part II, § 12). In other
words, the tree may be the cosmic center or axis, the deity, the maternal
womb from which the deity is born and the symbol on which he dies, the
source of enlightenment or of the knowledge of the opposites, or perhaps
the dispenser of healing potions. Often it is the embodiment of the dying
and resurrecting god himself, or of the hermaphroditic transforming substance; as such, it is the symbol of "new life" par excellence. This tree often
comprises seven planets or stages of the process (Plate VIII). Most of these
connotations are implied in the patient's representation of her delusions.
The function of the red, it should be noted, is to mediate between her own
differentiated mind (her flairs) and the crowd, thus suggesting once more
its role of relationship, Eros, and feeling. This relation of the central red to
the surrounding community in all colors has already been seen in Drawings
I, VI, and VII.

The progress of the "new life" was taken up again in the germination theme (Drawing IX), the corrective to her attempt to show herself at the center in red. Considering its place in the series, we are justified in regarding this as a differentiation and growth within the blackness, that "nigredo" already appearing in the form of baby and cancer and chaos. There are no personal associations or emotional contexts whatever to this image; thus it must be considered as a symbol, and its meaning must be elucidated through the method of amplification. The explicit description of the imagery of the evolution of the black motif can be found nowhere so clearly as in the alchemical system of projections, since, above all others, the hermetic philosophers experienced the same psychic problems of Western culture that confront the modern mentality—that is, the structuring of the dark aspect of the self that tends to be denied and repressed. The patient was following the classical procedure as reflected in this system, that the black primary substance should be divided into four elements in two pairs. This was often represented as the cleaving of an egg as a chaos.[50] Further differentiation of these four elements appeared in the patient's later fantasies about the political parties, also referred to in terms of the "new birth" and "new life." In alchemy the synthesized Stone was called "Son," "Round Thing," "Holy Embryo," "Golden Egg," or "Golden Child," the form of whose birth is similar to the fourfold or twelvefold wheel (see Part II, §§ 5, 18). The fourness and twelveness of the design in either the patient's or the alchemist's symbolism has solar connotations, as does the golden color (see Part II, §§ 1, 3, 14, 18).[51] The final fantasies of the patient bore this out, and there are innumerable symbolic parallels to demonstrate the archetypal basis of this identity of golden germ, child, and sun as the self (see Part II, § 31). Finally, according to the alchemists, the gold of the sun was found within the black substance because the "nigredo" was the black earth in which the gold was sown like the grain, spun into it by the rays of the sun circulating around it.[52] The "doodle," then, can be interpreted as a kind of diagrammatic anticipation of the ensuing steps of her fantasies.

Research has been made on the subject of these mandalalike "doodles" drawn by children. In an unpublished paper, Rhoda Kellogg makes a statistical analysis of these configurations, and finds that the child's manner of depicting the human figure evolves gradually out of these sunlike, mandalalike quadrated circles.[53]

In the eighth week the resolution of the whole psychotic regressive situation started moving vigorously—and, it must be admitted, as the consequence of the depressive, perturbed phase that the patient was experiencing at the time. Such an outcome is characteristic, since careful observation of a depressive process reveals that the "backward" or "downward" flow of libido has the effect of activating, in the blackness, values hitherto only latent and lost to consciousness. Fortunately, the patient clearly identified these activated values in her case.

Until now she had been living in the guise of her "gay and superficial mask," an effect of remaining entirely under the domination of the mother. The accompanying attitude to life was the one she expressed in the final interview—that fate managed everything and that she never had to plan things or think them through, because all was predestined. Such a feeling is characteristic of the infantile state in which all the world seems magically permeated by the mother and her influences, and which therefore tends to leave all responsibility in her hands. This state of mind is designated in analytical psychology by the term "provisional life," in that such a person cannot think of herself as being yet old enough to have an independent, self-determined life of her own; rather she gives an impression of never quite experiencing present realities for their present value, but always only in relation to a mythical future in which things will be different for her. The archetypal pattern underlying this basic orientation is known as the "Eternal Child," the *"puer aeternus"* or *"puella aeterna,"* who exists only in relation to the mother goddess. The ego—such as it is—of this kind of individual is similarly only an adjunct to the mother complex, since such an ego tends to remain in identification with the child archetype and to perceive the mother in identification with the mother archetype.

The patient now realized that it was imperative for her to discover herself—that is, her real individuality—and that this process of self-discovery entailed fighting away from her mother in a spirit of hatred. We can interpret this as meaning that tearing down the persona must go hand in hand with struggling free of her own mother complex and infantility. Her psychotic material had already demonstrated that the inner corollary of being the adored child of doting parents is the identification with the archetype of the Divine Child—the self. Analysis of the mother at this time would probably have revealed that this woman's spiritual potential of individuality was lodged in projection onto her child, and that the child would appear in her dreams as the representation of the self that should be entering the consciousness and the life experience of the mother. This is the counterpart of the daughter's receiving this projection and being overwhelmed by the archetype of the Divine Child—the self; thus "devoured" by the mother, the daughter remained cuddled in the maternal lotus in perpetual infantility, in absolute rulership, and in celestial innocence, until it became imperative to break this spiritual imprisonment.

This rule at the "center"—the "center of attraction"—was being overthrown, and the innocence—the suspension among the inert and undifferentiated opposites—put to a quick finish. The psyche accomplished this by bringing to birth a new entity out of its dark, chthonic side—the "new life," or the fourth party—and hell itself was unleashed for a while. These images might be considered only mild figures of speech except for the great intensity of the emotions about them, the tremendous fear, distrust, perplexity, self-reproach, and guilt, over the matter of her world rule and the revolt against her.

The potential of individuality was fostered by the husband, who, she said at another point, did much to bring her out and help her to mature and become independent. This same role was also assigned to the therapist; so both men were suspected of being delegates of the revolutionary party—psychologically they were. The mother was—naturally—the conservative party, standing firmest against any such change and opposing the husband's or the doctor's effort. Thus the masculine image (animus) was again the agent of discrimination and of self-discrimination, who would break the deadlock between the opposites which were thus far invested entirely in the parental authorities as in Drawing I. The separation and differentiation of the opposites are the initial act of consciousness, mythologically expressed as the eating of the fruit of the central tree, giving the knowledge of the opposites that thrust the first man and woman out of the innocence of the primitive paradise of Eden.[54] Preceding this discriminative activity in her, the pairs of opposites were bound together, and inertia held sway because of the lack of polarity; consciousness then remained primitive or infantile, and the opposites parental. But after this juncture, they became the "two sides to a person"—to her, the "masculine and feminine parts of me"—unconscious and conscious, by whose conjunction a third entity, the "new life," was brought to birth.

In Drawing X the husband animus is, then, the agent bringing, not only a discrimination of the opposites, but also a reconciliation of them under the rule of a third. This "third party"—or "new life"—is the "reconciling symbol" that intervenes in such situations of arrest and suspension of the libido between opposite polarities in deadlock and supersedes them both by embracing them, thus offering a way ahead for resumption of its progressive movement.[55] This is a kind of Hegelian dialectic, or—better—perhaps the Hegelian concept was derived from this kind of psychic foundation. But the reconciling symbol is incomplete if it represents only the union of the two sides of a conflict in a third, thus making a threefold pattern of wholeness (the green world with three parties of Drawing X); the threefold pattern has a tendency to lead over into fourness,[56] for the reconciling symbol contains the potential of the self.

On the last two days of the series the patient's ambivalent feelings of fear and confidence toward the new life or new party paralleled those about her husband himself. There was a great distrust because of all that he seemed unconsciously to imply to her, as bringer of the inner revolution against her infantile rule; yet there was also the assurance that he was liberating her and bringing her into her own. She knew the result was desirable—that an old authoritarian rule was to be sacrificed in favor of a new leveling and harmony, and that this meant that the "upper class," the mother's party, was to be destroyed. To her, this was synonymous with destroying the old superficial mask that her mother inculcated in her by false standards, the persona.[57] Thus the struggle was the classic one of animus against persona, directed toward bringing the ego to the experience of her true nascent individuality.[58] As antagonist and rebel against the conscious standpoint, he with the forces behind him is enemy to it; yet, as bringer of a new and improved state of development, he is redeemer to the psyche as a whole (see Part II, § 21). With this new influence, she said that she was becoming aware of great depths in her, "like the bottom of the sea," a classical image of the collective unconscious; this was the extent of the profundity of the animus-led movement from below, from the rebellious "lower classes," the dark reaches of the collective unconscious, as deep as the persona mask was shallow.

Such was the struggle in the arena of the personal psychology of the patient. At another level this struggle is the collective theme of the battle of the hero against the great mother to wrest from her the symbol or function of rulership that she hoards.[59] Until now the patient had identified herself with this central ruling function still lodged in the archetypal mother; so the struggle would naturally involve freeing the ego from this mother-bound state and setting up a central ruler that was not ego. As already mentioned, the use of these political symbols, of world dimensions and general import to all men, was valuable in getting the patient oriented to the collective, suprapersonal character of the issues with which she was embroiled at this point.

The patient's insight of the forty-seventh day, that the two rival parties are the masculine and feminine parts of herself, indicated the psychological nature of the third party, the "new life" and "new birth." She had said of the two that they were the father's and mother's parties, and the image related back to the opening delusions in which these two were the conflicting halves of the world, the father's and mother's sides being somehow associated with the sun and moon and suggesting kingship and queenship. The opposing halves of the cosmic circle and those of the family circle were recognized as representations of halves of herself in her state of division between contrary aspects; hence cosmos and parents were images of the self. Moreover, their union is a theme found universally in the various systems of projection of these archetypes (see Part II, §§ 6, 22, 26). The *hieros gamos* of classical mythology and its connections with fertility and initiatory rites have already been mentioned (see also Part II, § 27). In the alchemical system the "coniunctio" of Sol and Luna as King and Queen is an essential step in the procedure; from it issues the child as the forerunner of the goal, the Stone. The child born of the cosmic couple is a symbol of unity arising out of the tension of the opposites, as Jung has frequently pointed out, and thus it is an image of the totality or the self. In this case the patient depicted the pair in the classical colors—blue for male and red for female, but the child in black as a circle in the red square. It is dark, threatening, the rebellious "Communist" faction—thus the enemy; it might be called the devil aspect of the redeeming reconciler.[60] What good can come of such a foe? According to the paradise myth, it was the Evil One who propelled the first couple into their move toward consciousness and conflict between the opposites—thus their eviction from the protective mandala enclosure.

An evidence of the general validity of these issues was the surprisingly spontaneous emergence of the fourth party in the patient's mind as a necessary addition to the former three; this seemed to impress itself upon her autonomously without her seeing the sense of it, just as the other autochthonous contents of her delusions had. She was even incredulous that people could have four parts to their nature, and was ready to doubt, if the therapist agreed to the point, that he could be a real doctor or anything but insane himself! She was distrustful of these unconscious intuitions and the therapist's alliance with them. Yet they were extremely meaningful to her, and she realized that the problem raised by them was the great crisis that she had been pushing aside for many years, as difficult to fathom as it was deeply serious—the discovery of her own individual wholeness.

The necessity of the fourness of the group of parties had no connection with the need for symmetry of patterns, it should be noted, since her first experimental placements of the four were side by side and rather askew (Drawing XI). The number had occurred in studied fashion only in the germination mandala, and there she refused to make comment on any significance it might have; in Drawing II it was more a question of a reduplicated third. Rather, all the evidence given in the discussion of the symbolism of the individuation process urge the conclusion that the psychic factors with which the patient was attempting to cope were the same that humans have always had to find ways to formulate and that the alchemists particularly described ad infinitum in their extraordinarily copious system of projections. She distinguished four parties, as they separated out four elements, and both she and the alchemists found them inimical, in a state of strife until united together in the One, which both she and the alchemists expressed in the form of the quadrated circle (see Part II, §§ 18, 24). The text and its diagram cited above depicted almost the identical experience as the patient's in Drawing XII, this time couched in different terms (see Part II, § 20); there also the central circle was called "mediator, making peace among the inimicals." The patient described blackness when the four are at war, as the alchemists also said that the "nigredo" is an imperfect state in which the four are in a condition of enmity and chaos (see Part II, § 24).[61] That the sun emerges out of the blackness at the center into the position of rulership is true of both, as indeed it must be, since the comparative symbolism of the quadrated circle has demonstrated its solar and ruling nature. The sun thus becomes a quintessence, the binding of the four in a new unity without any one of them being destroyed thereby; on this point patient and alchemists insisted alike (see Part II, § 24).[62] The emergence at the center she called the "real new birth," as those philosophers also said of the birth that its form was like the wheel, the golden child being the gold and sun generated out of the blackness (see Part II, §§ 5, 31).[63] Its analogy to the Christ image, seen by the patient when it was suggested that the center is the position of the deity, has its parallels in alchemy as already noted.[64] The alchemists said that their Stone was like Christ, in whose body occurred "a most intimate binding" of the four elements hitherto in a state of "chaotic antagonism." It was their thesis that the First Adam was natural man, mortal, made of the four corruptible warring elements, whereas the Second or Last Adam (Christ)[65] was spiritual man, immortal, made of the one, incorruptible, pure essence uniting the four;[66] the unconscious psyche prompts man thus to express the emergence of individuality as a rejuvenation, by the death of the old and the birth of the new.

Thus the finding of the fourth factor appears to be nature's way, necessary to the progress of psychic synthesis. The patient made it quite plain that the place of the ego relative to the new fourfold center was a difficult question to comprehend; but the outcome made it equally clear that the end state obtruded itself into her awareness and led her toward its own ends. The weaving of the fantasy was propelled by truly autonomous influences, which had systematically ousted the ego from the central position and replaced it by an image that is universal but whose significance was hitherto unknown to the patient. Tibetan rites had the same purpose—of sacrifice of the "ego self" in favor of the "higher self" in the form of a cosmic mandala (see Part II, §§ 13, 28). This has been true of many such manifestations of this unconscious problem, in many different religions. In the psychotic process the patient did not undertake the venture by intention, but rather the sacrifice was imposed upon her by the same forces that constituted the original difficulty, the unconscious.

The paranoid mechanism was made clear in these events. The paranoid fear represents the threat to the ego, in its state of inflation, from the unconscious, in its aim to overthrow the ego from its dangerous identification with the ruling center, the self. The paranoid state was induced here by the fear of an involuntary sacrifice imposed by the unconscious upon the mother-bound ego unwilling to recognize and surrender its usurped role. Since the object of the fear was unconscious, it was naturally projected; first the mother, then the husband, and finally the Communists were all held in suspicion.

The patient's infantile prejudice first led her to expect that somehow the four parties would converge in herself, that the tremendous clash of powers would focus upon the ego as if she were still in the parental world. But as

soon as she represented this on paper, it seemed all wrong (Drawing XI, *a*);
she knew ego was not at the center—that is, it no longer felt that way to her.
Yet the point of convergence had to be at some functional center, therefore
somehow in the midst of the circle, though she sensed the parties as still
crowded in together side by side near the ego (Drawing XI, *b*). Simultaneously she recognized the impossibility that any powers as large as world
political factions should all meet within her ego self. Their strange quality—
of being somehow within and yet somehow much greater than she—
impressed her in such a way as to lead her now to conclude that therein was
an order of events in a realm of its own, to which she herself did not belong.
Only at this point could the "real rebirth" take place, which is the birth of
the golden, solar, divine center out of the darkness, bringing the four
opposites into union, in a totality comprising the deepest depths and the
uppermost authority—that is, unconscious and conscious.

As to the specific nature of the parties in terms of the patient's own psychology, the question was more difficult to cope with, especially as no actual
analysis was being done and the personal associations to the archetypal
material were not forthcoming in any consistent manner. However, she
did say a great deal about her former fear and hate of people and her present
delight in finding herself liked by them; at the same time she described the
qualities of the Socialist party as the one that strives for the brotherhood of
man and is "sociable" and that stands for the principle of the leveling of all
classes and parties. This party seemed to contain within itself the viewpoint
of striving toward the harmonious state that was actually reached in the
final solution. This was expressed in red, which might suggest that this party
represented the feeling function.

This function in her is the one that mediated between the two others.
It would enable her to live in relationships with her social community as
vital as those of the symbolic world community depicted in the diagram
of the new inner order. In other words, this function motivated the carrying
out of this inner potential into actuality, mediating between the inner world
and the outer, by conferring feeling valuations upon the latter. The sense
of reality depends upon this role of feeling to create meaningful connections
with the objective world, and these are cut across when feeling is withdrawn.[87] This function was the missing factor when her inner perceptions
were remaining only psychotic fantasies instead of becoming motivating
experiences, perhaps religious ones. The lack of this function probably
initiated the psychotic regression to activate the unconscious, and its appearance was a prerequisite to the setting in motion of the integrative process
and the consequent release from the psychotic disturbance. What made this
step in her development so extremely difficult was that this function needed
first of all to be experienced in its most intolerable, negative, shadow side—
in hatred of the mother and fear of her friends—before it could be accepted

to the point of being serviceable to consciousness for real discrimination of valuation, of liking and disliking, and of appreciating and depreciating.[68] In accordance with this trend, the imagery had to deal with the shadow situation of conflict and hate and strife before the enlightened reign of peace and harmony could emerge. Only by such disturbing acts of discrimination and differentiation could a sound ego consciousness be structured, capable of evaluating her surrounding world realistically and relating to it comfortably.

This final diagram (Drawing XII), then, portrayed a new fourfold center, designated as sun and deity and new birth, emerging as light from darkness, gold from blackness, peace from war, or unity from enmity, perhaps cosmos from chaos. Each of these aspects is a culmination of themes running through the whole series of images from the start.[69] The crucial observation here is that each aspect is also a classical element in the traditional symbolism of the self (see Part II, §§ 1–20). Therefore the patient's labors had all gone into evolving an image that was already preformed *in potentia.* Her struggle had been not toward creation of something new, but toward her new apperception of the most ancient of human experience. Since the apperceptions obtruded themselves into her consciousness without her quite realizing their significance, it must be said that the image was evolving and fulfilling itself under her observation from the onset of the psychotic eruption of unconscious contents. For the self apparently strives to manifest itself and realize itself in human experience, and directs the movements of the psyche toward its self-completion. As it was said of another bearer of this archetypal image, he who was born existed from the beginning.

10 CONCLUSIONS

The basic viewpoint of analytical psychology emphasizes the need for genuinely empirical study of unconscious material. This approach demonstrates that the symbols encountered contain profound meaning and represent developmental process. The material of the schizophrenic case was presented at first with a minimum of psychological hypothesis in order to bring out the factual nature of the symbolic process contained in the fantasies, and after this the material of the comparative symbolism was presented at first similarly without such hypothesizing, in order to indicate the universality of these phenomena and elucidate their meaning. Only then was the psychological theory given and its application in the interpretation of the material attempted. At this point it would be well to consider the nature of the whole discussion with reference to the distinction between data of observation and theory.

The essential fact, it should be stressed, is that the patient was preoccupied with the question of a center, identified with it when she was most psychotic and disidentified when least so, and spontaneously gave it the same general plastic form that the archaic psyche has always given it in various times and places, without knowing that she was doing so—that is, without having become acquainted with such symbolism before. Equally a matter of fact is that a spontaneous development of the symbol, with its differentiations, its correlative symbols, and its various attributes, took place during a period of weeks and described a process of synthesizing a fourfold center that was not ego. Furthermore, the theme of death and rebirth went hand in hand with rebellion against the parental domination and with new awareness of her own individuality. Equally factual are the experiences that other individuals and groups have had of these same psychic contents and processes, both in our culture and in many others, as seen in the comparative studies.

These objective events, it is suggested, constitute the data of observation. It has been shown here and elsewhere that it is possible to group and classify such data, and that regularities can be found thereby that make the data more meaningful than would otherwise be possible. The question of predictions is more difficult with such spontaneous phenomena, which can hardly be subjected to experimental conditions, but it can be justly claimed that the therapist's anticipation of the general nature of the patient's plastic representation of the center constitutes such a prediction. It might also be added here that he predicted an aimful process in the psychosis at a staff conference before he undertook the therapy of the case. Thus far it can hardly be disputed that the esoteric and archaic contents of the psyche can truly be handled by scientific method.

The entire last half of the discussion of the present case and the statement of theory and interpretation are not factual data, but are secondary to these as working hypothesis only. No claim can be made about the objective validity of these as it can about that of the observed phenomena themselves. It must be admitted, however, that the theory as constructed by Jung goes little further than is necessary to account for the regularities seen in the data of experience.

To be less coldly methodological in the evaluation of the material, such a spontaneous occurrence of mandala symbolism is a remarkable phenomenon with unescapable ethnological implications (see Part II, § 33). It is too often assumed that the unconscious imagery in fantasy is largely made up of material derived from the conditioning by the culture, that since the mind must be a *tabula rasa* at its birth all its contents must be learned from experience. Yet psychiatrists are continually watching psychotic delusions of death and rebirth and identifications with deities in which, though the themes may be familiar in the culture, the uses to which they are put in representing the psyche's movements are not known in the culture. In the case presented here, the endogenous nature of the imagery is made even more clear by the fact that the mandala is not a symbol known in this culture; if the patient had by any chance seen the symbol, she still would not have been able to elaborate its various connotations in such accurate detail. The difficulties encountered in exploring the symbol in the present discussion are evidence enough that the symbol is not generally known.

Rather do such phenomena urge the acceptance of the concept of an unconscious psyche with autonomous propensities toward self-representation, self-organization, and self-structuring. The inevitable conclusion is

that the self is a psychic center that is autonomous and nonego—an archetype that represents the organizing focal point of the total psyche. Concealed
in this symbolism lie problems so profound as to merit far more investigation than they have yet received. As a renowned explorer of the deep reaches
of psychic experience wrote long ago of this imagery,

Dante: "If only were the world
          Disposed as I perceive these wheels to be,
          What thou hast told me now would be enough....
          I must hear further ...
          For by myself I cannot understand."

Beatrice: "If thine own fingers cannot loose this knot,
          In truth it is no marvel—for the cord
          Has grown so hard for want of being tried."[1]

_____
[1] For notes to chapter 10, see p 164

PART II

I INTRODUCTION

Since the symbolism of the self is still almost entirely unfamiliar in the modern West, and since it nonetheless promises to be of central importance in the analysis and therapy of unconscious processes, it seems appropriate to present the historical data here in some detail.

The following may give the appearance of an elaborate search into the highways and byways of cultural expressions for merely alien and esoteric symbolic usages. The course of such an investigation might even seem labyrinthine in its turns and juxtapositions and groupings, but the thread to guide the reader is the concept of projection and systems of projection. Part I has shown to what degree these symbol formations can be endogenous in the unconscious of the patient; these collective representations need not be considered as only the product of cultural diffusion. Apparently, wherever man confronts the unknown, the unaccountable, and the mysterious in his world, he finds himself disposed to apprehend it in terms of the primordial images. For what is unknown equates itself with the unconscious, and what is unconscious tends to be symbolized. In consequence, where man has needed to induce fertility, to rejuvenate the year or the manhood of the community, to read his destiny in the stars, to account for his creation, to foster moral order and an organic society, or to further his own spiritual development, there he has tended always, for lack of better objective understanding, to use the language and practice of the archetypes. The problems of life that are most pressing and most generally valid tend to find expression in generally valid emotions and imagery. Thus, in magic, in ritual and myth, in folklore, and in various protosciences, the arrays of archetypal images are found ordered, elaborated, and externalized in the vegetation, the heavens, the cosmos, the ancestors, or the outward symbols of ritual. These are the systems of projection, and for the purposes of scientific study of the imagery of the unconscious processes they are source materials as instructive as the productions of modern men and women undergoing analysis.

Naturally, some violation is done to the material when a certain species of imagery is taken out of the context of the rest of the complete system of projection—for example, the mandala considered apart from the general Buddhist culture. This approach is under criticism by cultural anthropologists at the present time. On the other hand, it must be agreed that much is learned by the comparative method. The result is that when the topic is reexamined in its specific context, the full scope of its meaning and role is more lucid than it could otherwise have been, and details that might have received little attention assume their proper recognition and perspective. Although this method is not ideal, it is still useful and perhaps even unavoidable in the study of symbolism. An illuminating example of its counterpart—the fruits of the comparative knowledge brought into the study of a symbol within its whole context—is found in Jung's *Psychologie und Alchemie,* in which the goal of the nature philosopher's work is shown to be identical with the goal of the individuation process, the synthesizing of the self, the archetypes being projected into matter. In the present comparative study, a transection is made across various systems of projection to delineate the forms of the self in each.

The following discussion consists, then, of a compilation of data and comments to expand and elaborate some of the observations briefly mentioned in Part I.

2 THE SYMBOLISM OF THE QUADRATED CIRCLE

The symbol of the quadrated circle is so many-sided that it cannot be said to designate only one or only another psychological entity, but rather it seems to be suggestive of many things at once, now emphasizing one aspect, now another, and at times all of them at once. We cannot avoid violating the expectations of the rational intellect, then, in describing it, for its very nature consists of condensation and paradox. A somewhat bewildering heterogeneity of forms and meanings is regrettable but inevitable.

§ 1. The simplest form of the quadrated circle is the *sun wheel*, containing a cross whose four arms have traditionally represented the four cardinal points,[1] as in the Asiatic mandala the four are the four directions or four continents (see §§ 14, 28). None of the authorities quoted here claims that the sun wheel is the basis of the Asiatic mandala, but Cammann's argument that the mandala may be derived historically from the Han mirror (see § 14) seems to indicate that this is likely, since the latter was essentially a circle and cross with the sun at its center.

If this is true, the sun wheel can be shown to form the root symbol for all the derivative symbols based on the quadrated circle (fig. 1).

The sun has been represented as a spoked wheel in all parts of the world since earliest history.[2] It was of importance apparently as early as paleolithic times, as seen in the Rhodesian rock paintings.[3]

---

[1] For notes to chapter 2, see pp 164–167.

Figure 1. *a*. Diagram of sun wheel. *b*. Diagram of Han mirror.

Figure 2. Emblem of
Akkadian sun-god.

Figure 3. Emblem of
Akkadian sky-god.

Figure 4. Sun wheels. *a*. Mycenaean. *b*. Greek.

Figure 5. Sun wheels. *a*. Swiss lake dwellers. *b*. Gallic.

Figure 6. Sun wheels. *a*. Dakotas. *b*. Mississippi.

In early Sumero-Akkadian monuments and seals, the circle and cross designated the sun or sun-god Shamash (fig. 2).

The Maltese cross originated there as the emblem of the highest god, Anu (sky- or light-god), and of the king[5] (fig. 3).

The symbol was in common use from one to three millenia B.C., in the various civilizations centered in the Mediterranean, most significantly in Malta, Mycenae, and Etruria.[6] In Greece it was an attribute of Apollo, seen on his scepter or as the spoked wheel of his chariot of the sun[7] (fig. 4).

The Bronze Age of Western Europe has left remains in the form of coins and charms with the sun wheel and solar cross,[8] and the Gallic sun-god was pictured with thunderbolt hammer and eight-spoked solar wheel,[9] which signs are found also on his altars[10] (fig. 5).

In India the sun was represented as a cross and rayed disk, and the Rigveda speaks of the "golden wheel of the sun."[11] The Buddhist "Wheel of the Law" is similarly a thousand-spoked sun wheel that, after a baptism in the east, rolls through the four quarters. In China the circle and cross, in the form of the swastika, was adopted in the seventh century as the character for "sun," whereas the square with the cross signified "earth."[12] In the

Figure 7. The sun in Navajo sand painting.

Western Hemisphere the solar symbol was used by the Aztecs and the Dakotas, with the cross outside as it is with some of the Gallic ones,[13] and the grave mounds of the Mississippi have revealed more complex ones[14] (fig. 6).

Navajo sand paintings differentiate four kinds of light around the sun[15] (fig. 7).

The encircled crosses mentioned above are all pre- or extra-Christian symbols, and they naturally present to the inquisitive mind the question, What relation have these to the cross of the Christian faith? In the iconography of its first two centuries, the cross is not seen at all or only disguised in anchors, tridents, ship masts, perhaps, as some authors suggest, because considerable odium surrounded any mention of this instrument of criminal death prevalent in that day.[16] At the beginning of the third century, Tertullian tells us, it was common for Christians to make the sign of the cross on various everyday occasions; it was a gesture of benediction, fellowship, or even exorcism, and represented not the death on the cross but the person of the divine man and his victory over death.[17] At that time there appeared, on rare occasions, the first crosses in any iconographic form whatsoever—the *Tau* forms, closely related to the Egyptian *crux ansata* or Key of Life (fig. 8, *a* and *b*).[18]

At the close of the third century the sign began to find more frequent use, but in the form of a monogram designating again the person of the divine man.

In *c,* the monogram is made up of ΤΧ, the initials of the Greek name, Ἰησοῦς Χριστός; *d,* of Χρ, the first two letters of Χριστός; in *e* and *f,* by the addition of the cross bar, Christ on the cross was depicted; and in *g* and *h,* later simplifications (fourth and fifth centuries, respectively) designated the same.[19] At the beginning of the fourth century the monogram was made popular by the use to which it was put on the labarum of Constantine, here in the form of the *chi-rho.*[20] Only in the fifth century did the now prevalent Latin cross make its appearance, first on a tomb of an empress and later becoming more frequent.[21] At first the elongated Latin and the equilateral Greek crosses were interchangeable, but gradually each became the charac-

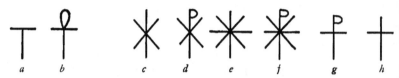

Figure 8. Earliest forms of the Christian cross.

teristic form in the usage of the Western and Eastern branches of the Church respectively.

Christ was not generally shown crucified on the cross until the Middle Ages; the two earliest examples of this theme, an illumination of a manuscript and an ivory bas-relief, were made about the sixth or seventh century. Only in the eleventh century was the dead or dying Saviour shown on the cross.[22] In the custom of the early church, "Jesus' head was placed before the cross, and this in the orb of the sun—and exactly at the point of intersection of the arms of the cross, thus at the place where one otherwise finds the lamb." This image of the lamb has historical connections with the sacrifice of the animal at the Jewish Passover, in which two spits were driven through the victim, forming a cross; Christ's sacrifice on the cross took place on this same festival of the spring equinox, and he was identified with the victim as the Pascal Lamb.[23]

It can be said, then, that the slow unfolding of the symbolism of the cross in Christianity indicates that there was ample time for the gradual accretion of significance from the network of neighboring cults, a process that is well established in regard to the beliefs about the Nativity and the Virgin Mother. More radical is the theory of Arthur Drews, who traces a development of these mythological themes from the earliest documents of the Vedic fire cult and its god Agni. There he finds a root symbol in the ceremonies that aimed, by a kind of sympathetic magic, to renew the sun daily at dawn and yearly at the winter solstice. He says that the cross (also the swastika) "is connected with the Fire Cult, and that both parts of the sign originally contained a reference to the pieces of wood (aranî) of which in most ancient times use was made to produce fire, has been placed beyond doubt by the investigations into the matter."[24] Thus he finds in the cross a sign of fire and of life, and suggests that "the Lamb encircled by the sun's orb refers to the ceremonial burning of the lamb at the spring equinox as an expiatory sacrifice and as a pledge of a new life. It appears the more plainly to be a figure of Agni (Agnus) since it is usually placed exactly at the intersection of the two arms—that is, exactly at the place whence the divine spark first issued at the kindling of the fire with the two araní."[25] Jung finds in this symbolism of fire boring a key to tracing the liberation of libido for cultural creativity through the work of the symbol.[26]

§ 2. The supreme *deity* or *divine man* has customarily been framed in the quadrated circle. The Eastern mandala is defined as a "symbolic geometrical diagram wherein deities are invoked"[27] and a "diagram of the universe serving as a frame for assemblies of deities or for their symbols," in which "the central circle frames either a chief deity who is considered as being the lord of the universe, or the symbol of such a deity."[28] The early custom of representing Christ in the sun wheel (cited above) showed him in this central position. He was not only at the center of the cross, however, but equivalent to the cross. The cross, according to Didron, "is more than a figure of Christ; it is in iconography Christ himself or his symbol"; he points out that "the cross has received a worship similar, if not equal, to that of Christ."[29] Farrar says of the cross that "it stood in the place of a portrait-figure as a symbol of the God-man," and that "to the members of the Church it represented their Master ... the whole faith—the person of Christ, his death for man, and the life and death of man in Christ."[30] The medieval figure of the enthroned Christ was represented in the midst of a circle with the signs of the four evangelists at the four points; this is analogous to the Egyptian designs of the four sons of the sun-god Horus standing on the lotus.[31] The prototypes of these designations of the evangelists is the image of the tetramorph in the well-known vision of Ezekiel, which is a mandala consisting of wheels with four living creatures with four heads (tetramorphs, with heads of ox, lion, eagle, and man) surrounding the central deity, whose throne was enveloped in fire radiating thunderbolts.[32] The Christian godhead was sometimes represented as fourfold, with the three persons of the Trinity and the Virgin as four figures in a central circle, surrounded by an outer circle and cross (see Plate X).[33] In the form of the rose the fourfold circle was centered in the figure of the Christ in Gothic cathedral rose windows.[34] Likewise, as lotus (see § 5) it bears the chief gods of several cultures: Vishnu, Brahma, and Buddha of India, Horus of Egypt, and Mithra of Persia.[35]

The concept of the "ideal man" as primordial or as divine survived from antiquity under the name "Anthropos," through the secret traditions of the nature philosophers. This figure embodied the principle of transformation (Mercurius as the transforming substance), with a round and square nature and a wholeness consisting of four elements. The Anthropos was often placed at the center of the mandala in alchemical iconography. Plate VI shows this figure at the center of the cosmic circle of the four elements. Plate VII depicts him at the center of the elements but also containing and uniting the four within himself; he is surrounded by the dual circle of sun and moon (cf. the corresponding circle in Drawing I). Plate V represents Mercurius as the cross itself in the cosmic sphere. This figure of the Anthropos occurs in many cultures, for example, the Egyptian Thoth, Greek Hermes, Hindu Manu, Chinese Chen-Jen, Western Mercurius, or Christian First and Second Adam or Christ.[36]

A most interesting variant of this transforming role of the ideal man is his function as initiator, as the ideal youth who carries out the sacred rite of initiation of the young men of the community (see § 27). The Greek "Kouros" ("youth") was such an idealized figure, first as Zeus and later as Dionysus and Apollo the sun-god, both portrayed within the rayed disk of the sun wheel.[37] Circular symbols were also characteristic of Dionysus.[38] Initiation has customarily involved identification with the deity who has the power of renewal and who has himself undergone it. Often the rite and this identification take place within the mandala enclosure (see § 27), as in both the Tibetan (see § 28) and Amerindian (see § 4) forms, in each of which the goddess is the model (in the former, the Goddess of Wisdom; in the latter, Changing Woman). The identification was dramatically indicated in the Isis mysteries: the initiant's "head was garlanded with a fair crown of spotless palm, whose leaves stood out like rays." After he had been "thus adorned as the sun and set up like to the image of a god, ... the people thronged in to gaze" upon him.[39] From this imagery was derived the later "solification" of the alchemists.[40]

Another aspect pertinent to the present discussion is the ideal man as king. In some cultures the ancients thought their ruler to be an incarnation of the sun-god, and the sun wheel has already been mentioned as his symbolic attribute in Asia Minor (see § 1). In India the king was called "Lord of the Universe" or "King of the Golden Wheel," his empire being the entire circle of the world quadrated by the four continents at the cardinal points, which he symbolically subdued at his coronation (see § 3). Buddha, as the paragon of enlightenment, was given this same title of universal dominion, the "Wheel of the Law" was his most characteristic emblem, and the accounts of his first actions at birth show an identity with those of the coronation ceremonies of the "Wheel Kings." When he attained his enlightenment at the Bodhi Tree, he was in the center of the mandala; the tree was surrounded by a large, round, horizontal stone wheel concentric with a lotus, called the "Diamond Throne" or "Thunderbolt Throne," thought to have appeared at the creation of the world at the center of the cosmos.[41] This ritual position was a heritage from former ages, when the spiritual aspirant—the Brahmin—would sit upon the wheel and turn it thrice around in the sunwise direction while a chariot race encircled him representing the rolling of the wheel around the center; by this action he "won" or "gained" the three worlds (earth, air, and heaven), thus acquiring the universal power of the Wheel Kings.[42] The post on which the wheel revolved was probably symbolically derived from the "sacred tree" or "world tree" as is suggested by their history (cf. § 12 and fig. 10 *a, b*),[43] and it is beyond doubt that these wheels were derived from the sun wheel.[44]

The halo carries much the same connotation as the wheel as a device to indicate a divinity or divine man or saint.[45] To be "holy" has a meaning equivalent to being "whole," as the derivation of the words reveals; (German "heil" means "whole" or "well," "heilig" means "holy," "heilen" "to make well or whole," "to heal").

The sacred presence at the center has sometimes been that of a deceased leader, whose venerated remains were enshrined in a reliquary or tomb. In more primitive societies these shrines are in the form of mounds, perhaps shaped by ornamentation into a sun wheel, or built in the pattern of the cross and surrounded by a circle of stones, as in the European Stone Age.[46] The Indian stupas (see § 16) were most often tombs or reliquaries (see § 27) in the form of three-dimensional cosmic mandalas to be circumambulated by the faithful. The central Moslem holy place in Mecca, the "Ka'abah," or House of God, is a square building surrounded at one time by a circle of 360 or 365 idols representing the days of the sun's complete cycle. The building is empty and is draped like a tomb; it is used for circumambulatory funeral rites, probably for the assurance of rebirth. The legend is that the structure was built by Adam, the Anthropos, as an exact copy of one he saw in heaven—a square built of four jasper pillars and a ruby roof encircled by angels (probably the 365 figures) circumambulating it.[47]

§ 3. The description of the Eastern mandala (cf. § 14) makes it clear that the quadrated circle represents a *cosmos and its central axis*. The mandala is defined as a "diagram of the universe," whose inmost circle is the center of the universe or world navel, or the "metaphysical Sun at the focal-point of creation";[48] its four directions are equivalent to the four continents of the world. The mandala, the temple, and the world share a common central axis and are merged in their significances by a mystic identification, in which the novice also shares during his initiation ceremony (cf. § 28).

A close analogy to this cosmic role of the design is seen in the West, where the circular zodiac in ecclesiastical architecture is placed on the floor at the crossing of the transept, that is, at the center of the cross formed by the structure; in China the zodiac around the T'ai-chi is placed at the center of the home, designating an identification with the cosmic axis (see § 1). The zodiac is, of course, a projection of unconscious cosmic and mythological contents into the heavens, and the horoscope is itself a twelvefold cosmic mandala, with a dark center and leftward circumambulation of the sun through the houses and planetary phases.[49] "A related idea," Jung notes, "is that of the identity of Christ with the [round] ecclesiastical year, of which he is both the stationary pole [at the center] and the life."[50] The Aztec calendar stone is similar to the mandala in pattern and meaning, embodying "a finite statement of the infinity of the Aztec universe," and surrounding the face of the sun-god at the center with a circular arrangement quadrated by a cross whose arms are cartouches depicting the four ages of the world.[51]

Hindu cosmogonic mythology conceived the world as mandala-shaped. Vishnu, floating on the cosmic waters, put forth out of his body "a single lotus, with a thousand petals of pure gold, stainless, radiant as the sun," with the God-Creator Brahma seated in its center with his four heads facing and controlling the four directions. Out of the lotus arose the world in a pattern similar to the mandala.[52] Egyptian representations of the cosmos also have a somewhat mandalalike composition. The cosmogonic myth related in Plato's *Timaeus* is a most instructive example. Here the dynamic factor that underlies all cosmic order, called the "world soul," is formed into a cross in the following manner: "The world's soul is made of two ultimate constituents: (a) the being which is undivided and always self-same; (b) the being which 'becomes' and is divisible in bodies. God first mixed these and made (c) a compound of the two.... Then he again mingled (a) (b) and ·(c) into one whole."[53] This substance is divided into two lines and a cross is made of them, and each is bent back into a circle and rotates. The Demiurge finally constructs the world's body within this structure of its soul. "This begins the 'unceasing and reasonable life' of the cosmos as an organism." Four elements are involved in its composition, and Taylor infers that Plato (if not Timaeus) believed that fire is at the center of the circles. The head of man was thought to be the dwelling of the immortal soul, which was like the soul of the cosmos, containing the same two circles forming the cross. The spectacle of the cosmic axis and the surrounding rings, in the mythical journey of Er into the realm of the dead, is described in Plato's *Republic*[54] (see § 32).

These circles of the universe represent the dynamic "order" of the cosmos that arose originally out of the chaos and must be sustained. The cosmic wheel is, then, the symbol of the organic integration of the universe, as a living principle in which the life of man also shares. For example, the Buddhist Wheel of the Law (Dharma), or Golden Wheel, embodies the same principle that the Vedic writings describe as Rita (rta), the Way. "As the basis of cosmic order the 'rita' rules the world of nature. The established facts of the visible world, but especially the events of nature that occur periodically, are fixed or regulated by 'rita' "; it "presents itself under the threefold aspect of cosmic order, correct or fitting cult of the gods, and moral conduct of man."[55] The sun is called the Wheel of Rita, with twelve spokes of the twelve months. Like the sun, the Golden Wheel was said to roll through the four quarters of the round world empire, over the four continents, following every movement of thought of the king, called "Lord of the Universe" or "King of the Golden Wheel." If the king is not reigning as he should and the people are not prosperous, the wheel then fails to roll and disorder threatens.[56] Jane Harrison has shown the analogy of this function of the Rita to that of the Chinese Tao and of the Greek Dike as expressions of the Way of cosmic nature and of man, all three being symbolized by the wheel,[57] to which a fourth example may be added in the Buddhist Dharma.[58] The zodiac is another representation of such an order, describing a cosmic periodicity and also believed to describe the pattern of man's psychic life.

The alchemistic nature philosophers were much influenced by Plato's imagery, and their mandala symbolism was primarily cosmic. Their transforming substance, the round and square image of fourfold wholeness (see §§ 2, 18), "is an analogy of the revolving universe, of the macrocosm, or a mirror-image of the same imprinted in the interior of matter. Psychologically, this concerns something like a mirroring of the rotating heavens in the unconscious, an image of the world, projected by the alchemists into their primordial matter"—that is, a microcosm and an image of the world soul as in Plato.[59] This transforming substance is Mercurius, which in Plate V is symbolized as the cross in the cosmic circles. The alchemists' symbol of the philosophic wheel (see § 18) "designates the ... circulating process.... It means by this the revolution of the universe as the model of the Work, and therewith also the cycle of the year in which the Work takes place"— implying the circular course of the sun.[60] The microcosm—man's psyche (projected into matter)—was felt to share in the same ordering process as the macrocosm—the universe—and the symbolism blends both these worlds.

§ 4. The mandala has functioned prominently as a *protective enclosure*. On the primitive level, the shaman or medicine man uses the magic circle to define the area into which he wants helpful spirits to enter and from which he means to exclude all other foreign agencies.[61] Among American Indian tribes this kind of protective circle is drawn or danced in healing ceremonies. Here the structure of the design becomes a well-elaborated mandala consisting of a circle and cross or swastika whose arms depict the four directions indicated by their guardian spirits; the patient or initiant is laid on the ground at the center, where the divine power is concentrated.[62] The use of the mandala in Tibetan initiation rites for the invocation of deities and combat with demons is described in section 28.

The protective and enclosing aspect of the mandala is displayed in its use for meditative concentration. The Tibetan Yantra form, for example, is "an instrument for contemplation. It should sustain concentration through the somewhat circular narrowing down of the psychological field of vision upon the center."[63] In it the outer circle of fire is said to designate the flame of desire, which must be held in by this form so that it will not be dissipated and thus work against the concentrating process; the square temple court inside the circle signifies "sacred seclusion and concentration."[164] This court is at the same time a garden, and it is said of it that "the whole diagram may perhaps represent the universe on the plan of a formal square garden."[65] This garden is a prevailing theme, known in the West among the nature philosophers as the "enclosed garden" or "rose garden of the philosophers"[66] and in the architecture of church and mosque as the cloister or closed court, always serving the same end of spiritual concentration.[67]

One of the better-known protective enclosures occurs in the myth of the first paradise—the Garden of Eden; it is represented as a garden because it also has the features and functions of the mandala. Its center is a world axis—though this is not expressly stated—for the tree of life is an image derived from older traditions of the cosmic tree, thought by Akkadians, Phoenicians, and Egyptians to be the central axis of the universe, an idea closely related to the axial world mountain of the Chaldeans;[68] in India also the central tree and central mountain are brought into close relation.[69] The garden has the familiar fourfold pattern, in that the four great rivers issue from it in the four directions. Within this garden the First Adam, whose name means "the man," (that is, the Anthropos [see § 2]) dwelt with his counterpart Eve as long as they remained ignorant of the fruit of knowledge. The garden, then, served to enclose primordial man in his innocence as a child of nature, a condition in which he could not remain once he had tasted of the fruit of consciousness, of awareness of the conflict of opposites, called the "knowledge of good and evil."[70]

The second paradise in this Judaic tradition is no longer a garden, but a city—the New Jerusalem of the Apocalypse.[71] It is a cosmos—a new heaven and a new earth—and a rather typical mandala, with its four sides with twelve foundations and twelve gates and its corners based on the circle of the zodiac;[72] at its center is the Lamb as the light of the world and the central tree of life again, this time with the twelve fruits of healing, referring to the circle of the year. This paradise is called the "Lamb's Bride," that is, the bride of Christ, the Second Adam or Anthropos. It comes, not as the beginning before the opposites were divided so that man might be aware of conflict, but at the culmination of the whole redemptive history where the division is healed again and the cosmos is under a reign of peace and reconciliation.

The city constructed on a cosmic plan was by no means unique in the vision of John, for the laying out of cities on the ground plan of the pattern of the mandala was customary in many parts of the ancient world. Ancient Roma Quadrata, for example, was laid out in ritual fashion, as were its later "coloniae." A large circular furrow was plowed about a central pit

Plate I. Quadrated circle as cosmic axis. Ceiling
mandala of Tibetan Buddhism.

Plate II. Sacred diagram. Buddhist mandala of northwest China.

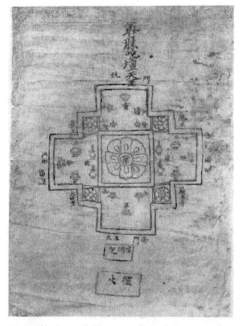

Plate III. Sacred diagram. Primitive mandala
of northwest China, used in healing ritual.

Plate IV. Han mirror of ancient China, with
TLV pattern.

Plate V. Cosmic diagram. The transforming
substance of European nature philosophy.

Plate VI. Diagram of the four elements. The
divine man of European nature philosophy.

Plate VII. Diagram of the four elements. The divine man as the world soul of European nature philosophy.

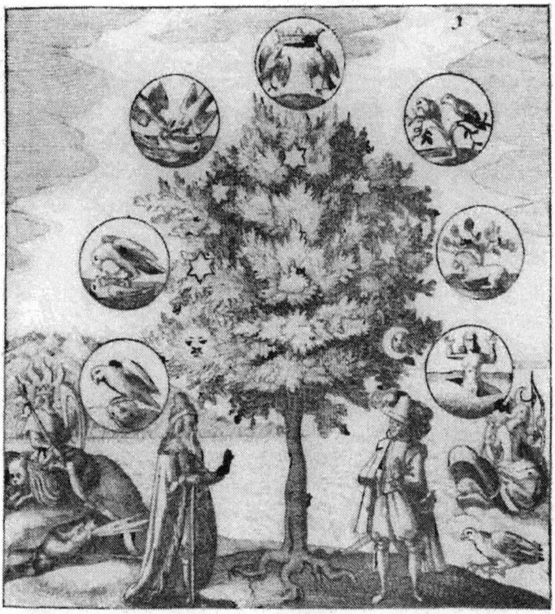

Plate VIII. Diagram of the transformation process. "The Tree of Universal Matter," indicating the seven stages of the Work of European nature philosophy.

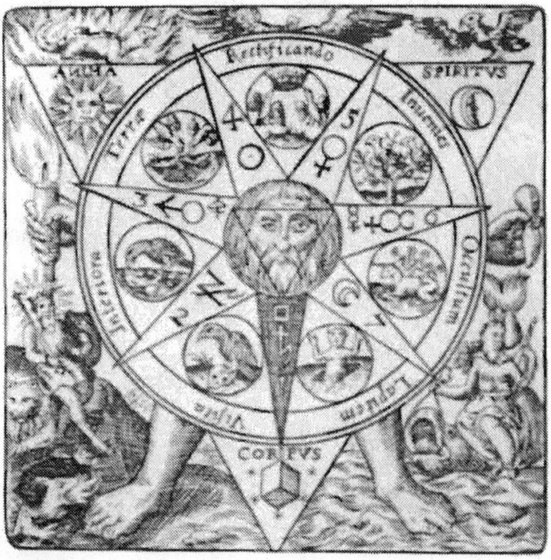
Rectificando
SPIRITVS
Invenies
Occultum
Lapidem
Visita
Interiora
Terrae
CORPVS

Plate IX. Diagram of the transformation process. "The Whole Work of Philosophy" as the squared circle, indicating the seven stages of the Work of European nature philosophy.

Plate X. The quadrated circle as godhead. The
Christian quaternity of the Trinity and Mary.

(mundus), where a building was consecrated to the spirits of the ancestors and the underworld. Accounts of the plan are somewhat confusing, but a square furrow and possibly crossed ones divided the circle into quadrants, thus creating a typical square walled town with gates in the four directions.[73] The same manner of city founding has been described in west African communities, and was probably prevalent over that whole region.[74] This plan is perhaps related to the primitive custom of arranging communities on the pattern of the circle and cross; a further suggestive fact is that the Egyptian hieroglyph for "city" is the circle and cross.[75] The mandala may delineate a kingdom as well as a city; the Han mirror designates by the square the Middle Kingdom—that is, China (see § 14). The Indian King of the Golden Wheel was Lord of the Universe, ruling the great circle of the earth quadrated at the cardinal points by the four continents, which he subdued ritually at his coronation and which the Golden Wheel rolled over at his behest if he was reigning by the virtue of the law (see §§ 1, 2, 3).[76] It may be that the essential feature of this aspect of the diagram is the organization of the community or society, perceived to be organically structured and integrated in the same pattern as the individual psyche, and similarly enclosed and protected from the boundlessness and amorphousness of the surrounding matrix of nature.

§ 5. The enclosing and protective aspect of the mandala has a corollary in its *maternal* character. The city has long been thought of as mother, as the word "metropolis" ("mother city") testifies. The heavenly city of the Apocalypse is also known as "Mother Jerusalem"; even more specifically, an early Gnostic text describes a typical mandala structure, with the god Anthropos at the center, as "the Mother-city (metropolis) of the Only-begotten."[77] The enclosed garden is another feature of the mandala related to the maternal element, the symbol being an attribute of the Virgin in Christianity.[78] More impressive, however, is the lotus as a maternal symbol, so widely associated with the mandala as to be justifiably considered an equivalent to it.[79] In India the cosmic lotus is the generative organ of the maternal procreative principle—the womb of the cosmic waters—and is personified as the Mother Goddess, the mother of all created things.[80] Their cosmogonic myth (see § 3) tells that Vishnu, as the Primordial Child floating upon the maternal waters, put forth out of his body a thousand-petaled gold lotus enclosing at its center the four-headed Brahma controlling the four directions. This lotus is called the "Goddess Earth," or "Moisture," out of which arises the mandala-shaped world.[81] In Egyptian art the lotus carries the child gods Harpocrates[82] or the four sons of Horus.[83] The Western parallel is the rose as symbol of Mary, which bore the young deity.[84] Dante says of her: "That fair garden / Blossoming underneath the rays of Christ. . . . / Here is the Rose, in which the World Divine / Became incarnate. . . ."[185] Later, Dante says of the Mystic Rose: "Within thy [Mary's] womb, that

love was re-enkindled / Whose heat has germinated this fair flower."[86] In
medieval hymns Mary is portrayed as flower of the sea or the calyx in which
the Christ nestles and rests hidden as a bird.[87] The Golden Flower of
Chinese Taoism serves a similar maternal function, called "seeding-place
of the diamond-body," which is likewise a "holy embryo"; this flower is also
called a city—"purple hall in the city of jade."[88]

In all these symbols the flowers are themselves mandalalike or are in-
corporated in the mandala, and the same is true of the Divine Child brought
forth in it. For example, in Western alchemical symbolism the philosophers'
stone was customarily thought of as a living child or germ being brought
forth from a mother (the hermetic vessel or "egg");[89] it was variously called
"round thing," "tender babe," "son of the philosophers,"[90] "orphan,"[91] the
"golden child" whose "form of birth is like the revolving wheel."[92] The
concept is related to the golden egg born as an embryo in the Golden Flower
of Taoism[93] or the Hindu golden germ as world egg (Hiranyagarbha) (see
§ 31).[94]

In Egypt the lotus is a symbol of the sun, supporting Horus as the Hindu
version holds Vishnu. It is held, however, in the hand of the goddess Hathor,
as it is in the hand of the Hindu Laksmi, and can be considered less as the
sun than the maternal solar matrix to which the sun retires for rebirth and
renewal of life, thus equivalent to the primordial waters. On Egyptian
sarcophagi the solar scarab emerges from a lotus between two goddesses,
representing "both the sun and the deceased passing through the tomb to
renew their existence," the solar rebirth symbolizing thus the human, and
thence "life in its eternal and unceasingly renewed essence."[95]

§ 6. Important among the universal features of the mandala is its duality,
as a representation of a *union of opposites,* these may be heaven and earth,
spirit and matter, god and goddess, and the hermaphrodite. The Eastern
mandala brings the round sky ($\male$) and square earth ($\female$) into relation (see
§ 14), and the closely related T'ai-chi shows the cosmic principles, Yang ($\male$)
and Yin ($\female$), in union (see § 23). Indian mandalas show Shiva ($\male$) and
Shakti ($\female$) in eternal embrace;[96] in Tibetan examples the circles are occupied
by pairs of deities in perpetual cohabitation called "Divine Father-Mother
(see § 32).[97] Similarly, American Indian sand paintings depict various
masculine and feminine pairs balanced in the central cross, made of the
male pollen and female seed.[98] Christian mandalas also portray the Holy
Trinity ($\male$) and the Virgin ($\female$) as a fourfold center (Plate X).[99] The two
paradises of the Judaic tradition remain true to form in this respect· in Eden
primordial man was differentiated into male and female, which were then
united; in the New Jerusalem were the Lamb and his Bride—that is, Christ
(the Second Adam) and Ecclesia (his bride the Church). Similarly, the central Tibetan Buddhist symbol—the "jewel in the lotus" (expressed in the
mystic phrase "Om mani padme hum")—has been shown to represent the

male and female principles in union, the lotus being the maternal goddess Padma and the jewel the supreme spiritual essence.[100]

Thomas Inman, in his discussion of the cross as derived from the sun wheel, makes a special point of the solar and lunar signs in the figures, indicating the concept of the mystery of the sexual conjunction of male and female powers as a fertility principle. Similarly, Drews argues that the Christian cross was related to the crossed sticks used in the ancient Vedic rites, namely, the cult of Agni the fire god (see § 1).[101] These fire-boring ceremonies were designed, by sympathetic magic, to renew the sun at dawn. A flame was ignited by the friction of sticks in a boring motion, a single male one being twirled where it penetrated the exact center of the cross formed by the two female ones, the araní. Typical nativity symbolism pertained throughout the rite, of especial interest here since it represents the Divine Child brought forth at the center of the maternal cross. The particularly impressive ceremony was held at dawn on the day of the winter solstice, the time most myths of that part of the world assigned to the birth of the god. "As soon as the spark shown in the 'maternal bosom,' the soft underpart of the wood, it was treated as an 'infant child.'" The ghrita, the juice of the cow, and the Soma, the juice of the plant, were poured over the fire, now raised on the altar; "from this time 'Agni' was called 'the anointed.'" Gods (kings) and herdsmen hastened to pay reverence; "the new-born Agni already had become 'the teacher' of all living creatures, 'the wisest of the wise.'" The end of the time of darkness and the beginning of the holy season were celebrated, and "Agni and the other Gods again returned to men, and the priests announced to the people the 'joyful tidings'...that the Light God had been born again."[102]

Conflict as well as union may be implied in the meeting of opposites in the mandala, as in one form of the Aztec calendar stone—the National Stone—which depicts the cosmic battle between the powers of light and of darkness, that "eternal conflict between the opposing forces of nature," all of which are summarized in the figures of day and night, according to Vaillant.

Hermaphroditic symbols are common in the writings of the alchemists. Their stone was called "rebis" ("thing of dual nature"), produced by the union of opposite principles—particularly spirit and matter—and an androgyne.[103] Mercurius, the personification of the transforming substance, was androgynous, as was the primordial matter.[104] Plate V shows Mercurius as the cross between sun and moon; the conjunction of Sol and Luna, or King and Queen, was an important step in the alchemical Work.[105] The Anthropos (see § 2) had a dual nature, associated with the Primordial Man of Plato, the Spherical Being who contained in himself both man and woman before their separation.[106] The same theme is seen also in the Upanishads, in the description of the Atman, the self: "He was...as large as a woman and a man who held each other in embrace. This his self (atman) he divided into two parts; from this arose husband and wife. He married her."[107] Adam was represented in the midst of the mandala as such a primordial man, differentiated into male and female persons who married.

§ 7. Finally, of some importance to the present discussion is the existence of the *healing* aspect of the mandala as well as its opposite—the *harmful* capacity as weapon or poison. Records show that the Chinese primitive form of the mandala, reproduced in Plate III, was probably used in healing ceremonies, since it refers to "Medicine Kings" (see § 14). Healing rites in American Indian sand paintings have been mentioned (see § 2). In the Chinese Taoist tradition the Golden Flower, of mandala pattern, goes through several transmutations through the body and finally produces an Elixir or Pill of Immortality.[108] Jung finds parallels between the Drug of Immortality of Christian dogma and the alchemical concept of the transforming substance (symbolized by the quadrated circle), as "Panacea" or "Medicina catholica," that healed the ignoble, sick metals and made them incorruptible.[109] But "the Tincture or Divine Water [forms of the Stone] not only performs beneficent works of healing and ennoblement, but acts as a fatal poison that penetrates other bodies as deeply as it penetrates its own."[110] In India the mandala is believed to be used by the god as a destroying weapon; it is said that the Buddhist "Holy Wheel may be likened to the Chakkra [wheel as discus] of Indra, the King of the Gods, which exterminates those against whom it is hurled.... For even so does the Holy Wheel of the Lord Buddha extirpate evil from the hearts of men."[111]

§ 8. According to tradition, the *numbers* associated with the circle give it certain different properties. The usual and complete mandala is the quadrated circle—that is, one with a fourfold pattern of a cross or other device. The number three and its multiples bear the connotation of incompleteness, of becoming, creation, and generation, or the rational spirit; the World Wheel of Buddhism is an example of this circle of incompleteness.[112] The fivefold mandala, on the other hand, signifies natural man, in his material and bodily aspect, suggesting unconsciousness as against wholeness.[113]

§ 9. *Circulation* or ritual circumambulation is an integral part of the symbolism of the mandala. In Asia the turning of the wheel was one of the ritual forms of worship, and Buddha was said to have "turned the Wheel of the Law," or rather, "set the wheel rolling onwards."[114] The Golden Wheel rolled over the four quarters of the universal empire; the Great Wheel Kings rolled their standards through the capital cities of the empire on the sacred wheel, symbol of the sun;[115] and Brahmins aspired to gain universal dominion by revolving on the wheel (see §§ 2, 12). The "Golden Flower" of Chinese Taoism was made to circulate to set in motion the transformation process called "putting the hand to" the mill wheel or water wheel.[116]

Similarly, in Western alchemy the process is called "opus circulatorium," and the "philosophic wheel" is made to turn to set in motion the distillation and hence the sublimation of soul and spirit from body.[117] Circumambulations are directed toward honoring or worshipping any sacred object or revered person and are customarily performed in the sunwise—that is, clockwise—manner.[118] The origin of these circulating motions is the revolution of the sun or the rolling onward of the sun wheel through the heavens.[119]

§ 10. One further aspect of the mandala (that does not have specific mention in the patient's material) is as *treasure,* denoting an esteem for the image of the self as an objective of highest possible value; most often this is represented by a precious metal or precious stone, emphasizing immutability, invulnerability, and incorruptibility. Gold is the classic designation of this quality. In the East the Golden Flower of Taoism, the Golden Lotus of Hindu mythology, and the Golden Wheel of Buddhism and Brahmanism are examples already mentioned; in the West a prime example is the alchemical Philosophers' Gold. In all these examples the golden sun wheel seems to be the basis of the imagery. It plays a part in such hero myths as the Nibelungenlied, in which the Rheingold is a golden ring wrested from the dragon's cave by the hero. Precious stones, particularly diamonds, are frequent expressions of this theme. The Diamond Body of Chinese Taoism, the Jewel in the Lotus of Tibetan Buddhism, and the Diamond Throne of Indian Buddhism have already been mentioned. In the West the New Jerusalem of the Apocalypse is a mandala made of many precious stones. The Navajo tribes make their sun wheel of turquoise, which is their most precious stone.[120]

Buddhist writings refer to the Treasure of the Wheel, that Golden Wheel or Universe Wheel of the monarch or the enlightened man. Significantly, they believe that the monarchs, of varying degrees of excellence, were Golden Wheel Kings if first rate, Silver Wheel if second, Copper Wheel if third, Iron Wheel if fourth rate, and their wheels ruled one less quarter of the world with each category.[121] This corresponds to the classical alchemical gradation of the metals.

§ 11. Mandalas have several simultaneous *levels of meaning.* The Buddhist mandala is a scheme of the universe and its central axis as well as of a temple and garden; it serves as an enclosure in which initiation is undergone; and finally, it is an inner representation of a state of the soul (see §§ 14, 15, 28). These all share an inward identification with each other as the center and fourfold structure of both the macrocosm and the microcosm. The term "Chakravartin" (or "Wheel King") designated the Universal Monarch, the actual temporal king who at his coronation subdued the four quarters by the rolling of the wheel; yet the term also is the title of any great spiritual leader who by the turning of the wheel gains universal dominion of an inward sort (see §§ 2, 12, 13). The New Jerusalem of the

Christian Apocalypse is a mandala that is a cosmos ("a new heaven and a new earth"), a city of the community of the redeemed, a place of healing ("the leaves of the tree were for the healing of the nations"), and an inner image of the state of salvation. There is, then, in both Buddhism and Christianity the concept that equates the attainment of enlightenment with the winning of a kingdom, and in each the great founder was called "King."

Kerényi says of the quadrated circle of the ritual city founding of the Romans: "The little worlds of men were to be drawn to the same ideal plan in accordance with which man 'knows,' mythologically speaking, that his own totality is organized, and which he also sees in the world at large."[122]

Figure 9. Sacred tree. *a*. Chaldean. *b*. Mithraic. *c*. Assyrian.

§ 12. Comparative mythology and iconography prove that the *sacred tree* is symbolically equivalent to the mandala or to its center.[123]

The significance of the tree as center reaches back to earliest history. Just as the mandala represents a cosmos (see §§ 3, 14), so the great cosmogonic trees—of Chaldea, of Eridu, of the Gilgamesh Epic, of the Hindu Vedas—expressed the form of the universe—the foliage as the heavens bearing jewels as the stars, the roots the earth.[124] The tree also serves as cosmic axis, as the mandala (see §§ 3, 14). Chaldean accounts describe the central World Mountain as a World Tree;[125] the Persian Haoma Tree or Nordic World Ash are central,[126] as are the Mayan and Omaha world trees, which are crosses.[127] The Buddhist Bodhi Tree has been depicted as emerging in the midst of the wheel of the Thunderbolt or Diamond Throne at "the center of the thousandfold cosmos."[128] In fact, the stylization of the sacred tree went so far as to reduce it to an ornate stump or pillar (fig. 9).

In Buddhist and Hindu imagery this pillar served as the support on which the ritual Holy Wheel pivoted horizontally (see § 2); the pictorial design sometimes shows the wheel vertically on the pillar as the tree of life.[129] This same theme is seen in early Christian art, in which the cross is equated to the tree[130] (fig. 10).

The Scandinavian world tree, Yggdrasil, is an example of a wheel-bearing tree. The Eddas say that it is the "chief and most holy seat of the gods.... Its branches spread over all the world and reach above heaven. Three roots

sustain the tree and stand wide apart [these reach into the three realms]....
But under the second root...is the well of Mimer, wherein knowledge
and wisdom are concealed. The third root of the ash is in heaven, and
beneath it is the most sacred fountain of Urd....There stands a beautiful
hall....Out of it come the three maids. These maids shape the lives of

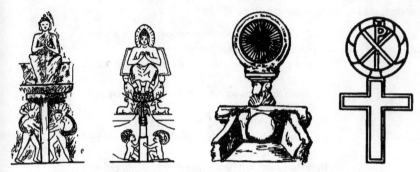

Figure 10. Sacred tree and wheel. *a*. Indian. *b*. Indian. *c*. Buddhist.
d. Early Christian.

Figure 11. Cosmic tree. *a*. Hindu. *b*. Scandinavian.

men and we call them the Norns." It is concentric with the world mountain
as the cosmic axis, and bears the world as a wheel. An illustration (fig. 11) in
a text of the Edda shows the circular plan of the concept and adds the
Ouroboros (the tail eater) in the enclosing ocean.[131] The configuration of
tree, well, and serpent is the classic pattern of the symbol in many cultures.[132]

As the mandala is basically the sun wheel, so the tree is often found in
this form. The Hindu cosmic tree is shown arising out of the World Egg;
it is concentric with the sun, and bears three suns as fruits (fig. 11).

An Assyrian design shows the palm tree as mandala wheel by depicting
the downward or upward view of it (fig. 12).

Goblet says of this rosette that it carries the same connotation as the lotus (which has often been associated with the tree), as solar matrix through which the sun is rejuvenated ritually (see § 5).[133]

As the mandala has its maternal aspect (see § 5), so the sacred tree is the simulacrum of the mother goddess Ishtar, Astarte, Cybele, Aphrodite, and others. A hymn of ancient Akkadian origin, probably between 3000 and 4000 B.C., represents the maternal tree as growing in the garden of Edin or Eden, said to be in the vicinity of Eridu:

> In Eridu a stalk grew overshadowing; in a holy
>   place did it become green;
> Its roots were of white crystal, which stretched
>   toward the deep:
> (Before) Ea was its course in Eridu, teeming
>   with fertility;
> Its seat was the (central place of earth);
> Its foliage (?) was the couch of Zikum the
>   (primaeval) mother.
> Into the heart of its holy house, which spread its
>   shade like a forest, hath no man entered.
> (There is the home) of the mighty mother who
>   passes across the sky.
> In the midst of it was Tammuz.
> There is the shrine of the two (gods).[134]

It has been noted that the lotus (see § 5) is the birthplace of the godling; so also were many of the gods born out of the tree as the mother—Tammuz, Attis, Adonis, Mithras.[135] This aspect, as the Tree of Life, designates the embodiment of the spirit of the vegetation that must be renewed yearly in ritual and its accompanying myth.[136] The tree has also a contrary aspect as Tree of Death, on which the god is sacrificed by hanging—Attis, Marsyas, Dionysus (as bull), Odin, or Christ.[137] The Christian cross has been considered the Tree of Death, and a medieval legend relates the identity of the trees of Eden and Golgotha.[138] Thus the tree is closely bound up with rebirth and initiation ceremonies (see § 27).

Also at the center of the mandala is another form of the sacred tree, the Tree of Knowledge in Eden, historically derived from the more ancient World Tree of the Chaldeans.[139] Similarly, the Zodiac Tree in the center of the New Jerusalem (see § 4), with its twelve fruits and healing leaves, was derived from previous tradition[140] and is essentially another form on which the wheel (of the zodiac) is placed on the trunk.

In the symbolism of alchemy the tree is again equivalent to the wheel, as shown in Plates VIII and IX, in which both the tree and the wheel represent the entire process by identical imagery; the tree bears the seven planets representing the steps of the Work, and stands between Sol and Luna, just as the wheel does. In alchemy the tree likewise is goddess, the female form of Mercurius as the agent of transformation,[141] essentially similar to the spirit of renewal of the year or of the vegetation; sometimes the tree is the bearer of the miraculous fruits, like the Zodiac Tree,[142] or of the wheel of the Work (fig. 13).

The patient's fantasies produced the most fundamental of these characteristics of the sacred tree—divinity, center, the pillar bearing the wheel, and an alternative to the mandala itself. By coincidence, the patient produced a palm, the most ancient and common of the sacred trees, thus lending added conviction to their mutual identity (see § 2).[143]

Figure 12. Sacred tree as rosette.

Figure 13. Alchemical tree and wheel. *a*. The philosophic wheel.
b. The hermetic transformation.

3 THE QUADRATED CIRCLE IN THE EAST

The mandala has attained its most evolved and refined expressions in the East, perhaps because of the great emphasis for many centuries in those cultures upon the deeply introverted discipline of the inner life. The Asiatic mandala has such complexity of background and forms that a detailed discussion of all its ramifications would be impracticable here. Rather, the discussion will be limited to its clearly functional usages. The florid, elaborate mandalas used as wall "banners" for "aids to meditation" (see § 4) are the less vital products of recent centuries and conceal much of the original symbolic intent of the image, as the historical derivation of the mandala reveals to a degree. The ceremonial manner of spontaneously creating the image in meditative practice throws still further light on the nature of the mandala as a dynamic psychic form. The ritual use in initiation, revealing even more of its psychological role, is discussed later with the various rebirth symbols.

§ 13. Since the Asiatic mandala occurs frequently in *Buddhism,* a few words of orientation to the fundamentals of this religion are in order. It is almost ironic to say of Buddhism that it is a system of projections in the sense that many other religions are, since the original teachings of Gautama made their chief goal precisely that of resolving projections. Yet the very construction of a system of formulations about the nature of the cosmos and of the mind involved the perception of things in terms of the primordial images. Underlying this doctrine is a peculiarly psychological viewpoint that throws light upon the significance of the mandala in Buddhism.

Arising out of the Hindu background, Buddhism divided into two main currents: that of the Lesser Vehicle of the Law, the Hinayana, going southward, and that of the Greater Vehicle of the Law, the Mahayana, spreading northward into China, Tibet, and Japan; it is the latter that is of interest in this study. Its aim is to attain, through enlightenment, liberation from the suffering engendered by attachment to the world; the name "Buddha" means the "Enlightened One." In this Greater Vehicle, the liberation does not imply a denial of this world and this life but only of certain illusions.

The rationale of liberation centers in the problem of the One and the Many, so familiar in philosophy (see § 24). The Self, known as the Buddha nature, is the one "universal principle of which all things are manifestations." It finds its existence not in any particular phenomenon, but in the totality of phenomena—therefore not in the separate ego, but in all minds. The illusion of the separateness of the ego and of phenomena is the creation of mind, and "results from a state of ignorance in the 'Universal Mind.' " In its blindness, Mind did not know its own nature. "Therefore in order to know and become conscious of itself it projected itself into forms and separate beings; it cast its shadow in order that it might see its own shape. This is a general proposition which is true of each individual; his mind reflects itself in an external world of forms and entities, for without these there can be no consciousness." A man's first step to enlightenment is the realization that this outer reflection "is no more than a shadow which indicates the state of the inner reality" of his own mind. On looking for his true nature there, "by penetrating to the very heart he will find the 'essence of Mind,' the Buddha-nature," or Self. The basic premise, then, is "that the One, being in a state of ignorance, differentiates itself into the Many in order to achieve self-knowledge, and further, that the Many suffer because they are ignorant of the fact that essentially they are the One."[1]

Gautama the Buddha achieved his enlightenment at the Bodhi Tree (see §§ 2, 12), which was a mandala wheel with thunderbolts and with a tree at its navel, located "at the center of the thousand-fold cosmos."[2] Here Gautama came to the realization that the self is not the ego but the totality of the cosmos. When an initiate practices the way to this goal, he produces from his mind the cosmic mandala around himself by active imagination, as described below. Any who attain the supreme enlightenment gain the title "Lord of the Universe" or "King of the Golden Wheel" (see § 2), a term derived from the role of the ancient Wheel Kings of India. In man's nature are four kingdoms, one of each of the four elements, and to him as King "his elemental subjects severally reveal themselves in their true nature and place in his hand the Sceptre (dorje, or thunderbolt) of Universal

---

[1] For notes to chapter 3, see pp 167–168.

Dominion over Matter. Then, indeed, is he Lord of Nature ... a Chakra-vartin, or Universal Emperor, God and Creator."[3] The foremost symbol of the faith is the Wheel of the Law, representing the Eightfold Path, which is the way of the Ending of Sorrow; this suffering world is represented in the sixfold World Wheel or Wheel of Life, which revolves in the unending sequence of rebirths "until the one who is bound on it breaks his own bonds through Enlightenment."[4]

§ 14. The term "mandala" carries the basic meaning of a circle, and refers customarily to the ritual or magic circle.[5] The *Buddhist mandala* is defined as "a symbolic geometrical diagram wherein deities are invoked,"[6] and as "a diagram of the universe ... serving as a frame for assemblies of deities or for their symbols."[7]

Cammann, in his discussion of the origin of the Tibetan mandala, argues that it has come down from the north, since the earliest examples are seen in China whereas in Tibet the image is a relatively late arrival, not having made its appearance apparently until the eighth century. He stresses that hanging a mandala on the wall is only a later custom, whereas originally there were two forms, those on the ceiling and those on the floor of temples, having different functions. He argues that "the principal type of Lama Buddhist mandala ... 'the ceiling mandala,' could very well have been derived from the 'TLV' (Han) mirrors which were hung—perhaps pattern-side down—from the ceilings of earlier Chinese temples and shrines."[8] Cammann explains the symbolic role of these ceiling forms: "The motives for placing the mandala in the center of the ceiling are practically identical with the metaphysical reasons for which the Chinese used to hang a mirror from the roof of their tomb vaults, and apparently their temples as well; it was in order to establish the axis of the universe-in-microcosm symbolized by the whole structure, and to indicate the supernal Sun, or Sun-gate, at its summit."[9] "The inner circle, or core, of each is the essential part.... On the Han mirrors this is emphasized by the prominent boss, which repre-sented ... the omphalos or center of the world. To the lamas, the center of the mandala has not only been considered as being the center of the universe, but more specifically as a representation of the metaphysical Sun at the focal point of creation.... Very possibly the Han mirror bosses had the same connotation.... On the mandala, the central circle frames either a chief deity who is considered as being the lord of the universe, or the symbol of such a deity."

In the earlier Han mirror (China, 100 B C. to A.D. 100) (Plate IV), the central boss is surrounded by an eight-pronged "cloud collar," and around this a square with a T-shaped gate on each side, as gates of the Middle King-dom at the center of the world, this being contained in a cross whose branches are the four cardinal directions, designated by guardian spirit ani-mals and depicting the wild lands beyond the pale of the Chinese civilization; the whole is enclosed in a large circle representing the rim of the dome of the sky.

In the later ceiling mandala (Tibet, after the eighth century) (Plate I) the central circle is surrounded by a circular pattern of an eight-petaled lotus or eight thunderbolts. "The important thing was not the actual device used but the number eight, or any multiple of four or eight, such a number having solar significance." This is enclosed in a square, known as "citadel of the earth," with T-shaped gates at the four sides, called "the gates of the earth," standing for the four directions designated by the four colors: North yellow, South green (or blue), East white, West red. (Sometimes the position of one or the other pair is reversed, depending on whether it faces up or down, of course). Finally, the circular rim of the dome of the sky encloses the whole.[10]

Intermediate in time between the mirrors and the mandalas are the so-called primitive mandalas, really incomplete ones, from the Chinese north-west, in which the square is outermost (Plate II), therefore lacking the enclosing dome that makes it a true mandala, or in which the square is enclosed in a cross only (Plate III). The latter was used as a charm against sickness, the name of a Medicine King being written at each of the four corners of the cross.[11]

§ 15. Zimmer's account of a Buddhist meditational rite indicates the *inward origin* of the mandala. The adept, in experiencing it, "develops out of and around himself an image of the world with the Mountain of the Gods, Sumeru (or Meru), in the midst. This is for him the axis of the world-egg, 'whose four-cornered and bejewelled body sparkles with sides made of crystal, gold, ruby, and emerald, the colors of the world's four quarters.'" The Hindu finds here the palace of the King of the Gods; the Buddhist, a monastic temple with four entrances and pointed roof like the stupa tombs. "Inside, the floor takes the form of a circle with an open lotus blossom, the eight petals stretching to all points of the compass. In it the contemplative sees himself standing in the form of Mahasukha (one of the great god Siva's manifestations), holding a female figure in his embrace. He sees himself as the 'highest bliss of the circles' with four heads and eight arms, and becomes aware of his own essence through contemplation. His four heads signify the four elements . . . and also the four infinite feelings . . . [the adept] causes rays colored after the four quarters . . . to proceed from the heads of Mahasukha, whose form he himself has taken in his mind's eye. The colors ensure that his feeling of universal compassion pervades the entire cosmos."[12]

In Jung's travels in India he obtained from a Lamaist confirmation of the inward and spontaneous creation of the mandala image. He was told that the ones in banners seen in cloisters and temples have no special significance, since they are only outer representations. The true mandala, it was said, is an inner image constructed through active imagination by the initiate lama. No one of these images is just like another, but all are quite individual. The true, inner mandala occurs only if there is a turmoil of the psychic center of gravity, or when a certain thought cannot be found and must be sought because it is not in the holy doctrine.[13]

§ 16. A discussion of the forms of the mandala would not be complete without at least a passing mention of the *three-dimensional forms*. One of these is the stupa (fig. 16), which is usually a columnar structure consisting in its upward ascent of a square (cube), a circle (sphere), a triangle (pyramidal), and crescent topped by a flame. Like some other forms of the quadrated circle, it is a monument to the dead or perhaps an actual tomb or reliquary.[14] Also like the mandala it represents a cosmos (see § 27),[15] the four elements depicted by the four forms and capped by the flame as the fifth, or *quinta-essentia*. The stupa is another form from which the mandala seems to be derived. Jung says of it that it "generally contains the square groundplan of a stupa. That this really signifies a building can be seen from the mandalas that are executed bodily. By the figure of the square, these convey the idea of a house or temple or of an inner walled-in space."[16] India was at one time dotted with many thousands of these stupas.[17]

Often a temple takes the shape of the three-dimensional mandala, an example being that at Boro-Budur in Java, where the initiant makes a spiral ascent through the various stages of spiritual development, culminating in a central apex at the summit as the goal of enlightenment.[18] Such a circumambulation was performed also around the stupas.[19]

Outside the Buddhist tradition, the Temple of Heaven in Peiping[20] is a typical cosmic mandala structure. This highest sanctuary of nature worship is laid out with geometric precision as a series of three circular terraces inside of square wall; both the outer circle and square are pierced by triple gates facing the four cardinal directions. Its middle stone is regarded as the central point of the universe; the surrounding nine concentric circles of stone blocks represent the nine sections of the cosmos, and the 360 pillars around the circles stand for the days of the lunar year (actually 354 days). The Emperor, as divine Son of Heaven, the only being worthy of entering these holiest of holy precincts, has made sacrifices here at the summer and winter solstices to induce the beneficient influences of divine order; this rite has been the principal token of his office for four thousand years and has given him the office of consecrated Sin Bearer, carrying upon himself to the sacrifice the sins of his people.

4 THE QUADRATED CIRCLE IN THE WEST

During modern times, the quadrated circle has dropped out of its generally accepted cultural role in the West. One of the few well-elaborated systems of thought revealing its meanings to the Western mentality was the protoscience alchemy, which positively teemed with primordial images and records of subjective experiences of unconscious activity, such as dreams, visions, and active imagination. The following comments are intended to outline the appearances and significances of the mandala image in this field.

§ 17. The study of the psychological *content of alchemy* is the study of a system of projections. At the time this protoscience flourished, the nature of matter was yet unknown. "Everything unknown is filled by psychological projection; it is as if the investigator's own psychic depths were mirrored in the darkness. What he sees and thinks he recognizes is, first of all, the facts of his own unconscious."[1] In alchemy the myriad unconscious contents are brought into interrelation in terms of process and sequences of processes leading toward final synthesis, all with some semblance of order and sense. In outline, it starts with a chaotic primordial matter or confused mass in which the elements have a corruptible relation to one another. Then there is a separation of these elements; the opposites fall asunder and, as male and female, or king and queen, unite in a "conjunction," followed by their death—the mortification or putrefaction. All this is the first phase—

---

[1] For notes to chapter 4, see p. 168.

the blackening or nigredo. The steps are in four main divisions, designated by four colors—black, white, red, and yellow or gold—including several kinds of chemical procedure and finally producing the perfect philosopher's stone or philosopher's gold, or tincture, reuniting the four elements. This final synthesis has the power to transmute other imperfect substances.[2]

§ 18. Jung summarizes the role of the *mandala symbolism in the alchemical system of projections:* "The quadrating of the circle is a symbol of the 'opus alchymicum' in that it dissolves the original, chaotic unity into the four elements and then brings them together into a higher unity. The unity is represented by the circle, the four elements by the square. The arising of the one out of the four results from a distillation or sublimation process, which runs in so-called 'circular' form . . . thereby 'soul' or 'spirit' is extracted in clearest form. . . . Spirit is the ternary (threefold) . . . the body is obviously the fourth. . . . The circular form represents in the Ouroboros, the dragon swallowing its own tail, the basic alchemistic mandala."[3] A fundamental formula was: "Make of man and woman a round circle and extract from this a square, and from the square a triangle. Make a round circle, and you will have the stone of the philosophers."[4]

The fourfold or twelvefold "philosophic wheel" is analogous to the Asiatic mandala in its significance as well as its form, in that it also is a diagram of the universe and is concerned with the evolution of spiritual life out of natural bodies (see § 28). In one system "the Redeemer constructs a cosmic wheel of creation with twelve containers (the Zodiac), which is used for the lifting up of the soul. This wheel is related in significance with the 'rota,' the 'opus circulatorium' of alchemy, which has the same goal, that of sublimation. . . . 'From the primary substance the wheel of creation takes its beginning, in that it leads over into the simple elements.' Enlarging on the concept of the 'philosophic wheel,' [one master] says that the wheel must be turned through the four seasons of the year and four points of the compass. . . . The wheel [is related to] the sun wheel which rolls through the quarters of heaven, and thus becomes identical with the sungod or sunhero, who suffers the passion of the difficult labors and of the self-immolation, as Herakles, or of imprisonment and dismemberment through the evil principle, as Osiris."[5] The wheel has been compared to the sun chariot, which dips into the sea (its death in the West), or to the circulating course of the sun, which is a line meeting itself again like the tail eater (the serpent biting its own tail), a sign of the deity and of the Work. The comparison has been made to the four-pointed cosmic wheels of Ezekiel, in which again the deity is at the center. The circular transforming substance "is an analogy of the revolving universe, the macrocosm, or a mirror image of the same, which is imprinted inside matter."[6]

Plates V to VII exemplify this alchemical mandala symbolism.

§ 19. The circulating wheel, then, was a symbol of the Work in the alchemistic quest, representing the rotation of the cosmos as a model of the process. The *inward and outward directions* of motion are sometimes stressed, evidently reflecting the ever prevalent influence of classical Greek philosophy in the thinking of the nature philosophers (see § 24). Boehme drew an analogy of the wheel of the philosophers to those of Ezekiel, saying: "We know that the spiritual life is turned inward upon itself, and the natural life is turned outward from and before itself." Then in the course of the Work, "the wheel of Nature turns itself from out inward; for the God-head dwells in the midst in himself and has such a form that man cannot paint it, but only a natural likeness. . . ."[7] In Empedocles' poetic account of the motions of love and strife in the great circle of creation, strife pushes away toward the periphery and separates the phenomena of nature whereas love draws all back into a unity at the center (see § 24).

§ 20. The above-mentioned *formula for the philosophers' stone* is elsewhere called the "Quadrangular Secret Wisdom": "In the middle of the quadrate is a circle with radiations (fig. 14).

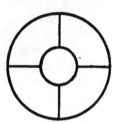

Figure 14. The four elements and their mediator.

Of it the Scholium explains: 'Divide your stone into four elements . . . and join together into one and you will have the whole mastery.' The circle in the middle is called 'mediator, making peace among the inimicals or elements' (namely, the four elements), 'for this alone (the mediator) effects the quadrating of the circle.' The circumambulation has its parallel in the 'circulation of spirits or circular distillation, which is from the exterior inward, interior outward: thus inferior and superior, meet together in one circle, and thus you no longer know what was exterior, or interior, or inferior or superior; but all are one in one circle or vessel. . . .' The division into four is the 'exterior': four rivers, which flow into and out of the inner 'ocean.' "[8]

Another text ("Rosarium") shows the same pattern in the form of a round fountain surrounded by a square with a star at each of the corners, which represent the four elements. Jung describes the meanings of the diagram: "Its content is the 'mare nostrum,' . . . a dark sea, the chaos. The vessel also is designated as uterus, in which the foetus . . . matures. Contrary to the quadrate, the basin is to be thought of as round, for it is the mother-abode of the completed state, to which the quadrate as an incompleted figure must still come. In the latter, the elements are striving away from one another, hostile to one another and must thus become united in the circle."[9] This again bears the marks of the Greek influence, specifically the roles of love and strife of Empedocles (see § 24).

§ 21. The essential feature of alchemy is transformation, of substances ignoble into substances noble, corruptible into incorruptible, striving into united, or natural into spiritual. At the heart of this process stands the figure of Mercurius, the Anthropos who, as chthonic revelation god and as spirit of quicksilver, plays the central role in the whole transformation process as its agent and its beginning and its end; he has a strikingly *double nature*. "As Mercury, he is particularly the sun, also related mostly to the gold. As quicksilver, though, he dissolves the gold and thereby extinguishes its solar brilliance.... Now he was a serviceable, helpful spirit ... assistant, colleague ... and now he was ... an evasive, deceiving, provoking elf driving the alchemist to despair, who had many attributes of the devil.... In the alchemistic series of deities, as Primordial Matter he is the lowest, as Stone of the Philosophers, the highest. The Mercurial Spirit is the leader and the misleader of the alchemist; he is his luck and his ruin."[10] His double nature is also expressed as hermaphroditic, and he represents the totality of all processes: he "stands at the beginning and the end of the work; he is the Primordial Matter, ... the Nigredo; ... as dragon he swallows himself, and as dragon dies and rises again as the Stone.... He is the play of (all) colors ... meeting of the four elements ... hermaphrodite of the beginning nature which separates out ... and unites in the 'conjunction'... matter and yet spirit ... cold and yet fiery ... poison and yet healing potion ... as symbol uniting the opposites."[11] These qualities, of course, identify the Mercurius symbol as an image of the self, which is both god and devil, creator and destroyer.[12] His representation in the quadrated circle has been cited above (see § 2) and illustrated in Plate V.

This figure is stressed here because of the light it throws upon the patient's case material in Part I. There the very dubious nature of the lowest and rebellious party, behind the husband animus, is a characteristic finding of the collective unconscious, especially in its paranoid trends. As Communist party, this image is naturally evil and dark in its connotations and an enemy of sinister and unpredictable intentions. Yet it has the redeeming effect of leading the transforming rebellion that aims at individuality. Here is a striking resemblance to the Mercurius image. This archetype of the transforming agency would be experienced in the woman's psychology as animus, which carries in it the potential of the self. That is, it would be the "leading aspect" of the self, through whose rebellious machinations the synthesis of the new psychic organization is fashioned in the form of the quadrated circle.

5 THE SYMBOLISM OF OPPOSITES

In the discussion of the aspects of the quadrated circle, many allusions were made to the differentiation and union of opposites. Not only is archetypal symbolism rife with the theme of opposites, but especially does it become familiar to those who take careful note of unconscious content in dreams and psychotic productions. The material of the patient described in the present study is perfectly characteristic in this as well as in other respects.

The imagery of light and dark, male and female, father and mother, sky and earth, heaven and underworld, spirit and matter, contains much hidden knowledge about the nature of the developmental processes. In it are integration and disintegration, progression and regression, elation and depression, hate and love, individuality and identification, freedom of consciousness and bondage to projection. The full range of its meanings merits long and arduous study. The following notes attempt only to call to the reader's attention a few of the multifarious modes of expression of the problem as a general human concern.

§ 22. The male and female pair of *cosmic rulers* as Great Father and Great Mother represent the opposite aspects of nature in many mythologies.[1] On the primitive level, many of these tell of a Father Sky and Mother Earth, such as the Greek Ouranos and Gaia or the African legend of the first cosmic pair who were locked together in a timeless embrace until forcibly separated when their offspring was brought to birth.[2] The more differentiated and re-

---

[1] For notes to chapter 5, see p. 168.

fined expressions of these figures on higher cultural levels are represented, for example, by the Greek Zeus and Hera, the Hindu Siva and Shakti or Vishnu and Maya, the Chinese Yang and Yin, or in Jewish mystical tradition Yahweh and Sophia. In orthodox Christianity, Christ and his bride the Church (Ecclesia) reign on high (as in Judaism, Yahweh's female counterpart is the people Israel) or the Trinity and the Virgin make a male and female pair or quarternity (Plate X).

The mandala often represents these various pairs in union (see § 6). This union is often an eternal sexual embrace, as in the Hindu Siva and Shakti or the early Tibetan Yab and Yum. In certain Tibetan writings the central

Figure 15. Chinese T'ai-chi.

deity of the mandala is found thus in eternal embrace and the pair is called "Divine Father-Mother" (see § 34). This union is related to the "heavenly marriage" of early ritual. For example, the "hieros gamos" was a Greek fertility rite in the spring festivals of rejuvenation of the year and its vegetation in which Zeus as the rain-bringing thunder unites with Hera as the fruit-bearing earth, the former represented as the thunder ax, the latter as the tree.[3] It is interesting to note that both tree and thunderbolt frequently appear in the mandala.

§ 23. The most subtle expressions of the imagery of the cosmic pair are in the Asiatic traditions. The Chinese *Yang and Yin* are symbolized in the T'ai-chi, closely related to the mandala. Cammann says of it: "Under the Han Dynasty ... some of the older ideas about the universe expressed by earlier philosophers began to be shown in picture form. The simplest of these, yet having the deepest meaning, was a simple diagram, a circle bisected by an S-curve, one half red, the other black. The red section represents Yang, the male element in the universe, source of light, life, and heat; while the black (for colorless) section represents Yin, the female element, from which come darkness, cold, and death. The complete symbol containing both represents the union of the spiritual and material in all things and is known as T'ai-chi, or Great Absolute. Around the T'ai-chi are usually grouped the eight trigrams (Pa-kua) ... each pair representing two of the chief phenomena of nature which were believed to have been created by the interaction of Yang and Yin at the time of the origin of matter, the principal ones being Heaven (pure Yang) and Earth (pure Yin). Later, an outer circle was added, made up of the twelve animals of the Asiatic zodiac....It (the T'ai-chi) is generally painted on the center of the roofbeam in the main hall of the large country houses, where this symbol of the axis or focus of the universe approximately marks the center of the home."[4] The T'ai-chi and Pa-kua[5] "together form a type of space-time diagram that is essentially akin to the mandala."[6]

The older philosophy to which the diagrams allude is well represented by Chuang-tse,[7] who had much to say concerning the union of opposites: "When subjective and objective are both without their correlates, that is the very axis of TAO. And when that axis passes through the center at which all infinities converge, positive and negative alike blend into an infinite ONE. [Cf. Yang and Yin in the axial T'ai-chi.] Therefore it is that, viewed from the standpoint of TAO, a beam and a pillar are identical [that is, horizontal and vertical]. So are ugliness and beauty, greatness, wickedness, perverseness, and strangeness. Separation is the same as construction. Nothing is subject either to construction or destruction, for these conditions are brought together into ONE."[8]

It is to be noted that although the Great Absolute is a cosmic axis uniting the contraries, the philosophy of the Yang and the Yin tells of alternations of ascendancy of the one over the other in circular fashion; when Yang is at the zenith and Yin at the lowest reach, then the seed of the Yin is born in the midst of the Yang and that of the Yang in the midst of the Yin, which then initiate the reversal of their positions.[9]

A similar alternation of polarities is found in the Hindu teachings. These tell, not of the usual single creation, but of a sequence of creations, successively brought forth and again resorbed, and in which then the eternal and the temporal hold sway over either phase. Zimmer explains of the cosmic pair that the Siva and Shakti "though seemingly two ... are fundamentally one, ... the Absolute has apparently unfolded into this duality, and out of them derive all the life polarities ... that characterize the phenomenal world ... the male being the personification of the passive aspect which we know as Eternity, the female, of the activating energy ... the dynamism of Time."[10] Certain Hindu mandalas represent Siva and Shakti in union as series of triangles facing upward and downward.[11]

§ 24. An analogous Western philosophy of the roles of the cosmic principles, as a pair of opposites that dominate contrary tendencies in the creative process, is found in Empedocles.[12] The same imagery pertains—the circle and four elements, the alternations of contraries: *love and strife,* and light and dark as sun and rain.

And these ([four] elements) never cease changing place continually, now being all united by Love into one, now each borne apart by the hatred engendered of Strife, until they are brought together in the unity of the all, and become subject to it. Thus inasmuch as one has been wont to arise out of many and again with the separation of the one the many arise, so things are continually coming into being and there is no fixed age for them; and farther inasmuch as they (the [four] elements) never cease changing place continually, so they always exist within an immovable circle....

For these ([four] elements) are equal, all of them, and of like ancient race; and one holds one office, another another, and each has his own nature.... For nothing is added to them, nor yet does anything pass away from them; for if they were continually perishing they would no longer exist....

Behold the sun, warm and bright on all sides, and whatever is immortal and is bathed in its bright ray, and behold the raincloud, dark and cold on all sides; from the earth there proceed the foundations of things and solid bodies. In Strife all things are enbued with form and separate from each other, but they come together in Love and are desired by each other.

... thus, then, in the firm vessel of harmony is fixed God, a sphere, round, rejoicing in complete solitude....

When Strife reached the lowest depth of the eddy and Love comes to be in the midst of the whirl, then all these things come together at this point so as to be one alone, yet not immediately, but joining together at their pleasure, one from one place, another from another. And as they were joining together Strife departed to the utmost boundary.

§ 25. The typical basic pattern of the myths of creation is the interaction between a *maternal chaos* and a paternal form giver. Among the earliest of the creation myths is the Babylonian account of the encounter of the world-creating sun hero Marduk with the maternal water monster of chaos Tiamat, whom he divided into two halves to make sky and earth.[13] Such a chaos is described in Hindu mythology as the cosmic waters ("the maternal, procreative aspect of the Absolute"), upon which sleeps the god Vishnu, out of whose navel arises the golden lotus that forms the world.[14] Plato's Timaeus calls this chaos the "Receptacle," a void that is a "matrix," and "nurse of all Becoming"; the Receptacle acts as mother, the eternal forms as father, and their child is nature, appearing first in the four elements.[15] The chaos is also an important factor in the alchemical system of images, where it can be recognized as the projected contents of the collective unconscious, out of which an order (cosmos) arises gradually through the various phases of the individuation process.[16]

§ 26. The content of the symbolism of the opposites, then, is apparently the psychology of differentiation and of integration, of separating the one into the many and uniting the many in the one. Any act of becoming conscious is the act of division of the opposites, thereby inducing conflict; integration requires their reconciliation on a higher plane of awareness. In terms of development, the first phase is that of the separation of consciousness with its several functions from its unconscious matrix and of its growing discovery of the outer world. The subsequent striving toward wholeness involves emotions expressed symbolically as the *longing for union* between the opposites, a drive that is erotic in the deepest sense and that is often represented in the unconscious imagery as sexual mating.

The heavenly marriage, the eternal embrace in the mandala, the differentiation of the primordial round man into man and woman and their reunion—all these themes are expressive of the same urge. In alchemical symbolism the role of the "coniunctio oppositorum" is paramount, expressed as a union between sun and moon, king and queen, spirit and nature, or the brother-sister pair.[17] Below, a little material is drawn from the *Divina Commedia* exemplifying the experience of the individuation symbolism which grew out of the erotic longing of Dante toward his lady Beatrice (see § 32).

Jung says of the individuation process: "If one wants to complete this exacting piece of work and bring it to realization, one must for better or worse come to terms with the animus or anima in order to open the way for a higher unification, a 'coniunctio oppositorum.' This is the indispensable requisite for wholeness.... The syzygy seems to represent at least a substantial portion, if not the two halves of the totality of the royal brother-sister pair, and so also that tension of the opposites from which the divine child emerges as the symbol of unity"—that is, the symbol of wholeness—the self.[18]

6 THE SYMBOLISM OF REBIRTH

If unconscious process can be said to have an essence, the theme of transformation might be singled out as the most representative. In ordinary circumstances the psychic organism is in a constant state of evolution and growth, which is the ever increasing differentiation of the individual personality from its inner and outer surroundings or matrices. During this slow unfolding and flowering, the self, being the unconscious potential of the personality, tends always and anew to find itself projected into now one containing form and now another. First, as in the patient's case, the projected self is carried by the mother, then by the father, subsequently perhaps by the homosexual ideal, or the group, and not long after by the heterosexual partner in the truly erotic bond. In later years other forms may attract the image: perhaps a way of thought or belief, a political credo or international concern, or some other collective structure. The self image might be more precisely delineated as a person's apperception of his identity in terms of his relation to the object holding the projection of the central archetype. At the same time that the ego is differentiating itself out of its unconscious matrix, the self is being extracted from its outward representatives. Transformation seems to consist of the change of the self image from an old form that no longer contains enough potential of growth into a new one that does. The age-old and widespread way of expressing this transition is in terms of rebirth.

Rebirth is the dying of an old form of the self and a bringing to birth of a new one. It might be said another way, that an old structure of the psyche is resorbed into its components and a new structure erected, or that perhaps an organization of the personality that no longer serves for further development is abandoned in favor of a reorganization.[1] At certain typical junctures in the course of life these changes tend to become major revolutions, and these are seen analytically as activations of the archetypal unconscious at these periods. In primitive cultures the *"rites de passage"* are the ceremonies ushering the individual from one phase of his communal life into the next, and they may be interpreted as the outward enaction of the typical inward events of the archetypal process at these universal points of transition.

Of these symbolic processes, the puberty rites of initiation are the most fundamental and also the most self-explanatory in their meaning, and subsequent rites retain some of their stamp. Catatonic schizophrenia abounds in symbolism[2] of the initiation process, and it occurs characteristically in adolescence, either during the second decade or, if the psychological work of this period of life is delayed or prolonged, in the third or even fourth decades. The following sections will attempt only to indicate how the schizophrenic symbolism relates to the generally valid forms and how in these the image of the self comes into play.

§ 27. The various *initiation rites* of primitive and ancient cultures are derived from one basic prototype, the puberty rite.[3] In all parts of the world, apparently, the principal features of the puberty rites consist of the boy's leaving his mother's keeping, his series of ordeals imposed by the elders to prove his mettle and thence his acceptance into the man's role, his symbolic death and resurrection or rebirth apart from the community, his later return to the community as newly born and renamed and without the slightest recollection of his former life of childhood, and his admission into the secret society of the men and introduction to their mysteries and mythology. The "death" may be by hazing, imitation killing, being devoured by a devil, or being passed through the jaws of a ceremonial crocodile. By giving up his former childish, mother-bound self in this "death," he then becomes identified with the totem self and thus an integral member of the male group who share this same "soul."[4] The rite has homosexual overtones, especially in the rigid seclusion of males.[5]

One of the theories attempting to explain the significance of these rites is of interest here because of its relation to the patient's notions. According to this theory, these ritual actions "are all connected with a primitive effort to assimilate the novices to the condition of spirits. When ... the dead are considered as exercising much power over the living, there will exist a natural desire [to do this] in order that the spiritual power appertaining to the dead may be obtained."[6]

As the civilization of antiquity emerged out of primitivity, the rite took

---

[1] For notes to chapter 6, see pp 169–170

on the more religious significance of a transformation of the mortal, worldly man into the spiritual, "enlightened" man aspiring to eternal life. At times the initiant identified with the deity who mythically possessed the power of renewal, and the rite was often associated with the rites of rejuvenation of the year and its vegetation. For example, in the Eleusenian mysteries of the Demeter cult of Greece, the initiant dressed as the goddess and joined a night procession representing the sorrowing search for her daughter lost to the world and held captive in the land of death; the central mystery was the revelation of the ear of corn as the sign of the miracle of renewal.[7] In the Attis mysteries in Rome, the process was even clearer. The death of the god was mourned at the vernal equinox, his effigy being hung on a tree and then buried, after which there was rejoicing over his resurrection; at the same time the initiant underwent this rejuvenation by being dropped into a pit underneath the sacrifice of the bull—the god himself with whom he symbolically died and whose blood drenched him—and then being greeted as a newborn babe and an incarnation of the deity himself.[8] The initiations in the cults of Attis, Tammuz, and Mithras were dramatizations of rebirth often held in caves.[9]

The relation of the rites of earliest Greek antiquity to those of primitives has been established, revealing the Divine Child—Dionysus or Zeus—as the initiant and the initiator in ceremonies following universal patterns and associated, as are those cited by Frazer, with spring festivals of the death of the old year and rejuvenation of the new and its tree spirit of vegetation.[10] It has been pointed out that the Tibetan initiation was likewise linked with the renewal of the year and vegetation (see § 28).

The sun wheel and mandala play a prominent part in many of these symbolic systems. The initiator in the Greek rites just mentioned was called "Kouros," that is, "ideal youth," and the prototype of this initiated youth was the god who had himself first undergone the process in the myth. Just as the divine Anthropos or ideal man was often shown in the mandala (see § 2), so this ideal youth, the divine Kouros, was represented in the sun wheel and later grew into the figure of Apollo or Helios the sun.[11] At the climax of the Egyptian Isis mysteries the initiant identified with the sun as the god, this "solification" (a later term) being demonstrated by the crown of palms encircling the head as the solar rays (see § 2).[12] In the Tibetan forms, the rite takes place inside the mandala (see § 28); in the American Indian, the boy is placed inside the sand painting (see § 4). In both, identification with the goddess is a feature. Complex systems of symbolism of seeking enlightenment are found in ancient customs in India, where Brahmins would gain dominion over the three spiritual worlds by sitting and turning upon the holy wheel at the center of a chariot race (see § 2).

More recently in India, the Tantric system designates the progressive levels of consciousness as "chakras," "circles" or "wheels."[13] These are seven lotuses in horizontal position and placed in vertical ascent, each of which represents a step upward through the body toward union with the spirit at the summit, and through the center of each passes the channel through which the Kundalini serpent rises; sometimes the structure is referred to as "tree." The chief levels of the ascent are identified each with one of the four material elements: earth, water, fire, and air, culminating in the fifth spiritual element, ether. This progression is symbolized in figure 16. This is the basic pattern of the stupa, the three-dimensional mandala (see § 16), and, characteristically, an image of the cosmos and the basic design of the temple. It is tempting to point out the analogy to the alchemical cosmic designs of the stone as square, circle, triangle, and conjunction of male and female.

Figure 16. Hindu stupa.

§ 28. An example of the *rebirth symbolism in the East* is found in Buddhism, revealing a specific function of the mandala image. The Tibetan ritual of Chod is linked to the ceremonies of death and rebirth of other cultures by the fact that it is not only an initiation rite but also a dramatization of the renewal process for the community. The latter is "performed for the purpose of expelling the old year ... through winning the aid of deities by means of human sacrifice (nowadays made in effigy) and thus safeguarding the crops and cattle and assuring divine protection for the state. ... Primitively, a sacramental eating of the flesh and drinking of the blood of the sacrificed one was probably associated with the rite."[14] The performance of the initiation rite in the presence of corpses of the dead, with encouragement of the novice to identify his bodily self with these,[15] is reminiscent of initiation practices of primitives, such as those of the Fiji Islanders described by Frazer.[16] "Chod" means "cutting off" or "sacrifice," and the rites are called "The Yoga of Subduing the Lower Self," that is, the sacrifice of the ego personality, represented by the body and its passions and predispositions, for the attainment of union with the divine consciousness.

In the earlier stages, a mandala is drawn on the ground and the deities whose powers are to be conferred on the neophyte are invited to be present and occupy the spaces reserved for them. If the inner illumination does take place, it is confirmed by seeing in the sky above the human drawing another, "true" mandala, similar to it but with the deities visibly present, conferring understanding. When the Chod ritual itself is undertaken, the initiant identifies with the goddess of wisdom at the center of the mandala, in which role he subdues the demons that represent the passions composing egotism. Then there is a dance in the four quarters representing the four continents around the central sacred Mount Meru, the cosmic axis. Finally, there is the "mandala of sacrifice," which the initiant contemplates and realizes to be his own body, visualizing his spinal column as center or Mount Meru, his four limbs the four continents, and his head the world of the gods; this body he offers up as a "fat, luscious-looking corpse, huge enough to embrace the universe."[17]

The aim is that the initiant see "the many as the One and the One as All, and knows the sole reality is mind," and keep his mind "in the equilibrium of the non-two state," that is free of the opposites (see § 13).[18] This ceremonial use is the function of the floor mandala as distinct from the ceiling variety; the former is employed as a "magic circle," the latter as a diagram to establish a cosmic axis.[19]

§ 29. *Rebirth symbolism in the West* still persists in Christian teaching and practice, though the original intent of much of the ritual has long since been lost to view. In the writings of Paul the point is made quite clear that baptism is the initiation of this faith, and he brings into his admonitions about it many of the classical features of rites related above.

It is well known to New Testament scholars that Paul gave greater heed to the authority of the inward experience of the Christ that appeared in his visions than to the Jesus for whom the apostles spoke[20]—that is, Paul's experience was primarily of the archetype.[27] In this spirit Paul writes, "I am crucified with Christ; nevertheless I live; yet not I, but Christ liveth in me: and the life which I now live in the flesh I live by the faith of the Son of God...."[28] It should be remembered that the early cross was in the form of the "tree" or of the encircled equilateral cross of the sun wheel (see §§ 1, 12, 30 *b*); therefore the crucifixion was the death of the deity at the center of the mandala as usual. To Paul, Christ was a kind of vehicle of the process of death and rebirth, as the god certainly was in the initiation rites of the Attis and Dionysus and Zeus cults already described (see §§ 2, 27). Paul says of the Christian initiation: "Therefore we are buried with him by baptism into death....For if we have been planted together in the likeness of his death, we shall be also in the likeness of his resurrection: Knowing this, that our old man is crucified with him, that the body of sin might be destroyed...."[23] The vegetation symbolism of planting and rising anew is, it will be recognized, more than the result of Paul's poetic sense; it was a real connection with the prevalent rebirth ritual of his day throughout the Mediterranean area.[24] As in the Attis mysteries, and others (see §§ 2, 27), the initiant identifies with the archetype in the perilous passage through death and resurrection, for the deity is the prototype or projection of the initiation process itself. Paul repeatedly insists on the inwardness of this deity. He says, "Always bearing about in the body the dying of the Lord Jesus, that the life also of Jesus might be made manifest in our body";[25] also, "For as many of you as have been baptized into Christ have put on Christ."[26] This Christ nature, then, somewhat like the Buddha nature, is a self that

is not the individual ego but a common life running through the entire
body of the faithful:[27] "For by one Spirit we are all baptized into one
body...."[28]

§ 30. Throughout the rebirth symbolism a major role is played by the
Great Mother, for it is generally in the return to her and passing through
her that man finds regeneration. There are some exceptions in mythology;
Zagreus, in one version of the tale, was passed through the thigh of his
father, Zeus, to be re-created. It can be said that as the child was born of
the mother into his boyhood, so at initiation he is born of the fathers into
his manhood; but also, as he was born of the physical mother once, so now
in rebirth is he born of the symbolic mother, the archetypal psyche. Perhaps
a way may be found satisfactorily to formulate these complex processes in
terms of the self:[29] The Divine Son is the self in a certain aspect; he is
reborn in the mandala, the self in another form, or in the Great Mother
or Great Father, also different aspects of the self and the main constituents
of the mandala. Mythology is full of accounts of the Great Mother who
creates and destroys, resorbs and gives forth again, and who is the very
vessel of rejuvenation. The patient's symbolism refers to elements that are
mythological equivalents of this figure as poisoner, destroyer, death, earth,
and sea.

(a) The goddess *poisons* and *destroys* in many myths. The Greek Medea
was a sorceress and priestess of Hekate who compounded a drug to make
Jason immune from fire and iron for a day and by her arts restored both
Jason and his father to youth. When the daughters of Pelias induced him
to submit to the same rejuvenation, Medea simply took his life. She also
dismembered her own brother in her flight with Jason.[30] The Egyptian Isis,
in her yearning after the world of the gods, plotted to wrest from the aging
Ra his power, which is magically contained in the name. She kneaded a
serpent of spittle and earth and put it in his way, and the feeble god was
reduced to utmost misery by the poison. When he called for "one with
healing words and understanding lips, ... Isis came with her craft, whose
mouth is full of the breath of life, whose spells chase pain away, whose
word maketh the dead to live." When she had learned the name, she
overcame the poison and cast it to the earth.[31]

Many of the ancient mother goddesses had a dual nature, promoting both
life and death, creation and destruction. The Greek Hekate, associated with
the moon, underworld, and night, was patroness of sorcery and necromancy
as well as of childbirth.[32] "Hekate, as Mistress of the spirits, warned the
Greeks that a threefold division would necessarily leave, side by side with
the ordered world of Zeus, a chaotic region in which the amorphousness of
the primitive world could live on as the Underworld.... Like Artemis or
Mother Earth herself, she was 'kourotrophos,' nurse and nourisher of all
those born after her."[33] The Hindu Kali was also associated with both life

and death. "The Goddess represents clearly enough by her feminine nature the life-bearing, life-nourishing, maternal principle; this, her positive aspect, hardly needs to be further emphasized. But the counterbalancing, negative aspect, her ever-destructive function, which takes back and swallows again the creatures brought forth, requires a shock of vivid horror if it is to be duly expressed . . . Kali: that is the feminine form of the word Kala, meaning Time . . . the all-producing, all-annihilating principle."[34]

Jung says of these threatening mother goddesses: "The mother is accused [that is, by members of her cult remonstrating over her cruel trickery] as if she were the cause of the man's flying to the mother in order to be cured of the wound which she herself inflicted. . . . Even yet a deep animosity seems to live in man because a brutal law has separated him from the instinctive yielding to his desires and from the great beauty of the harmony of the animal nature . . . among others, the incest prohibition . . . therefore pain and anger relate to the mother as if she were responsible for the domestication. . . . In order not to become conscious of his incest wish (his backward harking to the animal nature), the son throws all the burden of the guilt onto the mother, from which arises the idea of the 'terrible mother.' The mother becomes for him the spectre of anxiety."[35]

(b) These myths exemplify the prevalent association of the mother goddess with *death*.[36] In the Babylonian Gilgamesh Epic, the hero enumerates the murderous crimes of the goddess Ishtar,[37] who is also responsible for the mass destruction of the deluge.[38] Also the Babylonian myth of Marduk describes the great mother Tiamat's agents of destruction, poison, and horror. She "let them swell with the splendor of horror . . . whoever sees them shall die of terror";[39] but from the body of this chaos arises the creation of the cosmos. The child Dionysus was dismembered by the Titans at the behest of his stepmother Hera[40] and was subsequently reborn. Attis (Asia Minor), in the service of Cybele the mother goddess, died by self-castration under the mother tree; he was ritually brought to life again by the sacrifice of the priests' genitals, which had been placed in chambers sacred to Cybele.[41]

In Christian culture, a medieval legend describes Mary as the good mother accusing the Santa Crux as the evil one, "Cross, thou art the evil stepmother of my son, so high has thou hung him . . . Cross, thou art my mortal enemy."[42] The interrelation of the tree of life and the tree of death is brought out in a medieval legend that the cross was made from wood from the tree of the Garden of Eden.[43] Further instances of the death-dealing aspect of the mother are discussed at length by Jung.[44]

A description of the blackening or nigredo of alchemy is given by Jung. It is either a quality of the primordial matter, or chaos, or confused mass; or, if the separation of the opposites is already established and the masculine and feminine unite, their death follows with the corresponding blackening (mortification, calcination, or putrefaction).[45] The theme of death as a descent into the sea (unconscious) and union with the feminine is related to other hero myths of rebirth."[46] (Cf. imprisonment and death of the king's son in the womb of his sister at the bottom of the sea, in "Visio Arislei.")

(c) An example of the role of the *Earth Mother* in life and death is found in the Greek Gaea, who is known under the name of Demeter as the nourishing mother; also, "after death men were laid away in her deep bosom, whence they had first come, so that she presided over the host of departed spirits, and it was only natural that, under the name of Persephone, she ultimately came to be known as queen of the lower world."[47] The Greek Rhea or Cybele was also an earth goddess associated with vegetation and lover of Attis. Her priests castrated themselves and placed the organs of fertility in her sacred chambers "to advance the growth of vegetation, and to free themselves from eternal death by mystic union with the immortal goddess."[48] Caves, crypts, tombs, and catacombs are thus associated with the mother; "the burial of the dead in a holy place ... is restitution to the mother, with the certain hope of resurrection by which such burial is rightfully rewarded."[49]

The New Testament reflects ancient ideas about the analogy of rejuvenation of man's soul with that of vegetation: "That which thou sowest is not quickened, except it die. . . . So also is the resurrectiton of the dead. It is sown in corruption; it is raised in incorruption. . . . It is sown a natural body; it is raised a spiritual body. . . . The first man Adam was made a living soul; the last Adam was made a quickening spirit."[50] Frazer notes the analogy in ancient Egyptian practice: "In laying their dead in the grave they committed them to his keeping [Osiris, the corn god's] who could raise them from the dust to life eternal, even as he caused the seed to spring from the ground; ... the effigies ... were at once an emblem and an instrument of resurrection. Thus from the sprouting of the grain the ancient Egyptians drew an augury of human immortality."[51] Similar concepts of the transmutation of bodily matter into spirit or of releasing the spirit entrapped in matter are found throughout the alchemistic formulation of these processes.[52]

(d) Greek mythology and philosophy conceived of the *sea* as mother of all created things. Homer speaks of it as "the source of all things."[53] The Divine Child theme is closely associated with the maternal waters. In India it is believed that at the beginning of creation "this world was water, a single flood: only Prajapati could be seen, sitting on a lotus-leaf"; and Vishnu was asked, "How did this world, shaped like a lotus, spring from your navel in the lotus-epoch when you lay in the world-ocean?"[54] The Greek Apollo Delphinios was associated with the womb of the sea, Delphi ("delph" meaning "uterus"), and his attribute was the dolphin, the "uterine beast."[55] Zimmer says of the Hindu belief: "When the divine life-substance is about to put forth the universe, the cosmic waters grow a thousand-petaled lotus of pure gold, radiant as the sun ... the opening ... of the womb of the universe. . . . The waters are female; they are the maternal, procreative aspect of the Absolute, and the cosmic lotus is their generative organ. . . . It is personified as the Mother Goddess through whom the Absolute moves into creation" (see § 5).[56] The goddesses Isis and Mary are both of the sea, "Stella Maris."[57] Jung traces the derivation of words for "death" ("mara"), "sea" ("mare"), and "mother" ("ma") back to a common root.[58]

The fundamental pattern of the return to the mother in the form of the myth of the sun hero, including his descent into the western sea, his being devoured by a sea monster (mother), and his rebirth and attaining the treasure (the self), is thoroughly discussed and amplified by Jung.[59]

§ 31. As the archetypal mother is the usual agent of rebirth, so it is the archetypal child to whom she gives issue. The appearance of the *Divine Child* in the cosmic womb or lotus has been indicated in discussing Vishnu and Apollo.

It will be recalled that on the most primitive plane the initiated boy, on returning from his supposed death, is regarded as a newborn babe, endowed with a new name and retaining no recollection whatsoever of his former ways of life (see § 27). In this state he has sacrificed his boyhood individual soul and exchanged it for the collective totem soul, which he shares with the whole tribal group of men into whose society he has been ritually inducted.[60] He is at this point often regarded as the reincarnation of an ancestral spirit, these dead heroes being the deities of such cults.[61]

When the Greek and Cretan cultures were still primitive, they too apparently practiced such initiations. According to Harrison,[62] the Divine Child of their cults, Zeus or Dionysus, was the embodiment of the rite itself, the representative of all initiated youth, the Megistos Kouros, and as such was the projection of the collective emotion involved in these magical acts of rejuvenation.[63] Equally primitive was the Oriental ceremony of initiation in ancient Rome in the cult of Attis in which the initiant, after being drenched in the blood of the sacred bull in a pit, was renamed and given infant's clothing and fed on milk, thus becoming an incarnation of the deity or Divine Child; this ceremony took place at the spring festival of rejuvenation of the vegetation (see § 27).[64] These cults were matriarchal (that is, of matrilinear societies), centering in the Earth Mother and the fruits of her abundance (child) and the rain (father) that fertilized her.[65]

When the matriarchal order in Greece gave way to patriarchy, the sky god, Zeus, took the ascendancy and the divine son was Apollo, the sun. As Harrison has indicated, his name had earlier been Apello, derived from the words connoting "flocks" or "assemblies" (like "ecclesia") of those who could be "sharer in sacred rites," that is, those who were initiated.[66] He represents the later differentiated Greek consciousness with its clear thinking, the "day mind," as against the more primitive "night mind" of the earlier age so prone to magic, oracle, and dream.[67]

The Divine Child is the sun in many myths. The basic pattern is the rebirth process symbolized in the form of the Night Sea Journey, described by Frobenius and elaborated at length by Jung,[68] in which the solar hero is devoured by the sea monster in the west and is reborn in the east as the newly risen sun; he loses his hair in the passage, a classical feature of initiation rites.[69] Mention has already been made of the Isis mysteries in which the initiant appeared at the end crowned with leaves of spotless palm like the rays of the sun, with whom he was identified as deity (see § 2). The Egyptian deity Harpocrates (sometimes Horus) was the newborn sun child. The figure of Christ took on many solar attributes, among which was the date assigned to his nativity, December 25, the night of the winter solstice celebrated at the time by worshippers of the sun-god Mithras as the time of the rejuvenation of the light of the "Sol Invictus."[70]

In alchemical symbolism, the rejuvenation symbolism retains its solar properties. The philosophers's stone, the goal of the Work, was regarded as a living child or germ of divine nature brought forth from a vessel as mother. It was called, as already stated (see § 5), "tender babe," "orphan," "son of the philosophers," a "golden child" whose "form is like the revolving wheel." In the Chinese Taoist practice, the "golden egg" (Chin Tan) was born as a "holy embryo" in the Golden Flower (see § 5).

Similar to this image is the Hindu golden egg or germ (Hiranyagarbha, the world egg), also the aim of their transformation process. "He (the self) is also he who warms, the Sun, hidden by the thousand-eyed golden egg, as one fire by another. He is to be thought after, he is to be sought after"; also Hindus call the sun "final goal and safe resort."[71] The collective nature of the self is emphasized in this symbolism, the golden germ being described as a "collective aggregate of all individual souls," the body of the highest Brahma and a collective soul.[72] These attributes assigned to the self bear a remarkable resemblance to the patient's intuitions of germination, the many-eyed egg, gold, warmth, sun, and the collective soul.

The appearance of the Divine Child at the center of the mandala or lotus or cosmic womb has been discussed above (see §§ 2, 5, 30 d),[73] examples being the four sons of Horus and Harpocrates in Egypt, Apollo and Dionysus in Greece, and sometimes Christ in the West, as well as the alchemical, Taoist, and Hindu forms.

The general characteristics of the archetypal-Divine Child are summarized by Jung and Kerényi from mythology[74] as his miraculous birth (usually in a cosmic womb, whether lotus, floating island, cave, or other), his abandonment and being orphaned, and his extraordinary powers.

It will be seen from this brief presentation of some of the material how immensely complicated are the problems of the psychology of regression and of rebirth. These problems will not be undertaken here, except to mention that the so-called infantile "oceanic feeling" and "feeling of omnipotence" are properties of the child archetype as much as of the individual's infancy, and that the signs of the apparent reenaction of the infantile phases of growth are more characteristic of the relation of the reborn initiant to the archetypal mother and father. In these images and emotions is a subtle and misleading intermingling of regression and progression, of vestiges of the individual's past and germs of his future personality, of the most childish of cravings and the highest enlightenment of consciousness; technically, that is, there is a blending of the contents of complexes and of archetypes, of ego and of self, which do not allow themselves to be reduced to simple formulae.

§ 32. In the literature of both East and West are various accounts of *journeys into the worlds of the afterlife.* These accounts contain imagery of the unconscious and of death and rebirth.

In the *Divina Commedia,* Dante presents an account of a series of visions that portray in systematic order the symbols of individuation, the entire journey through the three worlds being a progress through a succession of circles designating levels of the depths and heights of spiritual development. The descent into the underworld and reascent to the spiritual goal culminate in mandala visions of rings, circles, and rose. The sequence is thus characteristic of the basic pattern of the initiation process, and is designated in time to coincide exactly with the days of the death and resurrection of Christ; once more, the initiant follows the lead of the archetypal prototype of the process.

In the *Paradiso* (Canto 28), Dante introduces the vision of the circles with his perception of it through the eyes of Beatrice:

> I saw, gazing in her shining eyes,
> Those snares which love had set to capture me.
> And when I turned. . . .
> I saw a point of radiating light,
> So piercing, that the eye on which it smites
> Must close perforce by reason of its glow.

Around this spin the nine concentric planetary rings of fire:

> And each of these
> Turned with a slower motion, as its number
> Was the more removed from unity.
> The more translucent flame was in that ring
> Which was the nearest to the pure scintilla—
> I think because it shares its truth the most.
>
> My lady, seeing I was sore distressed
> And anxious, now said: "From that single point
> Depend the heavens, and all that nature holds.
> Look on that circle which is nearest it,
> And know it turns so rapidly because
> It is spurred onward by its ardent love."

Beatrice, as bearer of the anima image,[75] is the moving and directing agent of the whole venture. Thus Dante's perception of the classical cosmic mandala pattern through her eye, itself a mandala symbol,[76] would be the coming to life of the central unconscious image of the self within this ardent love for her. This is an example of the potential of individuation contained in the emotions and images of the transference, through which love Dante apprehends the love that makes the cosmic order move, that is, the Eros that gives ordering to the self as the union of opposites (see §§ 24, 26).

Most notable among the last and highest of these images for the purposes of the present discussion are the visions of the mother goddess, of the circle and cross with the Christ, and of the final glory of the deity associated with the squared circle.

The Virgin Mother is seen as the rose in a garden and as the womb encircled by a ring of flame of love, and is praised by the souls as an infant would reach in love to its mother (Canto 23). Beatrice chides Dante for misdirecting his ardor:

> "Why is it that my face enamors thee
> So that thou turnest not to that fair garden
> Blossoming underneath the rays of Christ?
> Here is the Rose, in which the Word Divine
> Became incarnate."...

> Athwart the heavens there floated down a flame,
> Formed in a ring, as 'twere a diadem,
> That circled her, and then revolved around her. . . .
> "I am Angelic Love, that circles round
> The Joy Sublime that issues from that womb
> Which is the resting place of our Desire."...

This is the ritual circumambulation to honor the object or person at the center (see § 9). Then,

> Much as an infant, after it has sucked,
> Will stretch its arm toward its mother's breast,
> Because its love will flame up outwardly:
> Just so did every gleaming radiance
> Stretch upward with its flame, so that their love
> For Mary was made manifest to me.

The sun wheel, of red flames, appears in Mars and in it appears Christ; in it the opposites meet in equality and balance; finally in its midst the poet encounters his ancestor, appropriately likened to the root of the tree of the family:

> Those rays now formed the venerable sign
> Of quadrants joined together in a circle.
> Here memory transcends my faculties;
> For there upon the cross flashed forth the Christ
> So gloriously, that similies are vain. . . .

> So I began: "For every one of you,
> Love and intelligence became alike,
> As soon as the prime equality appeared:
> Because that very Sun which lights and warms you
> With heat and fire, has such equipoise
> That all similitudes are meaningless.". . . .

The ancestor steps forth and speaks, addressing him:

> "O leaf of my own branch, and my delight
> Ere thou didst come—I was thy parent root!". . .

Finally, the gaze of the poet tries to penetrate the blinding light of the godhead. In a circle he discerns a face, which he associates, classically enough, with the problem of squaring the circle (Canto 33):

> That very circle which appeared in Thee,
> Conceived as but reflection of a light,
> When I had gazed on it awhile, now seemed
> To bear the image of a human face
> Within itself, of its own coloring—
> Wherefore my sight was wholly fixed on it.
> Like a geometer, who will attempt
> With all his power and mind to square the circle,
> Yet cannot find the principle he needs,
> Just so was I at that phenomenon."

Less familiar to the Western reader is the account of the visions of the afterdeath state in the "Bardo Thödol," or "Tibetan Book of the Dead" (eighth century A.D.). This book contains instructions to guide the deceased through his experiences during the weeks following the leaving of the body. The order of events in this Eastern form is just the opposite of Dante's. The journey begins with the visions of heavenly Peaceful Deities, corresponding to the *Paradiso,* and as the deceased fails to grasp the meaning of his experiences step by step, he progresses further and further into encounters with hellish Wrathful Deities who threaten him with torment and destruction, analogous to the Inferno.

On each of the successive days immediately after death, the deceased is met by one of the benign deities enthroned in a circle. These deities are the rulers of the center and of the four directions or elements, which on the sixth day appear grouped in a mandala. They are called "Divine Father-Mother," being male deities in sexual embrace with their female consorts:"

Then from the Central Realm, called the Spreading Forth of the Seed, the Bhagavan Vairochana, white in color, and seated upon a lion throne, bearing an eight-spoked wheel in his hand, and embraced by the Mother of the Space of Heaven, will manifest himself to thee.

This central Buddha is described in the commentary as the "highest path to enlightenment" and as "a Central Sun, surrounded by the four ... Buddhas of the four cardinal directions, who dawn on the four succeeding days," representing the "One Truth surrounded by its four constituents or elements," and the source and creator of all phenomena.[78]

The four others grouped around the central Buddha represent the four cardinal directions, colors, elements, wisdoms, and psychological functions, and may evoke four cardinal sins:[79]

> The east:
> > white
> > water
> > mirrorlike wisdom
> > principle of consciousness
> > anger
>
> The south·
> > yellow
> > earth
> > wisdom of equality
> > touch
> > egotism
>
> The west:
> > red
> > fire
> > all-discriminating wisdom
> > feelings
> > attachment
>
> The north:
> > green
> > air
> > all-performing wisdom
> > volition
> > jealousy

Thereafter these same five figures appear as groupings of pure lights in the corresponding mandala patterns and colors, "glorious orbs of light ... emitting rays," being surrounded by smaller similar orbs in series of diminishing size.[80]

The sun imagery still predominates:[81]

From the hearts of the Divine Fathers and Mothers of the Five Orders, the rays of light of the Four Wisdoms united, extremely clear and fine, like the rays of the sun spun into threads, will come and shine upon thee and strike against thy heart.

The goal urged upon the deceased by his instructor is to recognize these apparitions as simply springing from his own mind:[82]

"It is quite enough for thee to know that these apparitions are thine own thought-forms."

and:[83]

These realms are not come from somewhere outside (thyself). They come from within the four divisions of thy heart, which, including its center, make the five directions. They issue from within there, and shine upon thee. The deities, too, are not come from somewhere else: they exist from eternity within the faculties of thine own intellect. Know them to be of that nature.

The deceased is thus enabled at any time to liberate himself from this bewildering succession of overwhelming or terrifying hallucinations by simply acknowledging their psychological origin and allowing himself to be received into the heart and love of the deity:[84]

Thou wilt merge into the heart of the Divine Father-Mother.... By thus praying, one recognizeth one's own inner light; and, merging one's self therein, in at-one-ment, Buddhahood (enlightenment) is attained: through humble faith, the ordinary devotee cometh to know himself, and obtaineth Liberation.

The ego thereby surrenders its blind misapprehensions of the nature of things and, through enlightenment, achieves a right relation to the self. As Evans-Wentz explains, "The after-death state is very much like a dream-state, and its dreams are the children of the mentality of the dreamer.... The *Bardo Thodol* seems to be based upon verifiable data of human physiological and psychological experiences ... that there are no visions of gods or of demons, of heavens or of hells, other than those born of the hallucinatory *karmic* thought-forms constituting his personality, which is an impermanent product arising from the thirst for existence and from the will to live and to believe" (see § 13).[85]

The psychology of the paranoid attitude to these unconscious contents, resulting in delusion and hallucination through their projection, is thus by no means new, and the advice given to individuals in the East is not unlike that offered the modern patient.

If the deceased persists in taking the attitude that perceives the apparitions concretely and with fear, then the characteristic paranoid terrors obtrude themselves in the form of mandalas filled with hideous "Wrathful Deities" who threaten to dismember and devour. These are understood to represent the same deities as the peaceful ones, but in their opposite, destructive aspect, emanating from the four quarters of the head, not the heart.[86] Their aim is forcibly to destroy the ego to bring about enlightenment, and liberation is still possible by the same formula of recognition.[87] "Power, which thus dissolves the world, is ever terrible to those who are attached to the world" (see §§ 13, 28).[88]

Rebirth through the womb into the world of phenomena is the consequence if the deceased fails in the foregoing trials.[89]

According to Evans-Wentz, there is a striking similarity between the various accounts of the last judgment and of purgatory in cultures as distant and disparate as ancient Egypt, Tibet, and medieval Ireland, and he finds them to derive from initiatory rites in caves.[90] Ancient Greece was no exception, and the last book of Plato's *Republic* contains the legend of the journey of Er to the land of the dead and back again.

Er lay slain in battle, but on the twelfth day he returned to life from the funeral pyre and told what he had seen. He had gone with others to a mysterious place where judges were seated. The just ascended on the right through two chasms in the heaven above; the unjust descended on the left through two chasms in the earth. Er was informed of the frightening behavior of this cave which retained the sinners for a thousand years at a time:[91]

They were just at the mouth, being, as they fancied, about to return into the upper world, but the opening, instead of receiving them, gave a roar, as was the case when any incurable or unpunished sinner tried to ascend; and then wild men of fiery aspect, who knew the meaning of the sound, came up and seized them . . . and threw them down and flayed them with scourges . . . carding them on thorns like wool.

On the twelfth day they came to the cosmic axis and the fiery planetary circles:[92]

They came to a place where they looked down from above upon a line of light, like a column extending right through the whole heaven and earth, in color not unlike the rainbow, only brighter and purer . . . In the midst of the light, they saw reaching from heaven the extremities of the chains of it· for this light is the belt of heaven, and holds together the circle of the universe, like the undergirders of a trireme. And from the extremities of the chains is extended the spindle of Necessity, on which all the revolutions turn.

It then described eight concentric revolving whorls like cups.[93]

Their edges are turned upwards, and all together form one continuous whorl. This is pierced by the spindle, which is driven home through the center of the eighth.

The spindle turns on the knees of Necessity; and on the upper surface of each circle is a Siren, who goes round with them hymning a single sound and note. The eight together form one harmony; and round about, at equal intervals, there is another band, three in number, each sitting upon her throne: these are the Fates, daughters of Necessity.

Subsequently the dead are given their choice of destiny in their next incarnation when they are born into the world again.[94]

These three examples, and there are many more, serve to illustrate the point that the symbolism of the afterlife, with its cosmic wheels and axis, is the symbolism of the unconscious and of the self, both so common in schizophrenia.

7 THE PSYCHOLOGY OF THE SYMBOLISM

§ 33. The question is still being asked by students of the various symbolisms of the world: Is the universality of the basic themes the result of *"cultural diffusion"* or of *"innate propensities,"* or of *"reinforcement"* of the first by the second? At the turn of the century, in the first flush of zeal to explore the whole world of comparative mythology and to account for the similarities found, each of the investigators posed the question. Goblet D'Alviella opens his account of the history of the cross and solar wheel: "It is not uncommon ... to discover the same symbolic figures amongst races the furthest apart. ... There are only two possible solutions: either these analogous images have been conceived independently, in virtue of a law of the human mind, or else they have passed from one country to another by a process of borrowing."[1] Likewise Simpson writes: "We are in the present day discovering symbols which have existed in most parts of the old world, and to which the word 'universal' has been applied; ... the wheel is one of these. ... One of the profound questions among archeologists is whether these symbols, rites, and customs had one origin in one original home, from which men radiated over the earth, carrying the first idea of these things with them, or if they sprang up in the different localities, and their similarity resulted from the mind of man being much the same in its various stages of progress. This uniformity, combined with the uniformity

[1] For notes to chapter 7, see p 171.

in the operations of nature, might have led to the separate evolutions of conceptions which bear a strong resemblance to each other."[2] In speaking of sun worship, Bloomfield says: "It is true, and it is an important truth, that the human race, endowed as it is essentially alike, is liable anywhere and at any time to incorporate in its beliefs the most imposing and deifiable visible object in all nature, the sun, the source of light and heat, seasons and vegetation. This is simple ethnological fact."[3] Frazer likewise leans to this view: "The modern student of comparative religion traces such resemblances to the similar and independent workings of the mind of man in his sincere, if crude, attempts to fathom the secret of the universe, and to adjust his little life to its awful mysteries."[4]

Cultural anthropologists and mythologists see these uniformities of the human mind and its images only as they are reflected in the outward and visible signs and inferred from circumstantial evidence. The psychologist and psychiatrist find themselves in the more favorable circumstance of being able to put these characteristics under direct scrutiny in the material with which they work from day to day. Even in the field of psychology and psychiatry there prevails a strong bias against accepting the principle of universality of unconscious expression.

§ 34. Since Jung's concepts of the archetypes and the individuation process are either so frequently misunderstood or not even clearly familiar, it is fitting, to account adequately for the present material, to summarize more extensively the psychological formulations of the factors involved.

Archetypes, like instincts, appear to be "systems of preparedness" that are common to the species, unlearned and autonomous, being likewise universal propensities toward reacting to typical life situations in ways that are specifically human. Jung says of them that they are "systems of preparedness that are at the same time images and emotions."[5] That is, instinct has one component in behavior, a pattern of response in physical activity, and another simultaneous component in imagery, a pattern of response in terms of psychical apprehension.[6] When the propensity is activated and both components come into play, they display considerable emotional tone, which is equivalent to saying that they are highly dynamic and that considerable psychic energy or libido is being channeled by them.[7]

It should be borne in mind that this theory does not by any means imply that such archetypal images are the sole concern of analytical psychology. On the contrary, the first and usually preponderant attention in therapy is given to analyzing the "complexes," those contents derived from personal experience, particularly of infancy and childhood. These are defined as emotionally toned groupings of psychic contents about a nucleus, part of which is endogenous, part formed by the experience of an object[8] (a mother complex is formed around the mother archetype and also around the experience with the personal mother on whom it is projected). When these are dissociated from the ego they are called "autonomous complexes," which can be pathogenic. They are not being further discussed in this study, because the self as an archetype is a content of the "collective unconscious" as distinct from the "personal unconscious," which is made up of complexes. In actual practice, the archetype tends usually to appear in projection and thus clothed in the contents of a complex.

The collective unconscious "consists of the sum of the instincts and their correlates, the archetypes,"[9] that is, the sum of the deposits or imprints of the experience of the ancestors, which have conditioned man to respond to his world in typical human ways. "The unconscious regarded as the historical background of the psyche, contains in a concentrated form the entire succession of engrams (imprints), which from time immemorial have determined the psychic structure as it now exists. These engrams may be regarded as function-traces which typify, on the average, the most frequently and intensely used functions of the human soul. These function-engrams present themselves in the form of mythological themes and images, appearing often in identical form and always with striking similarity among all races; they can also be easily verified in the unconscious material of modern man."[10] In speaking of their cultural expressions, Jung says: "The religious character of these [collective] ideas proceeds from the fact that they express the realities of the collective unconscious; hence they have the power of releasing the latent energies of the unconscious. The great problems of life are always related to the primordial images of the collective unconscious."[11]

The material of delusion or fantasy is thus understood to possess a certain quality of substantial actuality instead of mere symptomatic fictionality. The diligent elaboration of fantasy used in this method of therapy, and often appearing quite spontaneously in psychosis, is more like a recording process than a whimsical confabulating one. The effort "does not 'spin fantasy' out into empty space without plan and without support, which is to say that it does not play with its object. Rather, it tries to grasp the inner truth of images faithfully copied from nature. This activity is the conscientious, exact, and careful notation and expansion of the content accruing to consciousness from the unconscious."[12] "Even fantasy, the freest activity of the mind, can never roam the infinite ... but remains bound to the preformed possibilities, the primordial images or archetypes." For "the psyche is ... a precipitate of adaptation efforts and experience of the phylogenetic succession ... an ancient instrument, prepared for quite definite ends.... These adjustments are not merely accidental or arbitrary happenings, but adhere to strictly preformed conditions, which are not transmitted, as are perception-contents, through experience, but are *a priori* conditions of apprehension. They are ... form-determinants ... assigning a definite formation to the stuff of experience; so that we may regard them as images ... or inherited function-possibilities, which, moreover, exclude other possibilities, or, at all events, restrict them to a great extent."[13]

Creativity, as well as the work of fantasy, takes its place among the purposeful activities of the human soul. This deposit of all human experience is "not a dead imprint...but a living system of reactions and aptitudes determining the individual life in invisible ways.... From the living fount of the instincts flows all that is creative; hence the unconscious is not merely a historical conditioning, but also the very source of the creative impulse."[14]

At the beginning of his work of investigation in this field, Jung established the fundamental point of view necessary to its proper comprehension. He uses the example of *Faust* as a creative work, and that of the Schreber case as a delusional system. Of *Faust,* Jung asks: "What does the poet mean by his symbolic creation? Proceeding purely reductively, one discovers the final meaning in these universal human things, and demands nothing further from an explanation than that the unknown and complicated shall be reduced to the known and simple. I should like to designate this kind of understanding as retrospective understanding. But there is another kind of understanding, which is not analytic reduction, but is of a synthetic or constructive nature. I would designate this prospective understanding, and the corresponding method as the constructive method." The mind is a point of passage, on the one hand determined by its past but on the other determining its own future; therefore the mind offers a picture of the precipitate of the past and also a picture of the germinating knowledge of all that is to come. Of such delusions as those of Schreber, Jung thus says: "We must, from the 'objective-scientific' standpoint, reduce the structural fantasy of the patient to its simple and most generally valid elements.... But that is only half of the work to be done. The other half is the constructive understanding of Schreber's system [the subjective-symbolic standpoint]. The question is: What end, what freedom, did the patient hope to achieve by the creation of his system?"[15]

This recognition of the subjective validity of the products of fantasy led Jung to one of his most profound discoveries: that the study of a sequence reveals a process moving toward a goal, revealing a propensity toward psychic development and self-completion, and expressed in a complex array of images and functions which come into play in a more or less orderly pattern. Jung called this the "individuation process."[16]

This process is a spontaneous urge toward the fulfillment of the specific basic pattern of the individual, that is, toward totality and wholeness and differentiation of a person's innate potentialities, a quest directed not by the ego but by the instinctual, archetypal trend in the unconscious—the nonego. The individuation process is the psyche's most impressive creative activity. The unconscious shows itself to be a vast matrix out of which the various qualities of the personality emerge one by one, until late in life a certain degree of completeness of scope of the personality is reached in all its own uniqueness. These qualities appear first as unknowns in symbolic form, being potentialities little understood or trusted by the ego. The collective unconscious is this matrix, the sum of the archetypes, the propensities that canalize the libido into specific forms of expression by way of the symbolic image. In it the pattern of wholeness lies inherent, however much unrealized, not as a static image or ideal, but as an affect-laden, dynamic trend "leading towards the achievement of wholeness as towards a goal."[17]

The individuation process is seen in dreams or fantasy in sequences of archetypal symbols and their progressive development and interplay; being archetypal, these symbols are of mythological aura. Jung says of these images that they "portray the centralizing process, or the production [that is, the making conscious] of a new center of the personality. . . . I call this center . . . the 'self,' a term that is meant to include the totality of the psyche insofar as this manifests itself in the individual. The self is not only the center, but also the circumference that encloses consciousness and the unconscious; it is the center of this totality, as the ego is the center of consciousness."[18] It is a component of the psyche which, however much it may find its way into some esoteric collective cultural expression from the unconscious, makes it appearance in individuals only at unusual times when constellated by a situation of conflict, stress, puzzlement, or profound stirring, particularly in such turmoils as religious experiences or psychotic episodes.[19] The image is most clarified and significant to the personality when it appears during an inner search, as in an analysis,[20] or a quest for meaning going in depth beyond the limits of the known, as in the experience of the alchemists.[21] In other words, the image is experienced only at those times when the unconscious is activated in its deepest reaches. Thus the image is a phenomenon that, though of paramount importance and universality, cannot be studied in "normal" conditions, and is even not known to those researchers who do not probe into the content of deep psychic turmoil.

The image of the self is so little known to Western man that he has to approach an understanding of it with all possible readiness to admit his limitations of knowledge. Jung says: "What then we can ascertain about the mandala symbolism today is this: that it represents an autonomous psychic fact known through manifestations that are constantly being repeated, are everywhere to be met with, and are always identical. It seems to be a kind of nuclear atom about whose inner structure and final meaning we know nothing. We may also regard it as the real, that is, the effective, mirror image of an attitude of consciousness, an attitude that can state neither its aim nor its purpose, and whose activity, because of this renouncement, is completely projected upon the virtual center of the mandala. This cannot happen except under compulsion, and the compulsion always attaches to a life situation in which the individual does not know how to help himself in any other way."[22] That is, it appears in those life situations in

which the ego does not feel itself able to solve the problem or to comprehend the implications of its deepest divisions between the opposites, and
only a superior and more all-embracing viewpoint can hold the lead. "As far
as my experience informs me," says Jung, "it is a question of significant
'nuclear processes' in the objective psyche, a kind of picturing of the goal
that the 'purposeful' psychic process apparently sets itself without being led
to it by suggestion from without.... The goal that promises to bring 'healing' and completion, is beyond all measure strange to consciousness and
can find entrance into it only with the greatest difficulty."[23] This goal is the
establishment of a center around which the many contradictory contents of
the psyche can structure themselves in a pattern that is uniquely oneself
and that is then "the law of one's own being."[24] It is found "playing the part
of a concealed pole around which everything turns in the last analysis. Every
life is, at bottom, the realization of a whole, that is, of a self, so that the
realization can also be called individuation. For all life is bound to individuals who carry and realize it, and apart from them is unimaginable. But
every carrier has an individual specification and determination, and the
meaning of living existence consists in its realizing itself in these terms."[25]
This is an entelechy, the striving of the organism toward self-realization.[26]

The problem the psyche assumes in the pursuit of this objective is the
differentiation of itself from what is not itself, that is, from what are the
general properties of human nature and human culture, in other words,
from the inner and outer collectivities.[27] For although the unconscious is
part of oneself, it is also the whole accumulation of all that has developed in
it before and that is common property to all, so that it is of indistinct nature
and its limits are hard to trace. Thus Jung feels the self to be a circumscribed
area of the collective unconscious whose parts are selected by an agency that
is little known; individuation acts as a magic circle (see § 4) selecting and
rejecting what does and does not belong to the individual personality and
protecting the center from the boundless inner and outer collectivities. This
governing influence is needed whenever the forces of the collective unconscious are called up. A breaking in through the circle would be the obsessive
influence of elements of the collective that are not properly one's own contents,[28] whereas a breaking out would be the loss of self-identity by the
obsessive enslavement to the object through the passions accompanying
projection.[29]

That this center is nonego is emphasized by the qualities ascribed to it in
all its symbolism as something cosmic and divine and imperishable. Rather,
this central archetype is a factor felt to be of highest value and of numinous
quality, to which the ego is subordinate. Jung's choice of the word "self"
to designate this phenomenon is borrowed not from modern psychology,
where it means something quite different,[30] but from the Hindu concept of
the personal and superpersonal Atman.[31] Closer to the actual experience of

human beings is the expression in the intuitive terms of such a tradition, rather than making up a new intellectual concept that would stand every chance of leaving out some of the most important connotations because of its onesidedness. To the introverted, nonrationalistic view of the Hindu, the separateness and autonomy of the ego are to be recognized as "non-knowledge" or illusion, and the realization of the oneness of the "self" with all other beings and with the cosmic "self" is to be attained; one is then governed by a higher "knowledge" superordinate to the ego.[32] This view-point need not be taken by the psychologist as mere metaphysical and mystical speculation, thus probably to be dismissed, but rather as the spon-taneous experience of the components of the psyche as they actually happen to exist and to impress themselves upon the observant consciousness; that is, such ideas are determined by, and thus describe, the archetypes, man's means of apprehending his inner and outer worlds.

The relation of ego to self is difficult to understand, not only intellectually, but in the course of a direct experience of these two centers as during an analysis. The self is a paradox; it represents one's own uniqueness and totality, and yet has attributes of universality; it is oneself, and yet not identical with what one finds oneself to be consciously. The self is an archetype, and, as with all these contents of the collective unconscious, one relates to it but does not identify with it except at the price of severe inflation and damage to the integrity of the ego consciousness.[33] One learns, as man has always learned, to accept its organizing and directing influences as inner promptings from an inner source that is not ego consciousness.[34] This source is apperceived as "spirit," as compelling, as an autonomous focus of psychic activity that somehow has greater vision and wisdom than the ego can possibly have, since it represents, after all, an awareness of broader, more inclusive scope than the ego's.[35] Also, its qualities are felt to be superior, since they ·represent those that are the greatest potential of the personality's future—the contents that may, through their assimilation, go into making the more mature and richer personality that the ego conscious-ness may become during its further development and experience. Modern man is often unable to sustain the projection of this higher authority into a heaven above, but feels these powers to be somehow within. This trend of the modern mentality first became evident in the West during the Middle Ages, when such individualistic searchers after truth as Meister Eckehart said: "God must be brought to birth in the soul again and again."[36] Yet being thus within, to see how it cannot then be simply oneself brings difficulties.

Jung cites examples of the catastrophes that can result from the claim of the ego to be all: "The psyche harbors contents and is exposed to influences, the assimilation of which may be attended by serious dangers. The ancient alchemists ascribed their secret to matter itself; and neither Faust nor

Zarathustra is an encouraging example should we be tempted to embody such a secret in the personal ego. Our part, then, surely, is to repudiate the arrogant claim of consciousness to be the whole of the psyche, and to grant the psyche a definite actuality, even if we cannot grasp it with our present means of understanding."[37]

APPENDIX

DETAILED ACCOUNT OF PATIENT'S
HISTORY AND MATERIAL FROM
HOSPITAL RECORDS

The patient was a twenty-seven-year-old, married, white housewife whose hospital stay lasted seven and a half months. She was admitted in the spring with a *chief complaint* that two and a half months before admission she began slowly to be depressed and would have periods of agitation; she began then to accuse her mother and also her husband of poisoning her baby or herself, and she was fearful that something bad was going to happen. She had been admitted to another hospital first, where she was given electric shock treatment, and had responded with several remissions and relapses. She was transferred to the present hospital without essential improvement.

The *family history* was essentially noncontributory. The family was of English stock with a long history in this country, and people of means, mostly owners of businesses. The maternal grandmother, of southern aristocratic background, was a Christian Scientist and a domineering woman who stressed social standing a great deal; living with the patient's family till five years before entry, she had considerable influence upon the patient in her formative years. The mother was somewhat like the grandmother in her tendency to domineer and to determine her life and that of her family by superficial standards of social status; she was very closely attached to the patient. The father, a successful manufacturer, was more kindly and easy-going, showing an understanding and generosity to the patient in whatever difficulties arose. There were no siblings.

The *personal history* described left-handedness which was "corrected" by retraining to right-handedness in her early school years, also stuttering upon excitement. She was shy and seclusive in her pubescent years, and the father went out of his way to help bring her out. Otherwise she had many friends and adjusted well to them. At school she stood in the middle third of her class. After high school she attended a home economics course for a year. She took jobs in stores for two years thereafter, where she got on well; she left one because it aggravated her asthma, another at her mother's insistence because the work and friends were below her status. At the end of this time she married a man she had known for a year. The courtship was turbulent, with frequent upsets, and at the end he tried to back out of it, but she put pressure on him to marry her; he had impotency at first, and has been aware that her affection has been greater than his.

The *medical history* described a "nervous stomach" since earliest years and a tendency to asthma; these brought her to many physicians. She had an appendectomy at nineteen.

In *personality* she was an easy-going, out-going sort of person, getting along well with people and having many friends. She tended to have spells when she worried about herself and her nervous stomach. She was inclined to be immaculately neat about her person, though not her room.

The *present illness* began almost a year after the birth of her baby fourteen months before admission. Ensuing upon the delivery came an aspiration pneumonia which kept her in the hospital an extra three weeks, and following which she was unable to nurse the baby. The baby was thought to be a wanted one so far as the informants knew, but she seemed to show very little emotion toward it; it was later learned that the baby was an "accident" and that she and her husband were not quite prepared economically at that time to have a baby. The patient was a "model mother," conscientious and dutiful, but evidently raised the baby according to the book, with little feeling on her part. In the fall she became upset over a new budget that her husband set up, on account of their living beyond their means, she never having had to watch money this way before. A little later she began to be interested in Christian Science, to which cult both her mother and grandmother belonged, and spent a great deal of time reading their literature. In the early winter she came down with a laryngitis and had a faith healer come over to see her. However, her throat did not become any better and she became depressed that Christian Science was not helping her, and she finally had to call a doctor. By this time she was depressed, agitated, cried a lot, and had insomnia. She had been rabid about Christian Science and thought she had failed it when she called the physician. She then became convinced that her mother was trying to poison her. She said she could taste the poison in her food, and hear her parents putting it in her food before she ate it. She then accused the husband of doing the same thing. She then stated that she could smell strange things in the air which she said was poison. Finally she said that the family were trying to poison the baby and that she had poisoned the baby and that it was now dead. She was nervous and constantly worried about something. She began to accuse herself of other things, chiefly that she had sexual relations with another man before she married (this was not true). She had occasional clear days. Her antagonism was expressed toward her mother, father, husband, and herself, no others, and principally it was against her mother, least against her father. These periods of aggression alternated with periods of anxiety, in which she was afraid of something, but she could not name what it was. She was finally taken to a hospital and was given electric shock treatments. She responded to these quite well and was discharged after a series of four or five; however, in a few days she would again relapse and be readmitted. This was repeated several times, up to a total of 25 shocks prior to admission to the present hospital. Her psychiatrists had not troubled to listen to her fears or beliefs to establish rapport.

Physical examination on admission was essentially negative.

Her *mental status* was typical of that of a full-blown catatonic schizophrenia. She did a great deal of catatonic posturing and was negativistic and mute from time to time. Her appearance was somewhat disheveled, and she was apprehensive, confused, and preoccupied. She would go around the ward smelling the air for good or bad smells, her means of determining whether people were friendly or hostile toward her. She showed considerable anxiety, believing people to be after her because she had poisoned her baby and numerous other people; she also stated that she could hear gun shots in the distance and that they would blame her for killing people. She lay in bed erotically stimulating herself. There was considerable preoccupation with sexual matters; she stated she could poison the world with her "bad sexual thoughts," and worried over her sexual feelings toward former attendants, over her husband's sexual activities while she was in the hospital, over her marital life, and over the accusations on the part of the other patients that the doctor was in love with her. The complex delusions will be presented in full below. There were also auditory hallucinations. She was aware of being ill, and intended to stay until cured, assured that the doctor would cure her because of his love for her.

Treatment consisted of ambulatory insulin, given three times a day. On this regime she made considerable progress during the first two weeks and showed good contact with reality, becoming more communicative and cooperative and careful of her appearance.

THE DELUSIONS

2nd week: Condition: dazed, confused, withdrawn, thought fragmental.

She is convinced that she and her baby are being poisoned. Also people are watching her and saying bad things about her, and she cannot make out why, since she has not been bad. A patient whom she has known before must have been sent here to spy on her, and there is a sense that things are going on subrosa in which she is implicated but which she cannot understand. One of these is that she saw another person by the same name as herself in a passageway, whom she refers to as "the other Mrs. . . . ." (there being no such person). She is very upset over terrible thoughts about her father, since observing an exchange of glances between him and a male attendant at a former hospital, knowing him not to be "that kind of man" and yet full of thoughts about his supposed homosexuality.

3rd week· Condition: improving, more cheerful, lucid, coherent, but still bewildered by delusions.

Her head has been pounding, due to the ideas getting clogged up in her head that she has held back so long. She hears girls' voices during the night whispering, talking about her, and framing her up for a murder, because they do not like her.

She can control everything that happens around her, and is even able to make the sun and the moon go in and out or make the rain start or stop. She is being held responsible for everything that happens and is causing all the deaths in the world. So they feel she must be punished. Always she feels she does not know whether she is doing the right or the wrong thing, and is aware of the contradictions in her, the yes and the no, and her gay and quiet side.

It is strange here because everyone around her is living in the afterlife; she has already died and is resurrected. She feels there is no death; you cannot kill anyone; she has seen so many people who look alike. She was the one who caused all the deaths in the world; things are being put off, and she has one more day to live. People who are killed come back as something else. Death is a planting. Even if people are planted in a graveyard they come back again as resembling the same person; this is real. They killed her by poisoning but she is not dead. They do it by black pills. The smells are the reincarnation. Our bodies may die, but the thing that keeps us going never dies—it's the soul.

All the world is around her here in the hospital, watching her and waiting. She is holding things up by not making up her mind, and must choose. She was to have had a cruise with her father, and husband, across the Pacific, but she blocked that, too. He was in Dutch, like herself.

She has been thinking she was Churchill's daughter, and that she was neither male nor female but a hermaphrodite. This she does not like but feels it is impossible; only the older women look at her as if she were homosexual. There are an awful lot of dark halves of her here. Her mother-in-law is running the kitchen in the disturbed ward.

At the gate she has thought there was a whole line of traffic held up around the place because she could not make up her mind about the question. Her father was running for the presidency of a company in town, and for all these things; then anything she would say would disrupt his campaign (later she refers to it as running for President of the country). The whole world has come to see her and she has not wanted them to know who she was. Everything bad in the news has been caused by her. All the traffic has been tied up around the hospital in a circle while a huge vote was going on; they were all on her side due to a great murder, then they all turned against her and she hoped she would die. They could not kill her and she has kept coming back. She had such a terrible life and this is her punishment. She hoped no one could find her here, and if anyone should come in, she would hear pistols. Then she heard roosters. She hears shots, and knows thus that she is not doing it, but has friends. At night someone yelled, "How can you do all those terrible things?"; there were eight murders committed that night, it was awful.

Her father and Churchill have flown over in an airplane. In this election the whole world is divided into two sides, and she is in the middle, on the fence, there is father's side and mother's side, and the sun and moon seem connected somehow. She is at the center and the whole world is around her waiting for her to vote, to choose. She believes the radio broadcasts to be from the inside of the hospital, about her life, and the TV to be showing her. The only way her father can win the election is by a poem.

Because she was getting shots in her hip, a woman was saying of her that she was having an illegitimate baby. She fantasied that she was in bed and that people were going to send a colored man in to sleep with her. The other Mrs.—— (the patient's other, dark half) was making a sucker out of her by passing her baby to her.

She has loads of complicated ideas she was not able to tell anybody; she has been afraid to talk about the frightful ideas because they were not attractive. She cannot get them clear now; they were real pictures. She has had millions of ideas and is at the center of them. She tried to solve the problems, which she could do because she was an only child, horribly spoiled and self-centered. She is relieved and grateful to be able to talk about her ideas.

Drawing I· (21st day): Condition: improved, but withdrawn and moody; she now disbelieves many of her delusions.

"There were two sides once, Father's side and Mother's side; the sun and moon seem connected somehow. I felt I had control over the weather. I could control it in my indefinite mind. I felt responsible for the rain and sun. I guess I love me. I am in the center and people are all around me. I am in a circle; it's a yellow, a sunny color. Snoopy people are in black—they are very unattractive. I'll put me in.

"This is not going to be an actual picture. My ideas will be in diagram. I am two personalities, one dark and one lighter color. (She starts with the red and the black patches at the center, her gay and her quiet side.) People who stick up for me will be in nice colors. I'll put Father and Mother in bright colors; then there's my husband, like Father; these are the most important ones to me because they stick up for me. (Father and husband are green on the left, making two thirds of the circle, the mother in orange at the right.)

(The next circles depict her progress from ward to ward, and as she draws she rehearses the delusions she had at each, thus reviewing the whole psychotic episode.)

"I came in in a bright and sunny mood into the hospital, when I arrived. I'll use a brighter color (first ring in·yellow, the good ward). When I first got upset . . . then I was moved and I felt framed, because rules were broken . . . the newspapers upset me . . . people were talking about me . . . Now the colors are getting darker as I feel badly; the picture is getting gloomier (next ring in purple, representing OT and an intermediate ward). Then I went to OT and was nervous because I felt I was being blamed . . . felt that someone was murdered . . . I felt framed and had guilt. Then I went to —— (the disturbed ward) people did glare at me over there . . . I felt they were sarcastic . . . I'll put them in brown . . . Then I decided not to talk, and then I decided I had to give way and I wept a great deal and that helped. I'll have to start a new circle, the wild ideas at —— (the disturbed ward). Now we have mixed-up ideas around here in ——(the good ward). Colors do not mean mood now; now the colors mean the yes-no, I can't make up my mind. All the fancy ideas really arrived now . . . (recites further delusions, recorded above). (The ring of six petals in different colors are the mixed-up ideas). My mother's on one side of the fence and my father on the other side (herself on the fence in the middle); these thoughts were vague. Mother will have a gloomy color; I was against her then. I realize now that some of the things were not true about her . . . (The world is divided into the "mother's world" and the "father's world" in the next circle, in blue and red respectively.)

"Then we get to the part where I tied up all the traffic around the hospital. I'll make a green (grass) square around the whole thing and block the whole thing in. The traffic is in dots (of every color in the box). At first there were a few; I was a devil and I did something, what I don't know . . . There were bands of policemen here, in black (the 16 dots in the circle of the intermediate ward). My father was trying to get me out of here; he had arranged this group of people, who I thought were listening to everything I said. I thought my father was flying over —— (the ward). (She places four black figures in the petals of the mixed-up ideas, representing the four detectives the father placed here.) The traffic circle is multicolored, there are so many different people in the world. A few come, then I tie up the whole world because I am ruling them. Everyone lives in Utopia . . ."

(She places gates for entrance and exit at the upper corners, but does not think there are any at the other corners. At the left comes the traffic, which circles around, but also divides up as cars go in to different houses, and yet again also is trying to get up to her at the center. This is a great puzzle to her for she does not see how she can have it both ways. She feels she ought to make it come up through the lower part of the circle vertically to her, but the work is interrupted here.)

4th week: Condition· very cheerful, lucid, coherent, habits neat.

She continues to hear voices, especially whisperings at night, and also fears the strange odors she senses exuding from her body. Her former ideas retain their interest for her, but there is less pressure to talk of them.

She says of her changing from day to day, "I flit from flower to flower." She rehearses the fears of poisoning, and emphasizes that it first occurred when she told her father that her mother was poisoning the milk. She feels herself to be much like her mother and closely attached to her, but finds her dominating and snobbish.

Ideas about hermaphroditism and the illegitimate child predominate. She relates a former dream or delusion, that she was an illegitimate child, the mother and father had a big disagreement, he accusing her of flitting around, she accusing him of inability to produce a child because of his hermaphroditism. People joined sides over this. She feels the parents to be not congenial, though devoted. The mother would not go along with the father on his cruises, which a wife ought to do. She felt guilty because she could have freed her father by this poem, to go on the cruise. She was sent lately over to the men's gym, for exercise, instead of the women's, and that made her a man. She felt her ward was just for hermaphrodites.

She says, "I might as well be frank and come out with it· I enjoy talking to other men. I don't know whether it's right. I have this 17 or 18 year old attitude. If I were to have a date, I don't know whether I'd feel right or not. I feel guilty for having the idea . . . Maybe I'm too straightlaced. There are two sides of me, one is and one is not.

"That's what I want to get straightened out. I was getting the illegitimate baby through needles. They were trying to make me into a man over in —— (the disturbed ward). I was turning into a man day by day and the next minute I was having an illegitimate child. Which would the child resemble? In —— I was having children, one from the doctor in the other place. I felt he would always stick up for me; he said I would want to see him again in nine months' time."

(She has more to say about the theme of death and rebirth, and draws a diagram of her ideas in the form of contiguous vertical bars of color starting with black as the grave and getting longer and lighter as the new life increases, then back again cyclically) ...

"My afterlife is not thoroughly pleasant; first it was gay and also dark ... The very gay is yellow, but generally I work at getting more gloomy ... I think that one must get gradually very gloomy; now I am more cheerful again ... Now I cannot go black because black is the graveyard, and I am alive; but my body is dead in the graveyard. They thought I was dead in —— (ward) and I came alive. They were celebrating my funeral services, I was missing (she puts a white space between the cheerful yellow and the black). But they have not really killed me—I'm coming back again. You can tell because I'm going to come back in brighter colors, but not so bright this time ... My motto is, they can't kill me or anyone because we come back again. The actions in the afterlife may be different but you may not realize that you are repeating the life you led before. There are no real changes. Oh, you may come back in a different social setting, but the basic thing is always the same."

She sees now that she could not have tied up the whole world around the ward, it is not big enough.

She begins now also to express feelings of love for the therapist, which later on she reveals more fully in retrospect as a feeling that there is something spiritual about him, as if he "might be a saint or something."

She has the following dream (23rd day) "The two friends I've grown up with are in the dining room at —— (the second ward), and we're sitting around a table together. There's a question about where we should sit, and we eat different things. My grandmother on my mother's side was in the dream, and my mother's brother, who is actually dead, appears on the scene. Evidently the doctors have told him that he is going to die the next day of cancer of the throat. Incidentally my uncle actually died of heart disease."

Drawing II (24th day): Condition as last noted.

1) "I'm the center of attraction again, as in most of my drawings. This may be the same thing all over again as the last time. One friend (B) lived close to me; I'm (A) effervescent, but she's two-faced, the smooth-operator kind. The other (C) was a few blocks away, the tactless type, and she was a third party who always wanted B to herself. So there were three people and always one was in between. C is not on my side. (Tries a few colors, then sudden impulse.) Oh, I've got another idea, really have it now.

2) "Blue is the friend I'm not so fond of. The cheerful colors are red and yellow. The yellow is sunny, and the sun is important; yellow's the cheerful one, for me. Then my two friends are here in the story. I'm at the center of attraction in it, of course, as I always am (laughs). We're three friends, with me in green. This to show we've always grown together. (Impulsively) Oh, I'll put a circle around because we've always grown in the world together, that shows our life. I can see probably doodles have a good deal of meaning. Blue is the outsider (C)

here, and wants to have my friend (B) (orange) closer to her, so I'll show that before we get out of the world completely. But I'm not satisfied, I want the one on the right (B) shown coming over to the left to the blue friend (C)."

3 and 4) (Experiments with herself as blue-green but decides she does not like it at all. She then feels that she should be orange, and the green and blue her friends).

5) "Now I'm getting pepped up, I'm on the right track now O.K.... This is actually a life drawing now, with my friends. We'll have me as orange, definitely. And the friend on the left wants to bring my friend over to her side. The colors are right now, the way I want them. (She brings the friend over to the left, but it doesn't seem quite right yet) Now the circle.

6) "The red doesn't belong in this, I don't like it. I like the original one best after all; I'd done better with the first originally. I must show my dark and light sides. This is good now, this I'm really enjoying. These are my two sides, the yellow now with the green. And my friend (B) is orange, and she has two sides, too, purple and brown; we'll give her brown. The other friend is purple. Then we're enclosed in the world and it's done. We'll make a new world. This is fine, but there's something missing. We've all got two sides; the purple should be brown so I'll doctor it up. Even the blue must have a light side, even if I don't like her, but I'll just leave her. (with some violet). Now some people think of the world as square, and some as round. And the sun and moon, how about them? I'll make it square then; I may ruin it all. I'll put the square in a different color. Then the question is, what is it, the world? No, it's the future life! I'll put blue here (upper right); then one to rhyme with it (lower left). There's a darker side and a lighter side to the afterlife. It's a grey world (the circle) because it's a dark day. Then yellow, to balance, orange; so there's a light-light and dark-dark. Then the sun and moon, yes, the darker and the lighter side. I should try one with red tomorrow. The sun goes here on the left in orange (the triangle) and the moon goes at the bottom (the crescent) in yellow; one up and the other down."

Drawing III: (26th day): Condition as before, but greater apprehensiveness.

"The cancer might be connected with the uterus, that baby, you know. I want to show the cancer coming in. The square is the ward. The baby is large because it's a major thought. I'm making it dark because it's illegitimate. This is the cancer (black circle) at the center; that's a horrible thought! I'm not interested in dark colors—this dark blue, it's unpleasant to me. Then it would all be a black background; it's all very unpleasant, all gloom. There's nothing coming out. It would all be dark and you couldn't see anything.

"My uncle's a sad man and sensitive, not meant for the outside world; he's seclusive."

Drawing IV: (Same interview)

"This just comes to me as a black spot only, black with white thoughts that move. It's very hard to show, but it's *really* amazing; it's very interesting to me anyway, really very exciting. This is fascinating to me. It's like a river flowing It's not a solid black, but a myriad pattern; it's terminating rivers, like terminating insulin. (She becomes increasingly engrossed in the contemplation of this and somewhat dazed.) Then it would just go on like this through a whole square field (leaves it unfinished)."

Drawing V: Condition· She spends an incredibly long time discussing stomach symptoms and special diet. She states she has no more tendency to hear voices, and she does not think of it any more. Nor is she any longer concerned with her anxieties; she just feels tense.

"Today my mind cannot get going. Recently I am going into disagreeable colors, many blacks and all. When I'm in this low mood, I want to wear nothing but fiery, red colors; it's just the opposite to make myself cheerful.

"I was trying to tell someone my feelings of life and death . . . I just feel there is death of body—but not of mind and body. People may try to kill you but they cannot . . . I wish someone would explain religion. I think Christ could be any one of us, he is like the power within us. I think angels and visions can come to any one of us . . .

"A couple of weeks ago I thought I controlled the sun and the moon and the rain. I thought I had a divided nature, my 'yes and no' nature. Then there was my pregnant idea. I thought that everyone I saw in —— Ward was pregnant; then I began to feel pregnant, and that started me to worry. I thought the X-ray was testing me, and they were putting me in the pregnant ward. This was a 'new life' beginning in me."

(Here the therapist ventured the suggestion that the pregnancy was a symbolic idea, of something happening in the mind, and that Christ is also this, not that we all become Christs, i.e., identifying, but that we all have the Christ symbol in us. This she jumps at immediately as the idea she was meaning to express.)

"In church yesterday I thought of Christ being a symbol; he could be any one of us. That's why I think bodies are not real, only the mind, since Christ is in every one of us. I think that Christ was in the tomb and has risen—that happens to all of us. We can all be Christs.

"A long time ago I thought I was Godlike. Yet all my life I have been the center of attraction at home—that accounts for my feeling somewhat Godlike. I feel I have not enough outside interests; I have a vivid imagination and must express myself in some way. (Looking over previous drawings, I and II) I'm getting outside my circle, I'm getting other people in the picture."

She begins to draw the chapel pews in brown, "to show what is real and also my thoughts," also the altar which got her thinking.

"I am definitely interested in church and religion; they've been the center of my thoughts for the past few weeks. (She reviews her Christian Science background.) Looking at the altar I began to think about the resurrection. I thought it could be any one of us, it need not be Christ's life . . . I think we could all be killed and planted in a tomb. The reason we celebrate Christ's life is because it is an ideal life; we all try to imitate it.

"I don't think there's a heaven; we come right back again—everything is enclosed in life here . . . we cannot escape, since we come back to face it. Christ rises, but he does not go into heaven; he comes back as 'red,' a cheerful color. (She has put the tomb in purple as a rectangle, then a black area next to it as death; now she makes contiguous red and black triangles above.) Since Christ went through the suffering, he is like one of ourselves; therefore he is one of us. He is both cheerful and bad, since the world is like that.

"No one person can see the whole world, that's why there are so many people here, and that makes me realize how illogical my thoughts were to think that I was the center of the world. (She laughs to scorn this idea.) Christ needs a great many people to see the whole world. To put people in the drawing of it, they would all be of different sizes since some people give more than others." (She later associated red with "warmth, fire, blood, turmoil, feelings like love and hate.")

Drawing VI: (Same interview)

(She begins a second drawing, in red.) "I have to show the world, it is missing in the first. Looking back now I think the automobiles in the driveway (in Drawing I) were trying to show the world (of people); I'm going to show that now. People will have to be good and bad—where to put them I don't know. I wonder if it would explain it if I was to use Christ's life as the model, and Christ should be at the center—it is NOT ME. We should show what Christ is like because he is the example, he is just a symbol in all of us." (She only succeeds in getting herself into the periphery, in orange, and never does get to the other people.)

Drawing VII: (29th day): Condition: apprehensive, anxious, serious, delusional fears returning.

"I had a good cry this morning; I couldn't finish the drawing. I started crying when Mother came yesterday, and now I feel much better today after all the weeping. Today I want explanations rather than more drawings. I feel I can't do any more drawings; I'm trying to solve my own problems...

"I'm feeling guilty again; I feel like I'm being framed again...I feel the insulin is to blame...I get all these ideas which are bad ones. I know they're fantasy, and they're all on the same track; all are of framing me. I would rather do drawings during the interviews, I like to relax. There are such a myriad of ideas. I go through deep stages of depression with the insulin; the ideas are crazy.

"I told my mother that I wanted to be independent and away from her apronstrings, so I stopped my mother from bothering the doctors. I'm going to take care of my own life. My mother's done everything for me. My mother said... 'I was always trying to make you stand on your own feet.' I try not to be catty about my mother but I had to laugh—she would never let me be independent. She will always do everything for me ... Mother does a lot for me materially, but somehow she doesn't do the right thing. I don't care for social background, which my mother stresses. But she is a problem; I cannot break away from her; she'll also be a problem about getting my child away from her ... (She talks of how the mother is clever, impresses people, feels sorry for her neighbors who live in the country, likes old families, private schools.) ... I'm afraid my parents are going to take away some of my husband's independence and ambition and then they'll say. 'Oh, he's no good.' (She tries to do more on previous drawing.)

"I'll start a new drawing (a) to show my relation to my parents. I'm going to be the center of attraction, in red. My mother's in blue, and Daddy in green. (She draws a red circle surmounted by smaller blue and green ones.)

"Now we'll draw another one (b) showing how mother-love developed; I'm red with black; when I have problems to face, who comes to the rescue? MOTHER, of course! It's O.K. when I'm a little girl to get that help, but now

I want to be thoroughly independent and have my husband pay for all the expenses. Daddy always foots the bills.

"Now for high school. I'm going to grow up quickly. How do the drawings (c) look? Practically the same because Mother always took care of me ... Mother and Daddy helped me with homework and got me through school; I was never a good student. I was always helped with everything; I had problems.

"In Home Ec. school things started to grow ... I took Chem. and my family could not help me; so I got out of my problem by myself; now my parents couldn't help me. So I can't show them in my drawing (d), if I do I'll put them in the background. I'm there by myself. Now people are coming in as different friends and they will be in different colors. (It would look messy, so she tears the sheet and turns it over.) ...

"Now the war came along (e) and that should be in black. I guess now I'll show the shop; had a wonderful time there, all the girls were wonderful ... The shop's in a pleasant light violet color. This pleased Mother very much because it was more refined and Mother said I would meet more people of my own class. Then I got married, which is a very happy experience and very gay. The war's over now. Do you notice how the war is the center of attraction? The whole world is interested in it. It's black because of its very serious implications. It disrupted everyone's careers. I don't feel that this drawing is centered around me because I am a very small bit. The family's centered around me even after I'm married. I would have been happily married even without the material help of my family. The red is my marriage.

"Now I have to show how I get back to here. We bought the house but my father paid for it. My mother helped me plan for the interior. I don't know whether my husband is going to develop into a 'loafer.' (She has difficulty shaping a drawing of life after marriage.)

"Mother's in a blue square, and my husband and myself in red on the right, and Daddy in green on the left (g). But I want to separate us from Mother. Now, what I want is this (h), Daddy, in green, comes on this side of Mother, and we're away off here (to the right, separated from the mother by the father; this she executes with a triumphal flourish)."

Sixth week, early: Condition: Depressed, agitated, apprehensive, withdrawn, preoccupied.

They, especially her mother, are poisoning her and her baby, and she cannot see why. Why are they whispering about her? She is "at the center again" and everyone is interested in her and watching her and taking notes on all she says and does. She feels very mixed up, and things are going on which she does not understand at all, and she feels herself to be the cause of what is happening. They are accusing her and framing her and she feels guilty, because she is hurting other people and messing things up.

She feels she has a strange smell under her arms which everyone notices. She's suspicious of the pills (vitamins) they are giving her, and thinks they are changing her into a man. When they took her over to the men's side to get X-rays of her chest, she thinks they wanted to see if her chest showed changes, whether she has become more like a man yet or not. She cannot see the sense of that; she is "not so curvy as some," but she is a woman all right. She asks about hermaphroditism often, especially talking with her mother about it.

She is not sure that she wants to go home again because now she is in love with the therapist. Then she saw his photo in "Town and Country" in an army officer's uniform, but with someone else's name in the caption, so she is not sure whether he is a psychiatrist or not. She is not sure anyone is what they claim they are. She thought the therapist would understand her ideas and fears, but he has not yet explained to her what they meant, so he had better go ahead if he can.

She was told that before this could be done she should work along in the problems which she felt to be still unclear and that they would be explained later, but a minimal interpretation was given to the effect that the symbols in her delusions had to do with inner and not outer realities and that the squared circle was an image of her psyche, which was going through some profound changes.

Drawing VIII: (36th day): Condition: as above.

"At home they said I was nice, but at the dance no one paid any attention to me, and I felt very self-conscious. I guess it is flattery, we all like that ... We could put all the colors in the dance and I walk in as half and half again; I feel self-conscious. (The base is in four colors plus red.) I enter the floor (in two colors, red and green). You could design me as a tree. You see, there are parts of me, one part as quite cheerful and then I will have different-colored leaves ... The leaves are supposed to be dullish colors (green), yet I know that I am a small fish in a big pond. Now I feel that I have been very self-centered; I wonder, I don't know. I'm afraid I've been so all my life."

The crowd at the dance are looking at her and she feels herself at the center of attention, self-conscious and singled out, and rising above them. The leaves are her "flairs for different things," emanating like thoughts from the head.

Seventh week: Condition: Superficially cheerful and buoyant, but actually bitter and depressed.

She wants to let "bygones be bygones and accept the whole thing as a joke, just a huge laugh"; many people are trying to make her into a bad woman and put labels on her. It has to do with this homosexual business. She understands the poison to be "the hate that destroys." She is mixed up and has a thousand ideas. Yet all her life she has liked people. Her husband is through with her, and she has thrown her life away. She is responsible for breaking up people's lives. She is setting the people here free, and all the world is coming in here; she has been sent to prison for life. They think one person can run the world, and pick her to blame things on. She is alone against the world, because they do not understand her; she is the cause of the world's troubles now. The world depends upon her and she is weak, and has lost her confidence. They make her talk of love, and are doing something to her because they want to get rid of her. Either her mother or her husband is doing a job on her; she is suspicious of his past.

Drawing X: (45th day): Condition: Still apprehensive and fearful, but less depressed; she speaks with earnest zeal.

"It's just occurred to me that my husband was a Red, a Communist. You remember the voting between Mother's and Father's sides? Well, this red Communism is made up of the lower class (she considers her husband socially inferior). I overlooked it and now it's too late. He wanted to get rid of me so he could get on better. I never thought of it before—too busy. Mother was always trying to hold onto me, and I never could make up my mind about him. Please don't make me talk, I want to keep bottled up about it. (After some coaxing) I felt you were also behind this, as a Communist. It's an effort to rule the world. I ruled the world before and this is a revolt, and the people around here are trying to revolt. That's what it's all about. They want to become popular, and know the other classes. So there's a presidential election, and Mother's against Communism and my husband's for it. (She takes the pad to draw.)

"Both parties are optimistic, and bright colors; the Republicans and the Democrats; this is a fight for world power between two sides. Then a third party wants to come in, and that will even it all out, even both the parties. The Republicans are the upper class, the Democrats the lower; you belong to the upper, and my neighbors around here belong to the lower. The Communists are in green, off to one side, and I don't know what they will do. It's an envious green, which wants to destroy both the parties. Then they come over to take power (she draws a line from the separate green body to the two parties). Some are already here in disguise, of course; they come over and take the whole thing over. I want to know what this is all about; I'm very interested. It's half and half again, like me being in two halves. No party can really take it all over; it would be all one color. There are two sides to a person, like having two parties, that's the point. They've got to compromise. I can't solve it, I can't think. I guess the parties are inside (i.e., in the mind)." (Note that the colors used are the same as in Drawing VII, with red at the center.)

46th day· Condition: Greatly improved, free of depression and fear.

"I just haven't grown up yet (in reference to her relation with her mother). I'm always gabbing and superficial. I really have more to me. But I never knew myself, and I want to know. Why should I be in such a turmoil? I only pushed it aside before, and now I need to face it. I want to understand myself, but I wonder if it's such a good idea. With this Communist revolt, there are arms here, and the nurses are involved. I like the world just now, though I disliked it last week. I always had friends, but was never a leader. This could be a symbol of my feelings, this idea of Mother's and Father's sides. But I know something's going on."

47th day: Condition: As above.

"I guess my husband's O.K., as a matter of fact. But I'm still rather mixed up. I know my baby's all right now too (talks a little about this). I don't know what's real and what isn't. My ideas that I've been having seem ridiculous...I want some more interpretations of all this. (We talk of her mother problem and her effort to get freedom and maturity and self-identity.) Yes, I've had angry feelings toward Mother especially. You say I'm trying to push her out of my life but I can't seem to do it...I see what you mean about the symbols, not taking them concretely; the illegitimate baby was one. I've thought about the third party as a new life, a new birth, the masculine and feminine part of me creating a new baby. (She draws.) The blue is the masculine part; there is some masculine in me. Then the red is the feminine; I'm more feminine actually. Then in the center it's dark, that's the new birth."

Drawing XI: (50th day): Condition· Good, cheerful, friendly, sociable, free of fears and depression.

"I've been having many thoughts about this new life. I feel fear, but also feel confidence (she starts to draw, and hums as she does so). These are the two parties, and here is the third as a happy medium ... I don't understand this third party as the new life. It seems to me there should be a fourth, the Socialists; then you'd have the Republicans, the Democrats, the Communists, and the Socialists. (It seems this occurred to her overnight.) (She puts in a fourth.) There are the four, and they all remain and aren't destroyed. What does it mean? Are there four parts to us? I don't see how there can be. I get the feeling you're another patient, not a doctor. This is the crisis, the one I've always pushed aside before, but now I have to face it ... (More ideas of blame and responsibility for everything.) ... Now these are related and are all in the world together. And they always will be; there's nothing you can do about it. They must decide which it's to be. Each party thinks it is right. There will be a great clash, a fight (here she shows signs of great inner tension). Then the new birth comes from this. But they must learn to live together with one another, so no one party can win. This is all very serious indeed to me. This is the hardest lesson in the world. It's like a world war. (She is dissatisfied, then, with the representation, and tries a second.)

"They should be side by side, like this, not clashing, though the Republicans and Democrats do. (Where they came together in one point), I represented it up here because it's what's going on in me (i.e., ego is at point of junction). You know, I was never interested in politics before; isn't it funny! (She is asked what she feels would be the ideal state.) I'd put nothing on paper till I'm sure. It would be where they were all heading for one goal, all converging somehow."

Drawing XII: (51st day) · Condition: Best to date.

"I've always been sort of an extravert, and always have put on a superficial appearance, I've always shown sort of a gay surface, but those were not my real feelings ever. What's this about Jung's psychology? (She has been talking with other patients about this during the last day or two, but has stated she knew nothing of these concepts before.) I have a sense of great depths. It's the deep unconscious in me, like the bottom of the sea (of which she has just done a painting with four sailboats on the surface). Are these inherited symbols? ... I have a feeling I'm never going home. I just wonder if I'll ever get out of this alternation of up and down. I've told some of the patients my fears (the therapist's recommendation), and they told me they liked me; that makes me feel much better toward them now. I still have some fears, but I hated them all last week and agree with X—that this depends on my own attitude. As for my mother, I need to get independent of her. She's so social. I've taken after her, being so superficial like this. But my husband helped me broaden my interests. (She starts to draw.)

"The Republicans are Mother's upper class party. The Democrats are Father's; he doesn't care whether people like him or not. The Reds, that's my husband, the lower class and revolutionaries. The Socialists, they're on one level, a happy medium. They believe in the brotherhood of man, and they're sociable, all one class. We could call them North, East, South and West, and have different colors for each one. I just thought of it yesterday that way; it just came to me in that form. The West is China; the East, Europe; and then North and South America; that makes a round world, you see. So the North are the Republicans, in orange;

the South the Democrats, in green; the West the Communists, in grey; and the East the Socialists, in red. Then we have the center again—all the points are coming in there. We have to make it into a world again, and that's all there is to it. Is this all self-analysis again, I wonder? ... They all point in to the center, and we have the world. (She experiments with the design.) This is the best; there we have it! Like the points of the compass.

"The grey disturbs me, but it's the glad-dismal idea again ... There has to be a center to everything. It came to my mind, it's warmth. (What gives the warmth?) The sun does. No, it's the revolution. They have war first, then revolution. Then when it's quiet, it gets all warm and sunny. So here's the revolution, in all colors (at the center, in concentric rings); this is supposed to be dark then, too. They all come to the center for the revolution. They're all after the upper class, to destroy the upper and level it off. This is what I've been through. And now the sun shines. It was me at the center of convergence in yesterday's design; but it was at one side and that was wrong. I was looking inward more then.

(The therapist comments on the transformation of the center, that the sun is as the god at the center, where the ego had been.) "Yes, that's right, that's just like my idea at Easter. Christ is a symbol in us all, you know, and we can all be Christs. All people have a unity inside, the same experience in us all, common to everyone."

In associating to the colors the next day, she said:

Orange—Sunny, bright, cheer. Sun, wheat, flowers, marigolds, fire. She doesn't like to wear it.

Red—Warmth, fire, blood, turmoil, feelings like love and hate.

Green—Cool, grass and leaves, nature, growth. She doesn't like green on her.

Grey—Pessimism, rainy day, cool; nothing cheerful about it, but she likes it.

Blue—She likes blue, but left it out.

Purple—Purple cross, like "purple passion." Combined red and blue.

She associates thinking with orange, and feeling with red. Thinking is the most important to her, she says. Maybe it is the grey: it was never important to her until she was here. She always had gone on the assumption that fate managed everything and all was predestined, before, and she never did any planning or thinking things through.

THE LATER HISTORY

(In the ninth week the therapist, i.e., the author, reached the end of his period of work at this hospital, and had to leave the case.)

During the ninth week, it was noticed that the patient again began to show signs of marked pre-occupation and that she was very easily upset by the manic patients on her service. She again re-entered her deep catatonic stage. During the next few weeks she had her old delusional ideas that the baby was going to be killed; she again was the center of attraction and was going to be the cause of another world-wide war.

Throughout this entire month she showed marked reaction to the manic patients and this time the paranoid delusions took on a new twist. She stated that other patients were accusing her of wanting to divorce her husband and marry her doctor. This again created a great deal of conflict within herself. During the fourth month the patient had a series of shock treatments combined with ambulatory insulin, and she responded extremely well to this treatment. In this month, she was able to go home on short visits and plans at this time were being made to have her go home on visits and continue under the care of a local psychiatrist. It was during this time that she began to speak much more enthusiastically about her baby and her desire to be home to take care of her child. She also stated that she cared for her husband a great deal and that she thought he was the finest man living and that she was very fortunate to have him for a husband. At the end of the fourth month, while the patient was home, she unfortunately slipped back again into her catatonic schizophrenic stupor. She was re-admitted to the hospital and again put on electric shock treatments to which she had responded very well, and continued to remain good. During the sixth and seventh months the patient was getting shock treatments once weekly and starting in the seventh month, her treatments were reduced to one every two weeks. On this therapy the patient continued to make good progress and to hold her own, and stay in a world of reality. During the fifth, sixth, and seventh months, psychotherapy was chiefly pointed towards helping her make a re-adjustment to her home situation. She has strong obsessional qualities and these have not been disturbed, since it was felt that these were probably a defense against her schizophrenia. Problems of every-day life have been talked over from the viewpoint of a common sense, non-analytical approach. It has been the feeling of the staff that it is important that the patient return home in order to keep her marital status on a good level.

Since discharge, her family states they have never seen her better. She is a good housewife and mother, and apparently has made an excellent marital adjustment. From what we hear she is well-adjusted, comfortable, and happy, and is warmer in all her relationships.

NOTES

PART I

NOTES TO CHAPTER 1

INTRODUCTION

[1] For Jung's original and basic statement of the differentiation between prospective and retrospective understanding, and between constructive and reductive analysis, see his essay "The Content of the Psychoses," part II (1914), in Jung, *Collected Papers,* p 313.

[2] For definition of "symbol," see Jung, *Psychological Types,* pp 601 ff.

[3] For definition of "archetype," see *ibid ,* pp 211, 378, 476 For definition of "libido," see Jung, *Contributions to Analytical Psychology,* "On Psychic Energy "

NOTES TO CHAPTER 4

THE DEVELOPMENT OF THE PROBLEM

[1] Cf John Read, *Prelude to Chemistry,* pp 19–20

[2] See Jung's discussion of "The Relativity of the Idea of God in Meister Eckehart," in Jung, *Psychological Types,* pp 297–319

[3] For a definition of "religion" in the psychological sense, see Jung, *Psychology and Religion,* pp 5–6

[4] *Ibid ,* p. 43

NOTES TO CHAPTER 5

THE RESOLUTION

[1] For a definition and discussion of the reconciling symbol, see Jung, *Psychological Types,* chap v, see also Jung, *Two Essays on Analytical Psychology,* essay I, chap VII.

NOTES TO CHAPTER 7

AMPLIFICATION OF THE SYMBOL

[1] Jung, *Psychologie und Alchemie,* pp 141–142

[2] Evans-Wentz, *Tibetan Yoga and Secret Doctrine,* quoted in Harding, *Psychic Energy,* p 381

[3] Cammann, "Suggested Origin of the Tibetan Mandala Paintings," *Art Quarterly,* Spring, 1950, p 107

[4] A Tibetan Bon rite Discussed in Evans-Wentz, *op. cit ,* quoted in Harding, *op. cit ,* pp 396–399

[5] A Buddhist rite Discussed in Zimmer, *Kuntsform und Yoga in indischen Kultbild,* quoted in Jung and Kerényi, *Essays on a Science of Mythology,* pp 17–18.

[6] The "Yantra" form For details, see Jung, *Gestaltungen des Unbewussten,* pp. 190–194.

[7] Jung, *Psychologie und Alchemie*, p 142
[8] *Ibid.*, pp 336–337
[9] Quoted in *ibid*, p 182
[10] *Ibid.*, pp 187–189, 515–520.

NOTES TO CHAPTER 8

PSYCHOLOGICAL CONCEPTS

[1] Jung, *Contributions to Analytical Psychology*, "Mind and Earth," p 118.
[2] Jung, *Psychological Types*, p 211
[3] Jung, *Contributions to Analytical Psychology*, "Instinct and the Unconscious," p 251
[4] In 1914 Jung established this basic orientation in terms of "prospective understanding" and the "constructive method" See part II, chap 7
[5] Jung, *Integration of the Personality*, p 166
[6] Jung, *Two Essays on Analytical Psychology*, pp. 183 ff More fully discussed in Jung, *Integration of the Personality*, especially in chap IV.
[7] Jung, *Integration of the Personality*, p 96
[8] *Ibid*, p. 64
[9] *Ibid*, p 199
[10] Jung, *Modern Man in Search of a Soul*, p 30
[11] Baynes, *Mythology of the Soul*, pp 345–346.
[12] Jung, *Two Essays on Analytical Psychology*, pp 183–218.
[13] Jung, *The Psychogenesis of Schizophrenia*, quoted in Baynes, *op cit*, pp 39–40
[14] Jung, *Psychology and Religion*, pp 45–48.

NOTES TO CHAPTER 9

INTERPRETATION OF THE PROCESS

[1] A discussion of these statistics is in Boisen, *Exploration of the Inner World*, pp 38–57
[2] Fenichel, *The Psychoanalytic Theory of Neurosis*, chap 18.
[3] Jung, *Integration of the Personality*, p 111
[4] Jung, *Contributions to Analytical Psychology*, "Mind and Earth," pp. 120–128.
[5] Jung, *Integration of the Personality*, p 139
[6] For the dismemberment of Osiris by the dragon Seth, see Frazer, *The Golden Bough*, part IV, book 3, chap 1, for that of Dionysus Zagreus by the Titans, see *ibid*, part IV, book 3, chap V, see also Harrison, *Themis, A Study of the Social Origins of Greek Religion*, chap II The relation of the hero myth to the danger of psychotic fragmentation is mentioned in Jung, *Psychologie und Alchemie*, pp. 454–461 Cf also Jung, *Contributions to Analytical Psychology*, "On Psychical Energy"
[7] Jung, *Integration of the Personality*, p 146
[8] The relation of the two is briefly discussed in Adler, *Studies in Analytical Psychology*, p 12 See also Jung's essay in *Eranos Jahrbuch*, 1940–1941, pp 136 ff.
[9] Discussed in Jung, *Gestaltungen des Unbewussten*, pp 161, 223
[10] Jung, *Psychology and Religion*, p 105
[11] Extensive discussion of this vessel aspect is in Harding, *Psychic Energy*, chap XII.
[12] For a full discussion of the theme, see Jung and Kerényi, *Essays on a Science of Mythology*, part I
[13] Jung, *Psychologie und Alchemie*, pp 236, 400.
[14] See Jung, *Integration of the Personality*, pp 224–232
[15] *Ibid*, pp 37 ff
[16] Further mention of the gates in this connection is omitted, although the presence of two instead of the usual four is undoubtedly of significance.
[17] Jung, *Gestaltungen des Unbewussten*, p 216
[18] The term "Eros" is used to connote the general principle of relatedness and interweaving, as an opposite of the "Logos" principle of discrimination and differentiation (Jung and Wilhelm, *The Secret of the Golden Flower*, pp. 117–118, also Jung, *Contributions to Analytical Psychology*, pp 175–180)
[19] The same sort of thesis has often been held before. Cf, in Plato's *Symposium*, Aristophanes'

jesting tale of the primordial round man, self-sufficient until split into male and female halves, since then he has known love as the longing of each half for the other—that is, for its pristine completeness (Taylor, *Plato*, p 219) The jest has a more serious history, however, in its Vedic prototype, in which the Atman is described in somewhat similar imagery

[20] Although I know this to be in accord with Jung's concept of schizophrenia, I cannot find a discussion of this distinct point in his writings except for an early statement of the role of feeling and object relationships written in 1912, in Jung, *Psychology of the Unconscious*, pp 193 ff Baynes, *Mythology of the Soul*, p. 35, barely mentions it.

[21] The psychodynamics of these processes are discussed in detail in Jung, *Contributions to Analytical Psychology*, pp 34–44, see also Jung, *Psychological Types*, pp 607–610

[22] The patient's own associations to the colors in Drawing XII are in accord with this statement See also Baynes, *op cit*, p 440.

[23] That is, in the brown and purple of the dark side of each of the leaves representing the friends

[24] The interrelations of the symbols sun, flower, and gold are discussed in Jung, *Integration of the Personality*, p 117

[25] The term "spiritual" is discussed and defined in Jung, *Contributions to Analytical Psychology*, "Spirit and Life," pp 77–98, as an autonomous unconscious content representing a potential of superior consciousness, its relation to the self is discussed in Jung, *Symbolik des Geistes*, chap 1

[26] The activity of the transference in constellating and containing the imagery of the individuation process is discussed in Jung, *Psychologie der Uebertragung*, part 1 and pp 91–95

[27] Quoted in Jung, *Psychologie und Alchemie*, pp 61, 369, 372

[28] Jung, *Integration of the Personality*, p 240.

[29] *Ibid*, pp 259–260.

[30] For a discussion of this theme of the descent into the depths, see *ibid*, pp 241–246

[31] See Jung and Wilhelm, *op cit*, pp 12–16, 114–120

[32] Jung, "Ueber das Selbst," in *Eranos Jahrbuch*, 1948, pp 288–315

[33] Jung, *Phychologie und Alchemie*, p 532.

[34] Taylor, *op cit.*, p. 450, Ezekiel 1.

[35] Quoted in Jung, *Psychology and Religion*, p 43, from the Homilies of Origenes.

[36] John 15

[37] E g, Gilgamesh Epic, XI Tablet Langdon, *The Mythology of All Races*, vol v, p 221

[38] See Jung's discussion in *Psychological Types*, pp 297–319, citing Meister Eckehart and Angelus Silesius.

[39] Jung, *Psychologie der Uebertragung*, pp 117–119.

[40] Frazer, *The Golden Bough*, part vii, vol ii, pp 225–226, Harrison, *op cit*, pp 19, 118–126.

[41] In the alchemical system of projections, circulation produces distillation, sublimation, or generation of spiritual substances out of material ones See Jung, *Psychologie und Alchemie*, pp 178, 182

[42] For definition, see Jung, *Two Essays on Analytical Psychology*, pp 225–231, also Jung, *Contributions to Analytical Psychology*, pp. 168–169, see also Emma Jung, *Wirklichkeit der Seele*, pp. 296–354.

[43] Jung and Wilhelm, *op cit*, pp 116–117.

[44] Jung, *Two Essays on Analytical Psychology*, pp 200–203, 214

[45] The difference between these types of animus, the developed and the primitive, is discussed in Emma Jung, *op cit*, pp 296–354

[46] That is, the soldier and Christ are both implied in the representation of the center in Drawing XII, in the blackness of the warring agencies and the brightness of the harmonizing sun

[47] Jung, "Ueber des Selbst," *Eranos Jahrbuch*, 1948, p 299, Jung, *Integration of the Personality*, p. 25.

[48] Experiments performed by Lang, described in Jung, *L'Homme à la Découverte de son Ame*, p. 166.

[49] The best-known expression of this intuition is the concept of "Neikos" and "Philia" of Empedocles, *Fragments*, book 1 According to Hauer (lectures in Zurich, 1933), the notion occurred in ancient Hindu philosophy.

[50] The cleaving is described in Read, *Prelude to Chemistry*, p 104; the egg as chaos is described in Jung, *Psychologie und Alchemie*, p 278

[51] See Drews' account of the twelve, prevalent in antiquity, citing Jason, Iasios, Joshua, Jesus, also Helios and Mithra, as solar deities with twelve companions, in Drews, *The Christ Myth*, pp 135–139

[52] The gold was considered the image of the sun and of the deity—that is, the self—spun into matter See Jung, *Integration of the Personality*, pp 240, 246

[53] Kellogg, "Structure and Design in Preschool Art"

[54] A psychological interpretation of the paradise myth is given in Adler, *op cit*, pp 180–185

[55] This process is called the "transcendant function" See Jung, *Psychological Types*, pp 601–610; also Jung, *Two Essays on Analytical Psychology*, essay I, chap VII

[56] Jung, *Psychologie und Alchemie*, pp 224–227, Jung, *Gestaltungen des Unbewussten*, p 197.

[57] Defined and discussed in Jung, *Two Essays on Analytical Psychology*, essay II, part I, chap III, see also Jung, *Psychological Types*, pp 589–596

[58] Discussed in Jung, *Two Essays on Analytical Psychology*, essay II, part II, chap II

[59] Discussed in Jung, *Psychology of the Unconscious*, chap VII, also in Jung, *Integration of the Personality*, pp 242–246.

[60] The archetype of Satan, the "Adversary," is discussed at length by Schaerf in Jung, *Symbolik des Geistes*, pp 153 ff In the form of the "Antichrist," as the dark aspect of the self and opposite to Christ as the light aspect, it is discussed in Jung, "Ueber das Selbst," *Eranos Jahrbuch*, 1948, pp 302 ff

[61] Jung, *Integration of the Personality*, pp 239–240, also Jung, *Psychologie der Uebertragung*, pp 67–71

[62] Jung, *Psychologie der Uebertragung*, part II, chap I, also Jung, *Psychologie und Alchemie*, pp 178, 236–237, 570.

[63] Jung, *Integration of the Personality*, pp 240, 246

[64] Jung, *Psychologie und Alchemie*, p 532

[65] The First and Last Adam are mentioned in I Corinthians 15 44–47 and in Romans 5 19

[66] Jung, *Psychologie und Alchemie*, pp 570–571, Jung, *Psychology and Religion*, p 68.

[67] Baynes, *op cit*, p. 35.

[68] Jung, *Psychological Types*, pp 543–546.

[69] Sun Drawings I (implied only), II
Deity Drawings I, V, VI
New birth. Drawings III, V, IX, X, XI.
Gold Drawings II, IX
Blackness Drawings I, III, IV, V, VII (as war again), IX.
Enmity Drawings I, II, III, VII, X, XI
Cosmos and chaos Drawings I, II, VI, VII, X, XI

NOTES TO CHAPTER 10

CONCLUSIONS

[1] Dante, *Paradiso* (translated by Lawrence Grant White), Canto 28.

PART II

NOTES TO CHAPTER 2

THE SYMBOLISM OF THE QUADRATED CIRCLE

[1] Goblet D'Alviella, *The Migration of Symbols*, pp 13–14, Simpson, *The Buddhist Praying Wheel*, p 239.

[2] Discussions of the distribution and evolution of the symbol in thorough detail are in Hastings, *Encyclopædia of Religion and Ethics*, vol IV, pp 324–329, Goblet D'Alviella, *op cit*, chaps I, II, Goblet D'Alviella, *Croyances, Rites, Institutions*, vol I, chaps I, IV; Simpson, *op cit*

[3] Jung, *Integration of the Personality*, p 127

[4] Langdon, *The Mythology of All Races*, vol V, figs 44, 51, 61, 62, 68, 73

[5] Hastings, *op. cit.*, vol. IV, p 324.

[6] *Loc cit*, Simpson, *op cit*, chap xvi, Inman, *Ancient Pagan and Modern Christian Symbolism*, pp 15, 36, 41, 42, 61.

[7] Inman, *op cit*, p 61, Harrison, *Themis, A Study of the Social Origins of Greek Religion*, fig 148

[8] Simpson, *op cit*, chap xvi, figs 25–37, MacCulloch, *The Mythology of All Races*, vol iii, pl ii

[9] MacCulloch, *op cit*, pl iv

[10] Simpson, *op cit*, pp 251–254

[11] Hastings, *op cit*, vol iv, p 325, vol x, p. 214.

[12] *Ibid*, vol iv, p 326

[13] Vaillant, *The Aztecs of Mexico*, end papers, Hastings, *op cit*, vol iv, p 326

[14] Goblet D'Alviella, *The Migration of Symbols*, p 76.

[15] Wheelwright, *Hail Chant and Water Chant*, p 170

[16] Farrar, *The Life of Christ as Represented in Art*, pp 19–23, Hastings, *op cit*, pp 328–329

[17] Hastings, *op cit*, pp 328–329

[18] Farrar, *op cit*, p 25

[19] Hastings, *op cit*, p 329

[20] Farrar, *op cit*, p 25

[21] *Loc cit*

[22] Drews, *The Christ Myth*, pp 159–160.

[23] *Loc cit*

[24] *Ibid*, p 154

[25] *Ibid*, p 161.

[26] Jung, *Psychology of the Unconscious*, part ii, chap iii

[27] Evans-Wentz, *Tibetan Yoga and Secret Doctrines*, p 72

[28] Cammann, "Suggested Origin of the Tibetan Mandala Paintings," *Art Quarterly*, Spring, 1950, pp 107 ff.

[29] Hastings, *op cit*, p 328.

[30] Farrar, *op cit*, p 23

[31] Jung, *Psychologie und Alchemie*, p 286, Abb 101, 102.

[32] Ezekiel 1 and 10.

[33] Jung, *Psychologie und Alchemie*, Abb 233

[34] The derivation of these from the wheel symbolism is discussed in Simpson, *op. cit*, chap xv

[35] Goblet D'Alviella, *The Migration of Symbols*, pp 35–39.

[36] Jung, *Psychologie und Alchemie*, pp 189–190, 608–609, Abb. 64, 65

[37] Harrison, *op cit*, chaps vi, ix, figs 52, 136

[38] Simpson, *op cit*, p 164

[39] Apuleius, *The Golden Ass*, book xi, chap. xxiv.

[40] Jung, *Psychologie und Alchemie*, p 90.

[41] Simpson, *op cit*, pp. 43–48.

[42] *Ibid*, pp 68–73.

[43] Goblet D'Alviella, *The Migration of Symbols*, chap iv, plate ve, f.

[44] Simpson, *op cit*, chap v.

[45] Inman, *op cit*, pp 35–36

[46] E g, "Brug na Boinne", MacCulloch, *op cit.*, vol. iii, pl. vi

[47] Simpson, *op cit*, chap x

[48] Cammann, *op cit*, pp 107 ff.

[49] Jung, *Psychologie und Alchemie*, p 284, Abb. 100.

[50] *Loc cit.*

[51] Vaillant, *op cit*, p. 163, pl 52.

[52] Zimmer, *Myths and Symbols of Indian Art and Civilization*, pp 51–52, 146

[53] Taylor, *Plato*, pp 445 ff An interesting parallel to this concept is found in ancient alchemy in the "Axioma Maria," which states the formula that "the one becomes two, and the two becomes three, and from the third comes the One as the fourth," a ground plan for the Work, see Jung, *Psychologie und Alchemie*, pp 224 ff.

[54] Jowett, *The Dialogues of Plato*, vol ii, pp. 457–463.

[55] Bloomfield, *The Religion of the Veda*, p. 126.

[56] Simpson, *op cit*, pp 43–46, 267–270, Hastings, *op cit*, vol xii, pp. 736 737

[57] Harrison, *op cit*, pp 523–528.

[58] Simpson, *op cit*, pp 50–54

[59] Jung, *Psychologie und Alchemie*, pp 523–524, Abb 192

[60] *Ibid*, p 230, Abb 80

[61] Hastings, *op cit.*, vol. viii, pp 321–324.

[62] Wheelwright, *op cit*, pp 162 ff, 194 ff, and appendix

[63] Jung, *Gestaltungen des Unbewussten*, p 190.

[64] *Ibid*, p 191.

[65] Stein, *Serindia*, vol ii, p 975.

[66] Jung, *Psychologie und Alchemie*, Abb 84

[67] Jung, *Integration of the Personality*, p 140.

[68] Philpot, *The Sacred Tree*, chap vi

[69] *Loc cit*

[70] Genesis 2 and 3, Adler, *Studies in Analytical Psychology*, pp. 179 ff

[71] Revelations 21 and 22

[72] Jung and Kerényi, *Essays on a Science of Mythology*, p 18, quoting Boll, "Aus der Offenbarung Johannis"

[73] Jung and Kerényi, *op cit*, pp 15–16.

[74] Frobenius, *Monumenta Africana*, quoted in Jung and Kerényi, *op cit*, pp 24–26

[75] Jung, *Psycholgie der Uebertragung*, p 105, quoting Hocart, *Kings and Councillors*.

[76] Simpson, *op cit*, pp 43–46, 267–270

[77] Jung, *Psychology and Religion*, p. 70.

[78] Jung, *Psychological Types*, p 295

[79] Goblet D'Alviella, *The Migration of Symbols*, pp 35–39

[80] Zimmer, *op cit*, pp 90–92.

[81] *Ibid*, pp 51–52, Jung and Kerényi, *op cit*, p 67, birth of Brahma illustrated in Keith, *The Mythology of All Races*, vol v, pl xi, p 120

[82] Jung, *Psychologie und Alchemie*, Abb 52.

[83] *Ibid*, Abb 102.

[84] See discussion of vessel symbolism in Jung, *Psychological Types*, pp 285–291

[85] *Paradiso*, Canto 23.

[86] *Ibid.*, Canto 33

[87] Jung, *Gestaltungen des Unbewussten*, p 207, Jung, *Psychologie und Alchemie*, p 250 n

[88] Jung and Wilhelm, *The Secret of the Golden Flower*, pp 24–26, 33

[89] Jung, *Psychologie und Alchemie*, p 250 n.

[90] Harding, *Psychic Energy*, p 445

[91] Jung, *Psychologie und Alchemie*, p 434.

[92] *Ibid*, p 232

[93] Jung and Wilhelm, *op cit.*, pp. 25–26, 33.

[94] Jung, *Gestaltungen des Unbewussten*, pp 213–214.

[95] Goblet D'Alviella, *The Migration of Symbols*, pp 35–37.

[96] Zimmer, *op cit*, pp 146–148

[97] Evans-Wentz, *The Tibetan Book of the Dead*, pp. 105 ff

[98] Reichard, *Navaho Religion*, chap xiii.

[99] The symbolism of the masculine Trinity and of the relation to it of the fourth principle—that of the feminine and also of the evil—is an aspect of the general problem of the relation of the three and the fourth, or of spirit and matter. These questions are discussed at length in Jung, *Psychology and Religion*, pp 73–77, and in Jung, *Psychologie und Alchemie*, pp 224 ff, 236 ff

[100] Simpson, *op cit*, p 38

[101] Drews, *op cit*, p. 154.

[102] *Ibid*, pp 99–100

[103] Harding, *op cit*, p 445.

[104] Jung, *Psychologie und Alchemie*, pp. 434, 452.

[105] Jung, *Psychologie der Uebertragung*, chap v.

[106] Taylor, *op cit*, p. 219
[107] Jung, *Psychologie und Alchemie*, p. 216.
[108] Jung and Wilhelm, *op cit*, pp 24–25.
[109] Jung, *Psychologie und Alchemie*, p 425.
[110] *Ibid*, p 405
[111] Simpson, *op cit*, p 46
[112] Jung, *Gestaltungen des Unbewussten*, pp 197, 226.
[113] *Ibid*, pp 217, 227.
[114] Simpson, *op cit*, chap. iii.
[115] *Ibid*, p 56
[116] Jung and Wilhelm, *op cit*, pp 23–58
[117] Jung, *Psychologie und Alchemie*, pp 178, 518, Abb 80
[118] Simpson, *op cit*, Goblet D'Alviella, *Croyances, Rites, Institutions*, chap 1
[119] Simpson, *op cit*, chap 5, Jung, *Psychologie und Alchemie*, pp 514–521
[120] Wheelwright, *op cit*, p 170.
[121] Simpson, *op cit*, p 270
[122] Jung and Kerényi, *op. cit*, pp 13–14.
[123] Given in Philpot, *op cit*, Goblet D'Alviella, *The Migration of Symbols*, chap iv, Frazer, *The Golden Bough*, part iii, chap viii
[124] Goblet D'Alviella, *The Migration of Symbols*, pp. 155–163, Philpot, *op cit.*, pp 115–116.
[125] Goblet D'Alviella, *The Migration of Symbols*, p 156
[126] Philpot, *op cit*, chap vi
[127] Hastings, *op cit*, vol iv, p 329.
[128] Simpson, *op cit*, p. 46.
[129] *Ibid*, chap iii.
[130] Goblet D'Alviella, *The Migration of Symbols*, pp. 137–138.
[131] Philpot, *op. cit.*, pp 114–116.
[132] Harrison, *op cit*, p 431.
[133] Goblet D'Alviella, *The Migration of Symbols*, pp 61, 142, 150, 151
[134] Philpot, *op cit*, p 111, also Goblet D'Alviella, *The Migration of Symbols*, p 157.
[135] Goblet D'Alviella, *The Migration of Symbols*, pp 142–143.
[136] Harrison, *op. cit*, chap vi, Frazer, *op cit.*, part iii
[137] Frazer, *op. cit.*, part iv, vol 1, chap v, Drews, *op cit*, pp 156–158, Harrison, *op cit*, chap vi
[138] Hastings, *op cit*, vol iv, pp. 324–325, Drews, *op cit*, p 149.
[139] Goblet D'Alviella, *The Migration of Symbols*, chap. iv
[140] Philpot, *op cit*, chaps vi and vii
[141] Jung, *Psychologie und Alchemie*, Abb 231
[142] Jung, *Integration of the Personality*, pp 248, 264
[143] Cf the crown of rays in the deification of the initiant in the Isis mysteries (§ 2).

Notes to Chapter 3

THE QUADRATED CIRCLE IN THE EAST

[1] This discussion has been paraphrased from Watts, *The Spirit of Zen*, chap 1, pp 21–26
[2] Simpson, *The Buddhist Praying Wheel*, pp 46–48, quoting Hiuen Tsiang
[3] Evans-Wentz, *The Tibetan Book of the Dead*, p 10
[4] *Ibid*, p 17
[5] Jung, *Psychologie und Alchemie*, pp 141–142.
[6] Evans-Wentz, *Tibetan Yoga and Secret Doctrines*, p 72
[7] Cammann, "Suggested Origin of the Tibetan Mandala Paintings," *Art Quarterly*, Spring, 1950, p 107.
[8] *Ibid*, p 114.
[9] *Ibid*, p 113.
[10] *Ibid*, pp 107–119
[11] See also Stein, *Serindia*, vol iv, ch 00186–00187
[12] Zimmer, quoted in Jung and Kerényi, *Essays on a Science of Mythology*, pp 17, 20

¹³ Jung, *Psychologie und Alchemie*, p 142.

¹⁴ Simpson, *op cit*, pp 59 ff

¹⁵ E g , the "Sanskrit-Word Pagoda," Kunming, in Cammann, *Kunming Guide*, p 23.

¹⁶ Jung, *Integration of the Personality*, p 143

¹⁷ Simpson, *op cit*, pp 59 ff

¹⁸ Jung and Kerényi, *Essays on a Science of Mythology*, p 18

¹⁹ See account and diagram in Simpson, *op cit*, p 61, fig 13.

²⁰ Bredon, *Peking*, pp 132–141, plan of temple, facing p 134

NOTES TO CHAPTER 4

THE QUADRATED CIRCLE IN THE WEST

¹ Jung, *Integration of the Personality*, p 207

² Jung, *Psychologie und Alchemie*, pp 316–318, Jung, *Integration of the Personality*, pp. 208–209

³ Jung, *Psychologie und Alchemie*, pp 178–180

⁴ *Ibid* , p 182

⁵ *Ibid* , pp 515 ff

⁶ *Loc cit*

⁷ *Ibid* , pp 230–231

⁸ *Ibid* , p 182, quoting from the "Tractatus Aureus "

⁹ Jung, *Psychologie der Uebertragung*, pp 67–68.

¹⁰ Jung, *Psychologie und Alchemie*, pp 102–104

¹¹ *Ibid* , pp 400, 504.

¹² Jung, "Ueber das Selbst," *Eranos Jahrbuch*, 1948

NOTES TO CHAPTER 5

THE SYMBOLISM OF OPPOSITES

¹ For detailed discussions of the whole array of such cosmic pairs, see Frazer, *The Worship of Nature*, chaps ii, iii, vi, vii See also, for a briefer summary of the theme, Read, *Prelude to Chemistry*, pp 19–20.

² Frazer, *op cit*, chap v

³ Harrison, *Themis, A Study of the Social Origins of Greek Religion*, chap vi, Frazer, *op. cit* , chap ii

⁴ Cammann, *Kunming Guide*, p. 56.

⁵ For the interrelations of the T'ai-chi and Pa-kua with the cosmic concepts of the four directions, four seasons, and four elements surrounding the fifth element (earth), see Wilhelm and Baynes, *The I Ching or Book of Changes*, vol i, pp 315–333

⁶ Cammann, "Suggested Origin of the Tibetan Mandala Paintings," *Art Quarterly*, Spring, 1950, n 24

⁷ Taoist, expositor of Laotse, third century B C.

⁸ Ballou, *The Bible of the World*, p 507.

⁹ Wilhelm and Baynes, *op cit* , vol i, pp 319 ff.

¹⁰ Zimmer, *Myths and Symbols of Indian Art and Civilization*, chap iv, § 3

¹¹ *Ibid* , fig 36

¹² Nahm, *Selections from Early Greek Philosophy*, pp 130 ff

¹³ Langdon, *The Mythology of All Races*, vol v, chap ix.

¹⁴ Zimmer, *op cit* , pp 51, 90, chap ii, § 3.

¹⁵ Cornford, *Plato's Cosmology*, pp 177–188.

¹⁶ Jung, *Psychologie und Alchemie*, pp 433–447.

¹⁷ Read, *op cit* , pp 19–20, Jung, *Integration of the Personality*, pp. 242–243; Jung, *Psychologie der Uebertragung*, chap ii.

¹⁸ Jung, "Ueber das Selbst," *Eranos Jahrbuch*, 1948, pp 296–297

NOTES TO CHAPTER 6

THE SYMBOLISM OF REBIRTH

[1] Jung has recently elaborated his formulation of the psychology of the rebirth process in Jung, "Ueber Wiedergeburt," *Eranos Jahrbuch*, 1939 It brings his theory to date from his earlier attempts in which the incest motif and mother image were given greatest considerations (see Jung, *Psychology of the Unconscious*).

[2] See statistical study in Boisen, *Exploration of the Inner World*, pp 30–34

[3] Harrison, *Themis, A Study of the Social Origins of Greek Religion*, chap 11.

[4] Complete accounts of these rites are in Frazer, *The Golden Bough*, part x, vol 11, pp 225–278, see also Webster, *Primitive Secret Societies*.

[5] Webster, *op cit*, chap. 1.

[6] Frobenius, quoted in *ibid*, p 46.

[7] Jung and Kerényi, *Essays on a Science of Mythology*, pp. 188–214

[8] Frazer, *op cit*, part iv, vol. 1, pp 271–276

[9] Jung, *Psychology of the Unconscious*, pp. 375 ff

[10] Harrison, *op cit*, chaps i–iii, vi, Frazer, *op cit*, part x, vol 11, pp 225–278.

[11] Harrison, *op cit*, chaps vi, ix, figs 52, 136.

[12] Apuleius, *The Golden Ass.*

[13] Avalon, *The Serpent Power.*

[14] Evans-Wentz, *Tibetan Yoga and Secret Doctrine*, p. 285.

[15] David-Neel, quoted in Harding, *Psychic Energy*, p 393.

[16] Frazer, *op cit*, vol xi, pp 244–246.

[17] Evans-Wentz, *op cit*, pp 302–313, quoted in Harding, *op cit*, pp 393–399.

[18] Evans-Wentz, *op cit*

[19] Cammann, "Suggested Origin of the Tibetan Mandala Paintings," *Art Quarterly*, Spring, 1950, p. 107.

[20] Galatians 1, see also Drews, *The Christ Myth*, part 11, chap 1.

[21] Cf Drews, *op cit.*, the closing discussion

[22] Galatians 2 20.

[23] Romans 6 4–6

[24] Cf Frazer, *op cit*, part iv.

[25] II Corinthians 4 10.

[26] Galatians 3 27

[27] Romans 12 4–5

[28] I Corinthians 12 13

[29] Jung gives this considerable mention in the newly rewritten form of *Psychology of the Unconscious*, now called, in German, *Symbole der Wandlung*, p 558.

[30] Fox, *The Mythology of All Races*, vol. 1, pp. 112–115.

[31] Frazer, *op cit*, part 11, pp 387–389

[32] Fox, *op cit*, vol 1, pp. 186–188

[33] Jung and Kerényi, *op cit*, p 157

[34] Zimmer, *Myths and Symbols of Indian Art and Civilization*, pp. 211–215.

[35] Jung, *Psychology of the Unconscious*, pp 266–267.

[36] The patient's process reveals ideas of eight murders, suggesting perhaps that the unconscious resolves the personality in its eight components (four double ones) This number is standard in the symbolism of the structure of the conscious personality as well as of the self These eight components appear later in connection with the further ramifications of the theme that death is a planting and that resurrection is a new vegetation (Drawings II and VIII). We might also say of her "responsibility for all deaths" that the relations to her fellow men are also resolved away in the regression, "killing" being in this sense equivalent to "withdrawing libido from"

[37] Langdon, *The Mythology of All Races*, vol v, pp 28 ff

[38] *Ibid*, p 220

[39] *Ibid.*, pp 295 ff.

[40] Frazer, *op cit*, part v, vol 1, pp. 12–15.

[41] *Ibid*, part iv, book 11, chap 1.

[42] Jung, *Psychology of the Unconscious*, pp 302–303.

[43] Hastings, *Encyclopædia of Religion and Ethics*, vol. iv, p. 325.

[44] Jung, *Psychology of the Unconscious*, "Symbolism of the Mother and of Rebirth" and "The Dual Mother Role "

[45] Jung, *Psychologie und Alchemie*, p 318.

[46] Jung, *Integration of the Personality*, pp 241–245.

[47] Fox, *op cit* , vol 1, p 273. For the corresponding Hindu concept, see Frazer, *The Worship of Nature*, vol 1, p. 318

[48] Fox, *op cit* , p 276

[49] Jung, *Psychology of the Unconscious*, pp. 403–408.

[50] I Corinthians 15

[51] Frazer, *The Golden Bough*, part iv, book iii, chap. v, § 4.

[52] Jung, *Integration of the Personality*, pp 227–234

[53] Jung and Kerényi, *op. cit* , pp. 63 ff.

[54] *Loc cit.*

[55] *Loc. cit.*

[56] Zimmer, *op. cit* , p. 90.

[57] Frazer, *The Golden Bough*, part iv, book iii, chap vi.

[58] Jung, *Psychology of the Unconscious*, pp 282–283.

[59] *Ibid* , chap v, also Jung, *Integration of the Personality*, pp 242–246.

[60] Frazer, *The Golden Bough*, part vii, vol. ii, pp. 225–227, 275, 277, Webster, *op. cit.*, pp 46–47.

[61] Frazer, *The Golden Bough*, part vii, vol. ii, pp 237, 242–244.

[62] Harrison, *op cit* , chaps i–iii.

[63] *Ibid* , pp 38, 42–48.

[64] Frazer, *The Golden Bough*, part iv, vol. i, pp 271–276.

[65] Harrison, *op cit* , 492–498.

[66] *Ibid* , pp 440–441.

[67] *Ibid* , p. 443

[68] Jung, *Psychology of the Unconscious*, chaps. iv–viii.

[69] The word "Kouros" derives from "keiro," "to cut hair," and signifies "He of the Shorn Hair" Harrison, *op cit.*, p 337.

[70] Frazer, *The Golden Bough*, part iv, vol 1, pp. 302–305.

[71] Upanishads, quoted in Jung, *Gestaltungen des Unbewussten*, pp 213, 215.

[72] Jung, *ibid* , p 214.

[73] For illustration of Christ child, see Jung, *Psychologie und Alchemie*, Abb 42.

[74] Jung and Kerényi, *op cit* , chaps. i, ii.

[75] Defined in Jung, *Two Essays on Analytical Psychology*, essay ii, part ii, chap. ii.

[76] Jung, *Gestaltungen des Unbewussten*, pp 160–162.

[77] Evans-Wentz, *The Tibetan Book of the Dead*, pp 105–106

[78] *Ibid* , p 105

[79] *Ibid* , pp 108–118.

[80] *Ibid* , p 122.

[81] *Loc cit.*

[82] *Ibid* , p 104.

[83] *Ibid.*, pp. 121–122.

[84] *Ibid* , pp 125–126.

[85] *Ibid* , p 34.

[86] *Ibid* , pp. 131–151.

[87] *Ibid* , p 148

[88] *Ibid* , p xliv

[89] *Ibid* , pp 183–192.

[90] *Ibid.*, p 37

[91] Jowett, *The Dialogues of Plato*, vol ii, pp 457–458

[92] *Ibid* , p 459.

[93] *Loc cit.*

[94] *Ibid* , pp 460–463.

Notes to Chapter 7

THE PSYCHOLOGY OF THE SYMBOLISM

[1] Goblet D'Alviella, *The Migration of Symbols*, p. 11.

[2] Simpson, *The Buddhist Praying Wheel*, p 66.

[3] Bloomfield, *The Religion of the Veda*, p 104

[4] Frazer, *The Golden Bough*, part iv, vol i, p 302.

[5] Jung, *Contributions to Analytical Psychology*, "Mind and Earth," p. 118

[6] *Ibid*, "Instinct and the Unconscious," p 274.

[7] *Ibid*, "On Psychical Energy"

[8] *Ibid* pp 9–14, Jung, *L'Homme à la Découverte de son Ame*, chap. iv.

[9] Jung, *Contributions to Analytical Psychology*, "Instinct and the Unconscious," p 251.

[10] Jung, *Psychological Types*, p. 211.

[11] *Ibid*, p 272.

[12] Jung, *Integration of the Personality*, p. 166.

[13] Jung, *Psychological Types*, p. 378

[14] Jung, *Contributions to Analytical Psychology*, "Mind and Earth," p. 117.

[15] Jung, *Collected Papers on Analytical Psychology*, "The Content of the Psychoses" (1914), pp 338–343

[16] Briefly discussed in Jung, *Two Essays on Analytical Psychology*, pp 183 ff , more fully discussed in Jung, *Integration of the Personality*, especially chap iv

[17] Harding, *Psychic Energy*, p 356, summarized in *ibid.*, chap xi

[18] Jung, *Integration of the Personality*, p. 96.

[19] See Jung's essay on Bruder Klaus, translated and discussed in Gray, "Brother Klaus," *Journal of Nervous and Mental Diseases*, April, 1946, pp. 359 ff

[20] See Jung's illustrated observations and discussions of patients' mandala symbolism in Jung, *Gestaltungen des Unbewussten*, chaps iii, iv

[21] See Jung, *Psychologie und Alchemie*, part iii, chap. ii.

[22] Jung, *Integration of the Personality*, p. 64.

[23] *Ibid*, p 199.

[24] Jung, *Modern Man in Search of a Soul*, p 30.

[25] Jung, *Integration of the Personality*, p. 200.

[26] Baynes, *Mythology of the Soul*, pp. 345–346.

[27] Jung, *Two Essays on Analytical Psychology*, pp 182–218.

[28] Jung, *Psychology and Religion*, pp 104–106.

[29] Jung, *Psychological Types*, pp 272–297.

[30] Wolff, *The Threshold of the Abnormal*, chap xvi.

[31] Jung, *Integration of the Personality*, p 133.

[32] Aurobindo, *Isha Upanishad*, chap. v.

[33] Jung, *Psychology and Religion*, p. 104.

[34] *Ibid*, pp 45–49.

[35] Jung, *Contributions to Analytical Psychology*, pp. 77–98, Schaer, *Religion and the Cure of Souls in Jung's Psychology*, pp. 86–92.

[36] Jung, *Psychological Types*, pp 297–318

[37] Jung, *Integration of the Personality*, p 275.

BIBLIOGRAPHY

I

Works on Psychology

Adler, Gerhard *Studies in Analytical Psychology* New York, 1948.
Baynes, H G. *Mythology of the Soul* London, 1949
Boisen, Anton *Exploration of the Inner World* Chicago, 1936
Fenichel, Otto *The Psychoanalytic Theory of Neurosis* New York, 1945
Gray, Horace. "Brother Klaus." *Journal of Nervous and Mental Diseases* (April, 1946), pp. 359 ff
Harding, M Esther *Psychic Energy.* New York, 1947.
Jung, C G *Collected Papers on Analytical Psychology* New York, 1917
  Contributions to Analytical Psychology New York, 1928
  Psychological Types New York, 1928.
  Two Essays on Analytical Psychology London, 1928
  Psychology of the Unconscious. New York, 1931.
  Modern Man in Search of a Soul. New York, 1933.
  Psychology and Religion New Haven, 1938.
  Integration of the Personality. New York, 1939
  "The Psychogenesis of Schizophrenia " *Journal of Mental Science* (September, 1939).
  "Ueber Wiedergeburt " *Eranos Jahrbuch* (1939) Zurich, 1940
  "Der Wandlungssymbol in der Messe " *Eranos Jahrbuch* (1941). Zurich, 1942.
  Psychologie und Alchemie Zurich, 1944.
  L'Homme à la Découverte de son Ame Geneva, 1946
  Psychologie der Uebertragung Zurich, 1946.
  Symbolik des Geistes. Zurich, 1948.
  "Ueber das Selbst " *Eranos Jahrbuch* (1948) Zurich, 1949
  Gestaltungen des Unbewussten Zurich, 1950.
  Symbole der Wandlung Zurich, 1952.
Jung, C G , and C. Kerényi *Essays on a Science of Mythology.* New York, 1949
Jung, C G , and R Wilhelm *The Secret of the Golden Flower* London, 1935
Jung, Emma "Ein Beitrag zum Problem des Animus " In *Wirklichkeit der Seele.* Zurich, 1947.
Schaer, Hans *Religion and the Cure of Souls in Jung's Psychology* New York, 1950
Schaerf, R "Die Gestalt des Satans im Alten Testament " In *Symbolik des Geistes.* Zurich, 1948
Wolff, Werner *The Threshold of the Abnormal* New York, 1950.

II
Works on Comparative Material

Apuleus *The Golden Ass* London, 1910.

Avalon, Arthur. *The Serpent Power* London, 1935.

Aurobindo, Sri *Isha Upanishad* Calcutta, 1941

Ballou, Robert *The Bible of the World*. New York, 1939.

Bloomfield, M *The Religion of the Veda*. New York, 1908

Bredon, Juliet *Peking* Shanghai, 1922.

Cammann, Schuyler *Kunming Guide*. Kunming, 1945

"Suggested Origin of the Tibetal Mandala Paintings" *Art Quarterly* (Spring, 1950)

Cornford, F M *Plato's Cosmology* London, 1937

Dante Alighieri *The Divine Comedy* (translated by Lawrence Grant White) New York, 1948

Evans-Wentz, W Y *Tibetan Yoga and Secret Doctrines*. London, 1935.

The Tibetan Book of the Dead New York, 1951.

Farrar, F W *The Life of Christ as Represented in Art*. London, 1923.

Fox, W S *The Mythology of All Races* (Volume I. *Greek and Roman*), Boston, 1931

Frazer, J G *The Golden Bough* London, 1919.

The Worship of Nature New York, 1926

Frobenius, Leo *Monumenta Africana*. Weimar, 1939

Goblet D'Alviella, Eugène *The Migration of Symbols*. London, 1894.

Croyances, Rites, Institutions Paris, 1911.

Harrison, Jane *Themis, A Study of the Social Origins of Greek Religion*. Cambridge, 1912

Hastings, James *Encyclopædia of Religion and Ethics*. New York, 1911.

Hocart, A M *Kings and Councillors* Cairo, 1936.

Inman, Thomas *Ancient Pagan and Modern Christian Symbolism* New York, 1922

Jowett, B *The Dialogues of Plato* London, 1871.

Keith, A B *The Mythology of All Races* (Volume VI *Indian*). Boston, 1917

Kellogg, Rhoda "Structure and Design in Preschool Art" (mimeo) San Francisco, 1953

Langdon, S. H *The Mythology of All Races* (Volume V. *Semitic*) Boston, 1918.

MacCulloch, J A *The Mythology of All Races* (Volume III *Celtic*) Boston, 1918

Nahm, M C *Selections from Early Greek Philosophy* New York, 1945.

Read, John *Prelude to Chemistry* London, 1936.

Reichard, G A. *Navaho Religion*. New York, 1950.

Simpson, William *The Buddhist Praying Wheel* London, 1896

Stein, Aurel *Serindia* London, 1921.

Taylor, A E *Plato* New York, 1936

Vaillant, G C *The Aztecs of Mexico* New York, 1941.

Watts, Alan W. *The Spirit of Zen* London, 1948.

Webster, Hutton *Primitive Secret Societies*. New York, 1932.

Wheelwright, M C *Navaho Creation Myth* Santa Fe, New Mexico, 1942

Hail Chant and Water Chant Santa Fe, New Mexico, 1946

Wilhelm, R , and C F Baynes *The I Ching or Book of Changes* New York, 1950

Zimmer, H *Kunstform und Yoga im indischen Kultbild* Berlin, 1926

Myths and Symbols of Indian Art and Civilization New York, 1946

INDEX

INDEX

179

CPSIA information can be obtained
at www.ICGtesting.com
Printed in the USA
BVHW040840310820
587677BV00014B/382

9 781258 157715